Introduction: Law, Anthropology and History

Law as discourse

SALLY HUMPHREYS

Department of Anthropology, University College London

ANCESTORS

Law as social fact

ANTHROPOLOGISTS WILL RECOGNISE, in the choice of law as the subject of this second number of *History and Anthropology*, a stratagem familiar to students of kinship systems: citing common ancestors to legitimate a new, or renewed, alliance. The nineteenth-century scholars whom social anthropologists now regard as the founding fathers of the discipline — Bachofen, Maine, Fustel de Coulanges, Morgan, McLennan — worked in the borderland between history and law, as did some of the pioneers of the history of social institutions (F.W. Maitland). The influence of the German historical school in law, with its emphasis on law as the product of culturally patterned reactions to historical processes, marked out the territory on which historians and anthropologists now meet each other.

The idea that differences between societies and changes in social structure could be studied under the rubric of 'constitutional law' had, of course, a long history behind it before Savigny began to write. The ancient Greeks had compared different types of *politeia* (constitution), had written histories of constitutional changes, and had described the 'laws' (*nomoi*) of barbarian tribes. Montesquieu's *De l'esprit des lois* (1748) had rescued the analysis of constitutions from the antiquarians and given it a place in the new 'philosophical history' of the eighteenth century (cf. Momigliano, 1950). The nineteenth century had widened this perspective to include kinship and the family, economic institutions and, as Maine said, the whole 'view of life' of past societies. Though we look back now to the second half of the nineteenth century as the period when some of the basic principles round which modern academic disciplines organise their identities were formulated, we must remember that it was an age of holistic purviews rather than hard boundaries. Philosophy, psychology, economics, law, history and sociology were closely interconnected. The passage from unselfconscious assumptions about the nature of man and society to formal theory was taking place in parallel along

History and Anthropology, 1985
Vol. 1, pp. 241-264
0275-7206/85/0102-0241 $18.50/0

different axes of thought; changes in contemporary society, the educational system and the organisation of the professions provided a common background and plenty of opportunities for the exchange of ideas.

Law is, in all societies, one of the most explicit, concrete and institutionalised cadres of ethno-sociological discourse. The early stages of development of sociology and social anthropology were even more profoundly marked by its influence than the historiography of social and economic institutions. Durkheim simply takes it for granted, in *De la division du travail social* (1893) and *Les règles de la méthode sociologique* (1895), that laws represent 'social facts' in their most concrete and factual manifestation, and provide the best basis for an evolutionist classification of social structures and types of social solidarity. Through the influence of Durkheim on Radcliffe-Brown, it became a fundamental tenet of structural-functional anthropology from the 1920s to the 1950s that the anthropologist's task was to discover the 'rules' governing the structure of the society he or she was studying.

Living law and legal realism

This equation between the codified law of literate societies and the unwritten 'rules' discovered by the anthropologist was facilitated by developments within legal theory in the late 19th and early 20th centuries which built on the bourgeois opposition between the state and 'civil society'. Ehrlich (developing ideas earlier formulated by Gierke) emphasised the 'living law' made by corporate groups and communities in regulating their own affairs, and contrasted it with what English writers termed the 'black-letter law' of the state. The idea of 'living law' allowed minority groups to legitimate their claims to at least a limited autonomy in regulating their own affairs; it provided a framework within which customary law both in rural Europe and in colonial territories could be accorded whatever degree of recognition suited the ruling group.[1]

The contrast between living and black-letter law was not however used solely in dealing with relations between the state and marginal groups or 'backward' areas. In America, Roscoe Pound and the 'legal realist' school asserted that judges and courts were not merely mechanically 'applying' laws produced by formal legislative action, but were themselves engaged in a constant process of law-making. In the context of the empirical research into the activities of judges, lawyers, disputants and juries generated by this movement, the resemblances between African lineages and modern organisations, between village moots and western courts, appeared more significant than their differences. Karl Llewellyn, one of the leading 'realists', collaborated with an anthropologist in the study of Cheyenne 'law-ways' (Llewellyn and Hoebel, 1961; cf. Twining, 1973), and anthropologists were encouraged to look for analogues of Anglo-American legal practice and principles in small-scale communities.

Both the concept of 'living law' and the theory of legal realism still rested, however, on the assumption of a correspondence between legal rules and social structure. If the state's law failed to conform to the structure of civil society, it required reform; the non-correspondence was a problem of time-lag, a chronological hiccup. Only in Marxism, with its view of law as part of the ideological apparatus by which the ruling class reified its own perception of social relationships, was the relation between law and social structure recognised as a theoretical as well as a practical problem; and apart from Karl Renner's pioneer work (1904) on the representation of interpersonal relations of dependence as relations of property between men and things, this line of research has until recently received little attention in Marxist theory (see now Jessop, 1980; Hunt, 1982; Sugarman, 1983).

Rules or strategies?

Anthropologists arrived at a more critical attitude towards the relation between law and social structure only through a slow process. Malinowski was already, in *Crime and Custom in Savage Society* (1926), questioning the assumption that 'savages' invariably and automatically followed the 'rules', imprisoned in what Bagehot had called 'the cake of custom'. While his main aim was to demonstrate that Trobriand islanders lived in a close-knit network of exchanges and reciprocal obligations which made conformity to norms a matter of prudent self-interest, he also noted that they could choose between alternative norms potentially applicable in the same situation, and that deviance was certainly not unknown. Firth (1930, 1951) developed Malinowski's remarks on the possibility of choice in selecting and applying norms into a basis for the microanalysis of processes of social change; F. Barth (1966, 1967) and F. Bailey (e.g. 1969) went on to view social behaviour as a succession of 'transactions' in which each actor tries to maximise his or her own advantage, within culturally defined limits which were not very adequately situated in the theoretical model.

E.R. Leach's contributions to this trend in social anthropology are particularly relevant to the study of law. In *Political Systems of Highland Burma* (1954) he suggested that different social classes or status groups might base their actions and their interpretations of the actions of others on divergent models of their society's structure, dominant groups favouring hierarchical models and subordinate or relatively autonomous groups egalitarian ones. In *Pul Eliya* (1961) he scandalised the anthropological establishment by proposing to treat statements about the 'rules' of kinship as merely an idiom in which claims over land and persons could be asserted. Maurice Bloch followed up the latter point in 1971 in an article on 'The moral and tactical meaning of kinship terms' (cf. Moore, 1978:ch. 5), and returned to the problem of alternative indigenous models of social structure in his 1977 Malinowski lecture, in which he suggested that it is particularly in rituals that a static, hierarchical, rule-governed model of society is presented. This argument linked the Malinowskian tradition in British social anthropology with the Marxist conception of ritual as ideology. Bloch criticised structural-functional anthropologists for paying too much attention to ritual and taking too little notice of practical activity, and thus presenting too static and normative a picture in their ethnographic analyses.

A somewhat different and theoretically more radical — though less overtly political — attack on the view that it is the anthropologist's task to specify the 'rules' of the society he or she studies has come from Pierre Bourdieu (1977). Like Bloch, he argues that anthropologists have naively accepted their informants' normative statements at face value instead of recognising the tactical uses to which they are put; but instead of dividing social action, as Bloch does, into 'ritual' in which a static, normative model of society is presented and 'practical action' in which actors modify behaviour patterns in accordance with their interests and the lessons of experience, Bourdieu sees the relation between theory and practical action as problematic in all contexts. What we need, he claims, is a 'theory of practice' which takes account of the different ways in which actors formulate and cite rules in interpreting situations and in choosing and justifying their strategies, and which analyses the relation between different types of practice and the theories they generate. In such a theory rule-making would be seen as part of behaviour and not as the production of a meta-language in which behaviour is to be described and evaluated.

The Manchester School and the case-history method

This rapid survey provides a background against which to examine the more specialised work on the anthropology of law developed principally by Max Gluckman and the 'Manchester School' associated with him.[2] The focus on disputes and processes of dispute settlement, rather than on normative descriptions of social structure, which has characterised their work has two main sources. One is the idea, which has its roots in the Malinowskian tradition, that social change and areas of potential instability can best be understood and identified by focussing on disputes as evidence for changing norms, areas of ambiguity or uncertainty in social relationships, and attempts to control change. The other — a particularly strong influence in the case of Gluckman himself — is an interest in showing, as Llewellyn and Hoebel had done for the Cheyenne, that the basic principles employed in investigating and adjudicating disputes in non-literate societies are similar to those used in more developed legal systems (see especially Gluckman, 1965; cf. also Fallers, 1969). The Manchester school's 'case history method' (Epstein, 1967) presented structure in action, in the formation of alignments in specific situations of conflict, and showed how norms were explicitly or implicitly invoked in such situations.[3]

Dispute settlement as 'social drama'

Historians have drawn profitably on this line of anthropological research. Boyer and Nissenbaum (1974) produced an extended case study of the Salem witchcraft trials which clearly brought out the structural tensions in the community which lay behind them. Anthropologists' detailed analyses of village disputes and the gradual processes by which alignments crystallise and decisions emerge have helped historians to put flesh on the bones of early legal procedure: Peter Brown (1975) showed how in small medieval communities the ordeal provided a dramatic setting, a temporal interval and an apparent shift of the issue to be decided to the 'objective' question whether the blisters on the defendant's hand had healed or not, which allowed support and opposition to crystallise in an apparently less partisan fashion.[4] Wendy Davies, in this volume, uses dispute records as a point of entry into the analysis of social networks and power relations in early medieval Brittany, where respectable men with local knowledge (*scabini*), called on to help in adjudicating disputes, not only operate in a way which combines the roles of witness and juror, but may also be more closely involved with litigants as oath-helpers and guarantors. Their appointment to act in the public role of *scabini*, under the eye of the *princeps*, distances them temporarily from normal social relations as the ritual setting of the ordeal does in the previous example. In my own paper, below, which was influenced both by Peter Brown's study of the ordeal and by Victor Turner's concept of 'social drama', I argue that witnesses in Athenian courts are used not so much for the specific testimony they offer — which frequently evaded the central point at issue and was not subject to cross-examination — as to give the jury the impression that the litigant had solid support from those best acquainted with the facts of the case. In classical Athens the results of the process of crystallisation of local opinion which is so vividly described at village level by Gulliver (1963) had to be artificially re-created in an urban court; analogous phenomena seem to be visible in the 'people's courts' of communist China and Russia.

Colonial dialogues

Anthropologists of the Manchester school also challenged the assumption that colonial governments applying an 'indirect rule' policy were allowing customary law to continue to function unchanged. In "The Politics of Law" (1969) J.A. Barnes emphasised the conflicting pressures to which Ngoni chiefs presiding over Native Courts were subject, and the amount of new law-making in which they engaged while ostensibly 'applying' customary law. Elisabeth Colson (1975, pp. 77-80) has made the same point; it is now becoming much more widely recognised that the concepts of 'tradition' and 'custom', both in Europe and in the Third World, can be used by peripheralised groups to preserve a degree of local autonomy by legitimating their demands and their identity in a way acceptable to the dominant capitalist culture and its legal institutions.[5] There may well be complicity between the colonial government and a particular status-group in the subject population; for example, governmental instructions to British courts in India to respect Indian laws on questions of status, by treating Sanskrit texts as the most authoritative source for native law, greatly intensified the Brahminisation of Indian law (Derrett, 1961, cf. Rudolph, 1965).

Max Weber: law and power

The work of Max Weber on law received surprisingly little attention in the developments so far discussed. This is of course partly due to general neglect of Weber by anthropologists until the 1960s. More specifically, Weber was probably perceived as being mainly concerned with societies in which a professional corps of legal experts evolved, and with the processes of formal rationalisation which such groups tended to promote (cf. Fallers, 1969; Kronman, 1983). This orientation was not particularly apt to find favour with those who — like Llewellyn and Gluckman — stressed similarities between the legal reasoning of western lawyers and the principles and thought-processes employed in tribal moots; it was equally unpopular with Marxists, who were reluctant to come to terms with the complex model of a plurality of competing elite groups which Weber offered. The wider frame in which Weber's view of the emergence of legal specialists was set — which, as Gilsenan's paper here illustrates, was structured by the competition between central rulers trying to maintain the maximum of power over their subjects, and local power-holders trying to carve out their own domains of arbitrary power over their dependants and limit the central government's claims on them — received little attention. Weber's remarks on 'qadi justice', and his distinction between formal and substantive rationality in law, did not seem particularly relevant to anthropologists until Lévi-Strauss began to write about *bricolage* as a characteristic pattern of mythical thought, and the study of cognitive categories and the difference between implicit and explicit mental structures became a central concern of anthropologists and sociologists.[6]

Historians of law have also made little use of Weber. In part this is, again, just a particular instance of a more general neglect, but it is also more specifically due to the fact that much history of law has been written from the standpoint of the legal profession (Baker, 1971, may serve as a typical example). From this point of view law is seen as developing by its own internal dynamics. Lawyers, in administering and interpreting existing law, perceive its defects; they press for remedial legislation; this legislation, when administered in practice, reveals further inconsistencies, 'gaps' and contradictions; further remedial legislation is called for, and so the process continues. The effect of external factors and political pressures in bringing about changes in law tends to be played down,[7] as is the fact that what is presented as an effort to 'clarify' the law often has other effects as well. For example, the 'clarification' of property rights in 17th-18th century English law led to the delegitimation of use rights previously enjoyed by the rural population and the redefinition of the exercise of such rights as theft, poaching, etc. (Hay, 1975b; Thompson, 1975a; Sharpe, 1980). Paradoxically, this lawyer-centred approach can only celebrate the skills of the profession in analysing the defects of law by admitting that the drafting of legislation is often defective; this aspect of the model has been put to fruitful use by historians less committed to the lawyer's view and more concerned to stress the unintended consequences of legislation, as Nippel, Whitcombe and Gilsenan do here. The concern with the process of applying, interpreting and re-formulating law has certainly been a positive contribution. But it is hardly surprising that practitioners of this approach have turned a blind eye to Weber's view of law, which firmly situates their own practice as characteristic of the determination of legal experts to uphold their own status honour.[8]

Marxism and the Warwick School

The main challenge to the lawyer-centred view of the history of law, recently, has come from Marxist historians, particularly the school which grew up round E.P. Thompson at the University of Warwick (see Hay a.o., eds, 1975, and the bibliography cited in Nippel, below; Bailey, 1981; Sugarman, 1983). The main focus of their work has been on law as an instrument of coercion, developed particularly for the protection of property rights and involving the redefinition and repression of various forms of popular protest as crime. This aspect of their work connects it to a wider interest in popular forms of protest and social control (rough musicking, charivari) which has appeared in the work of the *Annales* school in France and those influenced by them, as well as in Marxist historiography.[9] The work of the 'Warwick School' has also been influenced by Michel Foucault's work on the history of the prison and other 'correctional' institutions (Foucault, 1975). This sympathy for popular action and concern with the cultural and ritual, as well as the political and economic aspects of social control is, however, accompanied in the work of Thompson and his students by an acute sensibility to the contradictions revealed when the working of the criminal law is studied in detail, to differences of opinion within the ruling class and to the ways in which the ideology of law and respect for 'due process' constrained its behaviour and could be used by defendants in their own interest (cf. Nippel, below; Thompson, 1975a, pp. 258-69; Ignatieff, 1983). They have highlighted the paradox that increasingly severe criminal laws, with the death penalty prescribed for an extraordinary number of offences, did not produce a corresponding increase in the number of executions. In some cases courts were reluctant to convict; but often, as Hay (1975a) has shown, death sentences delivered with maximum ritual solemnity were subsequently commuted to transportation. This apparent inconsistency, rationalised by a theory of the deterrent effects of 'exemplary' punishment of selected offenders (which, as Nippel shows here, was particularly problematic in the case of a collective offence like rioting), betrays more fundamental conflicts between the ruling class's image of execution and that of the watching crowd, which tended to turn the victim into a hero (cf. Evans, 1984).

The main points of contact between the anthropology and the history of law thus seem to have been, so far, the use made by medieval historians of detailed anthropological accounts of the functioning of village courts to help them flesh out their own conception of medieval institutions, and the fusion of a Marxist analysis of class conflict with an *Annales*-inspired sense of the significance of ritual and symbolic communication in the work of the Warwick School. Weber remains as yet little more than a shadowy presence waiting in the wings.[10] What new directions for collaboration or cross-fertilisation do the contributions to the present volume suggest?

LEGAL EVOLUTION: DEMISE OF A MODEL

New directions in western law?

It may appear surprising that the topic of legal evolution does not play a more prominent part either in the preceding discussion or in the papers which follow.[11] Their focus is on law as process rather than on macro-historical trends. There seem to be three main reasons for this, all connected with Western society's perceptions of its own institutions.

In the first place, nineteenth-century confidence in the superiority and rationality of western law has been invaded by doubt. We have become more aware that access to justice is unequal (Cappelletti a.o., 1978-9) and that the formal boundaries set up by modern legal systems generate substantive irrationalities (Humphreys, below). Experiments are being made with new types of dispute settlement procedure which may to some extent reverse the trend towards increasing formal rationality in court procedure and in the interpretation of law which has hitherto seemed characteristic of western history (cf. Sander and Snyder, 1979). Roscoe Pound's crusade against 'mechanical jurisprudence', calling for more creative interpretation of the law by judges, perhaps already indicated a change in the direction of the wind just at the period when Weber was singling out the growth of formal rationality in law as one of the key elements in the bureaucratisation of western society.

Ethnocentricity

Secondly, anthropologists are reacting against the idealisation of 'primitive' societies which theories of evolution tend to enshrine. Bloch, for example, emphasises that ritual and formal language can be used as instruments of social control in simple as well as in complex societies (Bloch, 1975, 1977; cf. Carlen, 1974 for a modern British parallel). Nineteenth-century evolutionists produced models which, as Kuper points out here in his article on Maine, were largely inspired by the preoccupations and experience of their own societies. The directions attributed to evolutionary change were projections backward in time of trends visible in Western society in the theorist's own day, or simply of tensions between opposed ideals and models of behaviour characteristic of contemporary society. Nostalgia for 'traditional' aspects and features of Western society which were felt to be vanishing, or which were no longer granted open recognition,[12] supplied materials for the model of 'primitive' society; and the picture of 'modern' society was also idealised, based more on ideology than on experience.

Louis Dumont has pointed out (1969, cf. 1975, 1977) that India often serves as a mirror-image of western culture. Accounts of Indian society emphasise the principle of ritual hierarchy and suppress the existence of competitive and egalitarian relationships, whereas ideological representations of Western society emphasise equality and play down the existence of hierarchy. In the colonial situation, evolutionary theories based on such dichotomies tended to work as self-fulfilling prophecies, since it was in the supposedly 'primitive' aspects of native culture that colonial governments were prepared to allow local custom more autonomy. Since British law had more or less abandoned the view of society as made up of hierarchically differentiated status groups (cf. da Cunha, below) and the regulation of religious affairs, the government of British India was prepared to respect the views of local legal experts on the Indian law of status.[13] On the other hand it did not seem necessary to consult local experts to discover whether the Indian law of contract differed from the British, and it seemed urgently necessary to reformulate the law of property along British lines.[14] Thus the view that Indian law was predominantly concerned with status and had little or nothing to say about contract was both generated by the observed shift from status to contract in the history of western law and confirmed by colonial practice, which produced a historical change from a law which dealt with both status and contract to a division of labour between two legal systems, one of which was supposed to specialise in the law of status while the other dealt with the law of contract.[15]

Similarly, one might argue that Weber's ideal-type of 'qadi justice' (Weber, 1922, II, p. 976; cf. Bourdieu, 1977, p. 16) highlights features present in all processes of dispute settlement (full knowledge of the litigants' background and a settlement which really 'fits' the individual case are always desirable) but which have failed to gain a place in western legal theory and thus have to be smuggled in through the back door in practice and representations of practice (Humphreys, below p. 354). Even Islamic theory, as Udovitch shows below, has some difficulty in making a place for respect for local custom and local knowledge.

The limits of 'rationalisation'. Law and medicine

What was perceived as a process of evolution in a progressive direction can also be seen, therefore, as a process of gradual delimitation, exclusion and suppression. The concept of 'law' as institutionalised means of settling disputes and solving problems of social order by discussion and human decision-making, and successive procedural refinements developed with that ideal in mind, have led to the outlawing of alternative institutions which may have had their own substantive rationality (such as rioting or witchcraft accusations) and to a deliberate refusal to recognise other phenomena which continue nevertheless to influence legal practice (such as status differences or 'local knowledge').

The next number of *History and Anthropology*, which will deal with medicine, will raise many of the same issues; the two fields have much in common. Both have their dramatic rituals and their acts of symbolic violence (spirit possession in some non-western medical systems, 'examination' and surgery; trials, penalties and 'exemplary' executions in law); both have their bodies of professional experts, their rites of confession, their techniques for tracing historical causality and apportioning blame. Medical anthropologists are becoming dissatisfied with an evolutionist perspective which dissects the medical discourse of other societies in order to extract for approval those propositions or practices which conform to western standards, rather than using it as a stimulus to recognising the limitations and scrutinising the silences of western medicine. Medical historians have shown how some of the basic features of the western concept of scientific rationality can be traced back to historically situated polemics between early Greek doctors and their rivals — priests of Asclepius or magical healers (Lloyd, 1979). Both in law and in medicine, openness to argument has been consecrated as one of the cardinal values of the western system (cf. Gernet, 1951; Elkana, 1981; Humphreys, 1984). In principle, change is easy, every new idea is fairly tested. But in practice, as we know, distinctions between what is relevant and what is not relevant are difficult to challenge. Those who have authority tend to defend the established boundaries and succeed in imposing their categories on the rest of society (Kuhn, 1962; Feyerabend, 1975; cf. Humphreys, 1978, pp. 272-3).

LAW AS DISCOURSE

Theory and practice

Pursuing the analogy between medicine and law, and drawing on suggestions made in the papers which follow, I should like to suggest that many of the false dichotomies introduced into the anthropology and history of law by evolutionary theory and by uncritical acceptance of western ideology might be eliminated if we look at law as a part of the discourse about good and bad states of society, as medicine is a part of the discourse on good and bad states of the individual. Such a view of law as "a fight between alternative definitions of rights" (Thompson, 1975a, p. 259; cf. Jhering, 1872), besides taking up the point often made before[16] that law is a form of ethnosociological reflection, has the merit of emphasising the combination of utopian and polemical elements in both legislation and court practice. At all levels we are dealing with competing attempts to impose models of what society should be on others.[17] Recent work on the sociology of deviance (e.g. Cicourel, 1967; Cohen, 1971) has indicated the fruitfulness of this approach, which can be more widely generalised.

From this point of view discrepancies between codified law and observed behaviour no longer appear as mysterious gaps between theory and practice (sometimes regarded as a defect and sometimes as 'functional') but as the result either of the use of different models of society by different groups (cf. Leach, 1954) or of silences in codified law which have traceable motives. Such silences may be due to incompatibility between local practice and the ideals of some part of the audience to which codified law is addressed, which may transcend local boundaries (cf. da Cunha, below; Cooper, 1980:70-1); or may correspond to a feeling that what is not being said is too obvious and universally recognised to need saying (Udovitch, below). Codification, as a form of rule-making, needs to be seen as an aspect of practice, a way of making assertions about social relationships, not as a description of practice or a blueprint existing on a different level of reality like a Platonic Idea. Codification turns a model of social relationships into a resource to be used in legal discourse and especially in court; this model is intended to appear as part of the real world, and therefore cannot be openly represented by those who formulate and use it as merely a model.

In characterising law as part of the discourse on society, I have three points principally in mind, which will be developed in turn: that we cannot draw precise definitional lines round 'law' but are dealing with a complex of ideas and institutions in which demarcation lines vary over time and between one group and another (cf. Foucault, 1969); that law combines speech with action and its study thus implies analysis of the power relations structuring speech (cf. Hirst, 1977, pp. 112f.); and that rules of law and legal arguments are formulated, approved and cited in specific historical circumstances.

Law and its opposites

From this point of view the problem of 'defining' law has no sense, not only because a definition is a tool which has to be redesigned for each job it is asked to perform, but also because even a single homogeneous group will contrast law with different opposing terms in different conversations: peaceful legal action versus illegal violence, the external authority of law versus the internalised standards of justice and morality, your revolutionary ideas versus my well-thought-out scheme for legal reform. It is an essential feature of the discourse that some categories of person (slaves, children, the mentally ill), and some actions, are excluded from it. Actions for which codified law and court procedure have no place, or which they penalise, derive new meanings from their exclusion: witchcraft accusations, in a colonial situation, may represent adherence to indigenous conceptions of morality (cf. Chanock, 1978); as has already been noted, 'tradition' and 'custom' are concepts shaped by opposition to the imposition of new models of legitimate behaviour. Violence or threats of violence may be either a way of expressing despair of reaching goals which the actor considers legitimate by legitimate means (Marx, 1972, cf. Thompson, 1975b) or a demonstration of power (Gilsenan, below). The domain of 'law', in the modern state, is bracketed on one side by the concepts of martial law and "official secrets" (Thompson, 1979), attempts to legitimate the use of force and arbitrary action, without 'due process', by the state, and on the other side by arguments about the legality of strikes, picketing, sit-ins and other forms of protest. It used to be claimed that law had evolved from self-help procedures and religious taboos; but in all societies for which we have evidence religious or moral taboos, public discussion and decision-making, and self-help are found alongside each other as alternative mechanisms for maintaining order (Humphreys, 1983). The study of 'law' always therefore demands consideration not only of phenomena which the institutionalised rules and procedures of law exclude or forbid, but also of those they ignore or pass over in silence: the successful economic transactions of slaves who have no power to make legally valid contracts, the careless attitude to written contracts adopted by businessmen as a sign of friendship (Macaulay, 1963; cf. Moore, 1978:59-65); images of heroic violence, from Achilles to the *mafiosi* of Sicily (Blok, 1974) and Chicago, or the beys of North Lebanon (Gilsenan, below); models of the just society presented by Aeschylean tragedy, philosophical utopias or detective stories.

Law always has an external source of legitimation in conceptions of power and conceptions of justice; the discourse includes these, and includes assumptions, never entirely explicit, about the nature of the person, of social relations, of knowledge (cf. Davies, Gilsenan, Udovitch and Humphreys, below; Rudolph, 1965; Garfinkel, 1967; Dumont, 1983:80-85; Geertz, 1983). To speak of a discourse does not imply a tightly-structured debate in which each speaker replies, point by point, to another. Such cohesion may be found in the arguments of legal experts, but not in the wider discourse of lay society. The conversation between lawyers and laymen may at times appear to be a *dialogue des sourds*, but traces of articulation can still be found. E.P. Thompson's analysis (1975b) of 18th century anonymous letters written by poor men who could find no legal channel of expression for their grievances shows how closely these threats of illegal action (usually arson) were tied to the official discourse of the law, both by their constant reference to justice and injustice and by the expression of their threats in the form of a kind of legal contract:

> Sir, we have inquired into your tithes and we have determined to set fire to you in your bed if you do not lower them. You receive from Fletching £500 a year, and give your curate only £100 a year, and you starve your labourers that works for you, you old canibal . . . You parsons have fleeced the country long enough. Strain, if you dare. You and your daughter shall be burned in your beds if you do. We shall tell all the people of the parish not to pay you, for we are determined and our names are legions of liberty. Deem this as friendly, and consider that we would not burn you up without notice.
>
> (Thompson, 1975b, pp. 315-6; cf. the following letter, signed 'Mahershalalhashbaz, Sec., and Jesus Christ, Cholera, Blood, Fire and Co. Extra Executors. Earthquakes, Panics and Co., Witnesses.")

To shift perspective deliberately, to move to and fro between the cadre defined by codified law, court procedure and the utterances of legal experts and the wider discourse to which they belong, is the only way to remain sensitive to the silences of codified law, the complicity between 'due process' and arbitrary violence or arbitrary acts of grace and mercy (Hay, 1975a), and the contradictions inherent in the ideals and demands to which law attempts to respond. Though the view that law evolves by an internal dynamism, as the straitjacket of legal rules never perfectly fits the Protean form for which it is designed and successive modifications only reveal new gaps, clearly exhibits the *parti pris* of the legal experts who produced it, it nevertheless has some solid basis; the attempt to satisfy contradictory ideals can produce a zigzag development in which a move in one direction will be followed by a compensatory swing of the pendulum. For example, the abolition in Britain in 1972 of the rule that jurors should be ratepayers was followed by the abolition of the requirement that the jury's verdict must be unanimous, and by new limits on the types of case for which jury trial is an option (Thompson, 1981; for similar examples from Athenian history, see Humphreys, 1983). Contradictions between the desire for order and the wish for consensus, between the desire for appropriate settlement of individual cases and for overall consistency and predictability, between the wish to control deviance and the demand that everyone should have freedom to justify his actions, are inescapable. Such contradictions can produce contemporary trends which appear to head in opposite directions: at present, while Western lawyers are exploring conciliatory modes of dispute settlement which take a wider view of the issue than courts do, third-world societies seem to be moving towards a narrower and more impersonal formulation of disputed issues (Colson, 1975, pp. 73-4). In many instances the opposing terms of the dichotomy may seem to correspond to opposed class interests, but the contradictions lie deeper than that. The ideals to which opposed groups appeal are often ideals which both accept. (Cf. Thompson, 1971; 1975a, pp. 258-69; and Nippel, below, on legalistic attitudes to the riot act shown both by magistrates and by rioters.)

Controlling the discourse

To characterise law as a discourse further implies, as I have said, that it is a combination of speech and action, of explicit claims and implicit messages. We have to ask who plays dominant and who subordinate roles in it, to whom it is addressed, how power is exercised, what means are consciously used to heighten its effectiveness and what kinds of covert persuasion it embodies.

Access to law may be restricted either according to status or according to skill. At the extremes, the very powerful may consider themselves above the law, while slaves are by definition below it. In the Breton society described below by Wendy Davies, peasant claims are settled within the village while the disputes of more powerful men have to be aired before a wider public. The same law may have different meanings at different social levels (Grace and Wilkinson, 1978:274-283). The size of the sum at issue in a civil case, or the penalty to be paid in a criminal one, often determines whether full public trial or a more summary procedure is used. Where legal experts exist, it is clearly in their interest to monopolise the discourse of law as effectively as they can, by impressing the lay public with their specialised skills and command of technical language and literature; the form their claims take will depend on the distribution of power in each society and the legal elite's relations to other elite groups. In classical Athens, expert speech-writers composing pleas for clients to deliver to mass juries had to employ their skills in making the litigant sound artless and inexperienced; in Rome legal experience was an integral part of political life, but the custom that a magistrate acting as judge consulted an informal council of *jurisprudentes* allowed some Romans to develop a special penchant for rather technical legal issues.

Courts, however, are ideally supposed to represent the general public; if elite domination is too patent their legitimacy becomes questionable. Roman magistrates sat in public and the crowd had ways of indicating its opinion (Nicolet, 1976, ch. 9). Where the public is given a role as jury, control may be exercised through techniques of selecting jurors (Thompson, 1981; cf. Davies, below: *scabini* chosen to act as jurors had to be 'suitable'; cf. Geertz, 1983, on Islamic witnesses), or through procedural rules defining what the jury is allowed to hear and the theory that it should confine itself to questions of 'fact' rather than of 'law' (cf. Humphreys, below).

Wendy Davies' paper also serves as a reminder that the discourse of law can flourish without law-codes or law-books; and, one may add, that where laws are written down they are often not easily available to the majority of those whose affairs they claim to regulate. Jack Goody (1977) has remarked that in the early stages of literacy writing is often used mainly for making lists, mapping and defining areas of knowledge; early law codes are lists of misdemeanours and penalties which give an impression that order has been imposed on social relationships. (The criminal code of 18th century England was perhaps not so very different.) The public announcements made by prosecution associations in 18th-19th century England certainly aimed to deter criminals from attacking the property and persons of their members, but they also proclaimed to the members themselves and their peers their definition of wrongdoing and determination to combat it — a determination which was not always pursued to the point of prosecution and conviction (see Shubert, 1981, and cf. Curtis and Speck, 1976). The legislators of British India often had their eye on the British rather than the Indian public in drafting their laws, and the legislators of 19th century Brazil were concerned to make a good impression in Europe even if it meant dealing inadequately with local practice (da Cunha, below). The discourse of law is not necessarily addressed primarily to law-breakers.

Analysis of the ways in which the discourse of law is controlled necessitates consideration of the relations between law and 'ritual' — which are complex. The symbolic trappings which perhaps immediately spring to mind seem to be used largely to reinforce the message that legal procedure represents Society, imposing order in place of deviance. Hay (1975a; cf. Nippel, below) has argued convincingly that the insistence of the English upper class in the 18th century on the death penalty for a startlingly large number of offences was mainly due to the place occupied by the ritual of sentencing, clothed in impressive symbolic furnishings, in the discourse of law and order; once the sentence had been pronounced, the peroration was over and the unofficial, extra-legal, unpublicised and (from the victim's point of view) unpredictable machinery leading to reprieve and transmutation of sentence could be set in motion. Gluckman takes a wider view, in remarking on the function in small-scale, face-to-face communities of ritual in signalling changes of role and transitions from private to public dealings (Gluckman, 1962; cf. Humphreys, 1978, p. 251; Brown, 1975). Gernet has suggested (1951) that the formalism of early Roman and, to a lesser extent, Greek law may be due to a lack of confidence in human decision-making unless it was confined between narrow limits. One can indeed see the Roman *legis actiones* — the formulae which had to be correctly pronounced before a magistrate would accept a case — not merely as a symbol that 'due process' was being performed, but as an extreme instance of a very wide class of procedural rules designed to limit what can be said in court. Such rules tend to work in favour of the educated litigant or the person who can afford to hire a lawyer, although they have often ostensibly been introduced as 'safeguards' for the defendant (cf. Humphreys, below). Any formalisation or ritualisation of speech limits what can be said (Bloch, 1975), and the technical speech of legal experts is well adapted both to intimidate the layman and to keep the argument running in the approved channels. The discourse about society is a Pandora's jar which it is dangerous to open too widely, and pressures towards closure, limitation and formalisation are seldom absent.

Consciousness of the utility of such means of control, though seldom admitted in openly cynical terms, nevertheless lies near the surface; those who gain advantage from them have some awareness that when a legal ritual is staged they are the dramatists and actors and the lay public is the audience. Other modes of control lie deeper, shaping the perceptions of the principals in the legal drama as much as those of actors with only walk-on parts. There are topics on which the legal discourse must be silent, either because its internal contradictions have to be covered up; or because to state its basic assumptions openly would be to expose them to discussion, critical scrutiny and the risk of rejection; or because the practice of law requires concealment of its nature as a discourse.

Contradictions and silences

A law-code, or accumulated set of rules and precedents, is a model of what society should be, not a mere random set of responses to practical problems. It embodies ideological tensions which often appear as a discrepancy between 'theory' and 'practice'. What is ideologically coherent in the legal discourse appears as 'theory', while discordant elements are relegated to the status of mere 'practice'. Thus contracts between freedmen and their ex-owners in 19th century Brazil, and traditional relations between Indian zamindars and their dependants, were not officially recognised in codified law because the model of social relationships which dominated 19th-century European law had no place for rural relations of dependence (da Cunha and Whitcombe, below). The history of the concept of 'customary law' needs study; it has two faces. It can be used by local groups in maintaining some independence from central government but it also, at least from the 19th century onwards, has allowed such autonomy only a provisional, limited and transient status; while it legitimates deviance from the dominant model imposed by the law of the state, it also implies an unequal relation between law and custom.[18] Customary law is not recognised as a model of society (except where the concept is introduced as the basis for a new law-code), but is seen as a mere aggregate of practices which people unready for change are reluctant to discard.

Modern Anglo-American law has concentrated much of its ideological effort on the elaboration of procedural rules and the concepts of 'due process' and 'fair trial'; contradictions often appear between the ritualised performances of the courts, the public face of law, and the unofficial practices which go on outside court: compromise, plea bargaining, police procedures, the granting of pardons in earlier periods and the condoning of the debts of zamindars in British India (Humphreys, Nippel and Whitcombe, below).[19]

Reference has already been made to the reification in laws and legal practice and in structurally related forms of social discourse of basic sociological assumptions: conceptions of normal honest social dealing (Udovitch), of the person (Humphreys), of status honour and the nature of power (Gilsenan), and of property rights (Whitcombe). Reification has to proceed tacitly; one does not constitute a world by discussing definitions.[20] Legal practice must present itself as legitimate at base (cf. Campbell, 1974); particular laws and judgments can be questioned, but to admit openly that law is a selective and often tendentious discourse, characterised by unequal power relations, would at the least imply radical changes in practice.

STRUCTURE AND HISTORY

My final point is particularly relevant to the question of the relations between history and anthropology. Law as discourse, as a combination of speech and action, is inherently historical and political. Laws are drafted and passed at particular moments in time in response to historically conditioned conceptions of society and its needs (cf. Moore, 1978, pp. 9-13; Humphreys, 1983); they are 'applied' and interpreted in particular cases. The concept of a legal system into which all these laws and interpretations are integrated is itself part of the practice of law, part of the status ethic of legal specialists; whether their practice is sufficiently consistent to make the concept useful for analysis is an empirical question which has to be asked afresh for each society.

To treat law as a part of the discourse about society does not therefore call for a static, synchronic description of a system or a language, but for an analysis of historically situated acts and utterances. In the study of myth, the application of structural analysis has, inevitably, led to the question why a particular version of a myth appears at a particular point in time[21] (Vernant, 1974:177-94; Vidal-Naquet and Le Goff, 1974; Lawrence, 1964), to a demand for an interpretation of myth as speech rather than as language (da Cunha, 1981). In general, those anthropologists who undertake historical research for themselves seem to me to be doing so out of dissatisfaction with synchronic analysis and the wish to understand the specific historical experience and processes out of which contemporary ideologies and configurations of power have emerged (cf. e.g. Gilsenan, below; O'Brien, 1971; Blok, 1974; Cole and

Wolf, 1974; Davis, 1977:ch. 6; Geertz, 1979; White, 1980; Kahn and Llobera, 1981; Peel, 1983). They assume that studying history involves studying events, conscious political decisions and power struggles, how actors interpret the logic of their own situations (Jarvie, 1964).[22]

This political interest on the part of anthropologists implies a certain danger that historians interested in anthropology and anthropologists interested in history may sail past each other in opposite directions, like ships in the night, without noticing it. For historians the interest in anthropology has come principally from the tradition of synchronic description of social institutions and *mentalités* particularly associated now with the *Annales* school. The polemical dichotomy between political *histoire événementielle* and the *longue durée* history of structures and *mentalités* introduced by the founders of the *Annales* to legitimate their enterprise is in danger of becoming canonised.[23] It is surely time to reunite the analysis of structures and systems with the historical actor's experience of social life as a series of events and choices (Bourdieu, 1977). *Montaillou*, one of the classic products of the *Annales* school (Le Roy Ladurie, 1975), seems to me from this point of view a sad example of opportunities missed; while Le Roy Ladurie provides a fine structural-functional analysis of the culture and social system of a late medieval village in the Pyrenees, he gives the reader little sense that his source is a document produced by an event involving intense political conflicts and a growing consciousness of schism between opposed world-views. The records of the inquisition carried out in 1318-1325 by the bishop of Pamiers, Jacques Fournier, in search of Albigensian heretics in Montaillou and neighbouring villages could also have provided materials for a case-study in the sociology of deviance and in the processes of local-level politics.

Contradictions in culture are sharpened by such events and become more visible in the historical record, rising to the surface of the social discourse (cf. Comaroff and Roberts, 1981); processual studies reveal the politics of culture in action. The passing of the Riot Act in 1715 also, as Nippel's article here shows, set in motion an intensified series of confrontations and debates in which the contradiction between the image of the state as wielder of supreme power (and therefore justified in quelling resistance by armed force) and the image of law as expressing the will of the people (and therefore adequately enforced by gentleman magistrates assisted by 'loyal citizens') became too patent for comfort. Similarly, it is by a study of historical process that Elizabeth Whitcombe reveals the contradictions generated by the British government in India's redefinition of the status and rights of the zamindars, tax-farmers under the Mughals, in terms of land-ownership.

Although it may be possible to predict some of the ideological stances likely to be taken up in such conflicts, comparative theory cannot map out their probable trajectory completely. Only detailed historical analysis of the genesis, interrelations, power bases, interests and social experience of competing classes, class fractions and elites[24] can explain how they will interpret each others' actions and structure their own discourse. If, as maintained here, some of the contradictions visible in the discourse of law are intrinsic to human society and not merely characteristic of specific class situations and modes of production, then one can not necessarily predict which ideals will be espoused by a ruling class and which by a subordinate class in any historical situation. Structures cannot be understood without the events and processes which produced them.

Notes

1. Ehrlich, 1913; Gierke, 1868-1913. On customary law see Moore, 1978:13-15, 20-21, and Chanock, 1978.
2. Gluckman has had a decisive impact on the anthropology of law in the U.S. as well as in Britain, though other influences can also be traced. Hoebel's attempt (1954) to develop the analysis of legal principles into a wider formulation of 'cultural postulates' (a fusion of Llewelyn's interests with the culture-configuration analysis of the Boasian school) represents an extreme example of the tendency to identify culture with 'rules'.
3. The work of the Manchester school also raised questions about the definition of 'law', since Marwick's study of witchcraft (1965) and Turner's account of Ndembu divination (1961) both presented processes of investigation and dispute settlement through 'social drama' in many ways analogous to the activities of courts. Problems of definition were much discussed in the 1960s but now receive little attention. See Moore, 1978: ch. 4; Comaroff and Roberts, 1981.
4. In other societies the shift of ground may be from substantive to procedural issues: Strathern, 1974:314-316. Where the judge or jury lacks local knowledge, the assumption may be that one of the court's main problems is to make good this deficit: see Davies, Humphreys and Udovitch, below, and Humphreys, 1983.
5. Cf. MacGaffey, 1970; Chanock, 1978; Fallers, 1979:62f.; Geertz, 1983:208ff. For parallel trends in the treatment of ethnicity see e.g. Ingold, 1976:ch. 21; Viazzo, 1983.
6. Cf. e.g. Bernstein, 1971ff.; Douglas, 1975; Bourdieu, 1977 (p. 16 on 'qadi justice'); and the papers by da Cunha, Udovitch and Humphreys, below.
7. See Thompson, 1975a:250; Sugarman in Sugarman, 1983:246-249. Even Veall, 1970, ostensibly concerned with a popular movement for law reform, lays much stress on the part played by lawyers in the movement; and the *Social History of Law* of Harding (1966) still concentrates largely on the process of legislation. The American legal realist movement, though claiming that law must respond to changes in society, represented an attempt to use sociology as a new basis for the lawyer's claim to know not only what the law is but also what it should become. In calling for a sociological jurisprudence, Pound had no intention of entrusting legislation to sociologists.
8. The adequacy of the lawyer-centred approach of course varies with the degree of power and autonomy acquired by legal experts in each society or period. It seems to me possible that Weber's interest in status honour and its role in legal history was partly influenced by Jhering, 1872.
9. Hobsbawm, 1959; Rudé, 1964; Hobsbawm and Rudé, 1969; Thompson, 1971, 1972; Tilly, 1975; Davis, 1975:97-151; Burke, 1978.
10. Weber has been used by anthropologists analysing constitutional history (Smith, 1960) and in the literature on modernisation (e.g. Eisenstadt, 1973); Geertz, 1979, and Gilsenan, 1982, are two modern Weberian studies which touch on developments in Islamic law.
11. Note Kuper's critical treatment of Maine's evolutionist theory, and Humphreys' rejection of evolutionist explanations of the role of witnesses as supporters in Athenian courts.
12. Tönnies' 'Gemeinschaft' and 'Gesellschaft' (1887) can be seen as aspects of western society

existing in complementary tension rather than the beginning and end of an evolutionary process.

13. As noted above, the assumption that expertise in law was the same in India as in Britain introduced considerable changes to the advantage of the Brahmans. With similar obtuseness British lawyers in India convinced themselves that in redefining the status of the zamindars they were merely codifying existing rights (cf. Whitcombe, below).
14. See Whitcombe, below. Her paper suggests that the reform was not as functionally indispensable as its authors assumed.
15. Cf. Derrett, 1961; Rudolph, 1965. Maine's later works (1871; 1883:ch.1) show much greater awareness of the changes introduced into Indian law by British rule.
16. E.g. Barkun, 1968:92; Fallers, 1969:ch. 1 and 314-317; Moore, 1978:7.
17. Cf. Aubert, 1966; Curtis and Speck, 1976; Elton, 1977; Hall a.o., 1978; Ignatieff, 1983:193. Hunt, 1982, argues that Marxists should cease to regard treating law as an ideological justification of property relations and treating it as a coercive means of suppressing working-class protest as alternative approaches, and try to arrive at a unitary theory encompassing both consent and coercion.
18. Moore, 1978:13-15, 20-21; Geertz, 1983:208ff. Distinctions between legislative and 'administrative' activity are also used: see Moore, 1981.
19. The harshness of the law in the 18th century was, however, also sometimes mitigated by using punctilious legalism as a means of rejecting charges: Hay, 1975a; Nippel, below. In the case of the zamindars the contradiction was incorporated into the legal code.
20. Where legal experts exist, it is a delicate matter to determine the threshold between concepts which have to be defined and assumptions which are taken for granted. One might paraphrase Dumont (1975:155) and say "The law-making creature does not like the making of law to be understood."
21. As one asks why, in the history of ideas, a theory appears at a particular time (cf. Kuper, below) or, in medicine, why a particular diagnosis is produced in a particular context (cf. *History and Anthropology*, II.1).
22. This conception of history may owe something to the way history is still taught in schools, and something to the more obviously political interests engaged in history-writing in new nations; but its main source is dissatisfaction with a comparative theory based only on synchronic studies.
23. See the discussion of the *Annales* and their influence in *Review* **1**, 3-4 (1978), especially the paper by Wesseling; also Clark, 1983; Ignatieff, 1983:193. French anthropologists of course have been associated with *Annales* for some time, but in Britain and the U.S. there has been little contact until recently and it is the macro-historical, rather than the synchronic aspects of the school's work which attract attention. Even Vansina (1978) who cites the *Annales* as offering a model for a less political type of history, still devotes considerable attention to individual decisions and historical configurations of power.
24. Note, for example, in the papers in this collection, the differences generated by the Ottoman state's predominantly military concern with North Lebanon, the British government in India's preoccupation with revenue, and the Brazilian government's interest in the effective control and exploitation of a large and underpopulated hinterland.

Bibliography

Aubert, V. (1966) "Some social functions of legislation" *Acta Sociologica* **10**:99-110.
Bailey, F.G. (1969) *Stratagems and Spoils*, Oxford: Blackwell.
Baker, J.H. (1971) *Introduction to English Legal History*, London: Butterworths.
Barkun, M. (1968) *Law without Sanctions. Order in primitive societies and the world community*, New Haven: Yale University Press.
Barnes, J.A. (1969) "The Politics of Law" in *Man in Africa*, M. Douglas and P. Kaberry, eds, London: Tavistock, pp. 99-118.
Barth, F. (1966) *Models of Social Organisation*, London: Royal Anthropological Institute (reprinted in Barth, 1981:32-47).

Barth, F. (1967) "On the Study of Social Change" *American Anthropologist* **65**:661-669 (reprinted in Barth, 1981:105-118).
Barth, F. (1981) *Process and Form in Social Life*, London: Routledge and Kegan Paul.
Bernstein, B. (1971ff.) *Class, Codes and Control*, I-III, London: Routledge and Kegan Paul.
Bloch, M. (1971) "On the moral and tactical meaning of kinship terms" *Man* **6**:79-87.
Bloch, M. (1975) "Introduction" in *Political Language and Oratory in Traditional Societies*, Bloch, ed., London: Academic Press, pp. 1-28.
Bloch, M. (1977) "The Past and the Present in the Present" *Man* **12**:278-292.
Blok, A. (1974) *The Mafia of a Sicilian Village, 1860-1960*, Oxford: Blackwell.
Bourdieu, P. (1977) *Outline of a Theory of Practice*, Cambridge: University Press (original French ed. Geneva: Droz, 1972).
Boyer, Paul, and Nissenbaum, S. (1974) *Salem Possessed. The Social origins of Witchcraft*, Cambridge, Mass.: Harvard University Press.
Brown, P.R.L. (1975) "Society and the Supernatural: a medieval change" *Daedalus* **104.2**:133-151 (reprinted in Brown, *Society and the Holy in Late Antiquity*, Berkeley: University of California, 1982:302-332).
Burke, Peter (1978) *Popular Culture in Early Modern Europe*, London: Temple Smith.
Campbell, C.M. (1974) "Legal Thought and Juristic Values" *British Journal of Law and Society* **1**:13-30.
Cappelletti, M., a.o., eds (1978-9) *Access to Justice* I-IV, Milan: Giuffré.
Carlen, Pat (1974) "Remedial Routines for the Maintenance of Control in Magistrates' Courts" *British Journal of Law and Society* **1**:101-117.
Chanock, M. (1978) "Neotraditionalism and the customary law in Malawi" *African Law Studies* **16**:80-91.
Cicourel, A. (1967) *The Social Organization of Juvenile Justice*, New York: Wiley.
Clark, Stuart (1983) "French historians and early modern popular culture" *Past and Present* **100**:62-99.
Cockburn, J.S., ed. (1977) *Crime in England 1550-1800*, London: Methuen.
Cohen, Stanley, ed. (1971) *Images of Deviance*, Harmondsworth: Penguin.
Cole, John W. and Wolf, Eric R. (1974) *The Hidden Frontier. Ecology and Ethnicity in an Alpine Valley*, London: Academic Press.
Colson, Elizabeth (1975) *Tradition and Contract: the problem of order*, London: Heinemann.
Comaroff, J.L. and Roberts, S. (1981) *Rules and Processes. The Cultural Logic of Dispute in an African Context*, Chicago: University Press.
Cooper, Frederick (1980) *From Slaves to Squatters*, New Haven: Yale University Press.
Cunha, M.C. da (1981) "Eschatology among the Krahó: reflection upon society, free field of fabulation" in *Mortality and Immortality*, S.C. Humphreys and H. King, eds, London: Academic Press, pp. 161-174.
Curtis, T.C. and Speck, W.A. (1976) "The Societies for the Reformation of Manners. A case study in the theory and practice of moral reform" *Literature and History* 3:45-64.
Davis, N.Z. (1975) *Society and Culture in Early Modern France*, London: Duckworth.
Derrett, J.D.M. (1961) "The Administration of Hindu Law by the British" *Comparative Studies in Society and History* **4**:10-52.
Douglas, Mary (1975) *Implicit Meanings*, London: Routledge and Kegan Paul.
Dumont, L. (1969) "Caste, Race and 'Stratification': reflections of a social anthropologist" in *Social Inequality*, A. Beteille, ed., Harmondsworth: Penguin, pp. 337-361.
Dumont, L. (1975) "On the Comparative Understanding of Non-modern Civilizations" *Daedalus* **104**, **2**:153-172.
Dumont, L. (1977) *Homo Aequalis. Genèse et épanouissement de l'idéologie économique*, Paris: Gallimard.
Dumont, L. (1983) *Essais sur l'individualisme*, Paris: Seuil.
Durkheim, E. (1893) *De la division du travail social*, Paris: Alcan.
Durkheim, E. (1895) *Les règles de la méthode sociologique*, Paris: Alcan.
Ehrlich, E. (1913) *Grundlegung der Soziologie des Rechts* (Eng. tr., *Fundamental Principles of the Sociology of Law*, Cambridge, Mass.: Harvard University Press, 1936).

Eisenstadt, S.N. (1973) *Tradition, Change and Modernity*, New York: Wiley.
Elkana, Y. (1981) "A Programmatic Attempt at an Anthropology of Knowledge", in *Sciences and Cultures. Sociology of the Sciences*, E. Mendelsohn and Y. Elkana, eds, **5**:1-76.
Elton, G. (1977) "Introduction: crime and the historian" in Cockburn, ed., 1977:1-14.
Epstein, A.L. (1967) "The case method in the field of law" in *The Craft of Social Anthropology*, Epstein, ed., London: Tavistock, pp. 205-230.
Evans, Richard (1984) "Öffentlichkeit und Autorität: zur Geschichte der Hinrichtungen in Deutschland 1794-1939" in *Historische Kriminalitätsforschung*, ed. Heinz Reif, Frankfurt a.M.: Suhrkamp.
Evans-Pritchard, E.E. (1949) *The Sanusi of Cyrenaica*, Oxford: Clarendon Press.
Fallers, Lloyd, A. (1969) *Law without Precedent. Legal ideas in action in the courts of central Busoga*, Chicago: University Press.
Feyerabend, P. (1975) *Against Method*, London: New Left Books.
Firth, Raymond (1930) "Marriage and the Classificatory System of Relationship" *Journal of the Royal Anthropological Institute* **60**:235-268.
Firth, Raymond (1951) *Elements of Social Organisation*, London: Watts.
Foucault, M. (1969) *L'archéologie du savoir*, Paris: Gallimard.
Foucault, M. (1971) *L'ordre du discours*, Paris: Gallimard.
Foucault, M. (1975) *Surveiller et punir*, Paris: Gallimard.
Garfinkel, H. (1967) "Some Rules of Correct Decision that Jurors Respect" in Garfinkel, *Studies in Ethnomethodology*, Englewood Cliffs, N.J.: Prentice-Hall: 104-115.
Geertz, C. (1979) "Suq: the Bazaar Economy in Morocco" in *Meaning and Order in Moroccan Society*, C. Geertz a.o., eds, Cambridge: University Press, 123-313.
Geertz, C. (1983) *Local Knowledge. Further Essays in Interpretive Anthropology*, New York: Basic Books.
Gernet, L. (1951) "Droit et prédroit en Grèce ancienne" *L'année sociologique*, ser. 3, 1948-9: 21-119 (reprinted in Gernet, *Anthropologie de la Grèce antique*, Paris: Maspero, 1968, 175-260).
Gierke, O. (1868-1913) *Das Deutsche Genossenschaftsrecht*, I-IV, Berlin: Weidmann.
Gilsenan, M. (1982) *Recognising Islam*, London: Croom Helm.
Girard, R. (1972) *La violence et le sacré*, Paris: Grasset.
Gluckman, Max (1962) "Les rites de passage" in *Essays on the Ritual of Social Relations*, Gluckman, ed., Manchester: University Press, 1-52.
Gluckman, Max (1965) *The Ideas in Barotse Jurisprudence*, New Haven: Yale University Press.
Goffman, E. (1963) *Stigma*, Englewood Cliffs, N.J.: Prentice-Hall.
Goody, J.R. (1977) *The Domestication of the Savage Mind*, Cambridge: University Press.
Grace, Clive, and Wilkinson, Philip (1978) *Sociological Inquiry and Legal Phenomena*, London: Macmillan.
Gulliver, P.H. (1963) *Social Control in an African Society*, London: Routledge and Kegan Paul.
Hall, Stuart, a.o. (1978) *Policing the Crisis: Mugging, the State and Law and Order*, London: Macmillan.
Harding, Alan (1966) *A Social History of English Law*, Harmondsworth: Penguin.
Hay, Douglas (1975a) "Property, Authority and the Criminal Law" in Hay a.o. eds, 1975:17-63.
Hay, Douglas (1975b) "Poaching and the Game Laws on Cannock Chase" in Hay a.o. eds, 1975:189-253.
Hay, Douglas, a.o., eds (1975) *Albion's Fatal Tree*, London: Allen Lane.
Hirst, Paul (1977) *On Law and Ideology*, London: Macmillan.
Hobsbawm, E.J. (1959) *Primitive Rebels*, Manchester: University Press.
Hobsbawm, E.J. and Ranger, T., eds (1983) *The Invention of Tradition*, Cambridge: University Press.
Hoebel, E.A. (1954) *The Law of Primitive Man*, Cambridge, Mass.: Harvard University Press.
Humphreys, S.C. (1983) "The Evolution of Legal Process in Ancient Attica" in *Tria Corda, Scritti in onore di Arnaldo Momigliano*, E. Gabba, ed., Como: New Press: 229-256.
Humphreys, S.C. (1984) review of L. Gernet, *Anthropology of Ancient Greece* (Baltimore: Johns Hopkins, 1981) *Man* **19**: 177
Hunt, Alan (1982) "Dichotomy and Contradiction in the Sociology of Law" in *Marxism and*

Law, Piers Beirne and R. Quinney, eds, New York: Wiley: 74-97.
Ignatieff, M. (1983) "State, Civil Society and Total Institution: a critique of recent social histories of punishment" in Sugarman, ed., 1983:183-211.
Ingold, T. (1976) *The Skolt Lapps Today*, Cambridge: University Press.
Jarvie, I.C. (1964) *The Revolution in Anthropology*, London: Routledge and Kegan Paul.
Jessop, Bob (1980) "On Recent Marxist Theories of Law, the State and Juridico-Political Ideology" *International Journal of the Sociology of Law* **8**:339-368.
Jhering, R. von (1872) *Der Kampf um's Recht*, Vienna: Manz.
Kahn, J.S. (1981) "Mercantilism and the emergence of servile labour in colonial Indonesia" in Kahn and Llobera, 1981a, 185-213.
Kahn, J.S. and Llobera, J.R., eds (1981a) *The Anthropology of Pre-Capitalist Societies*, London: Macmillan.
Kahn, J.S. and Llobera, J.R. (1981b) "Towards a new Marxism or a new anthropology?" in Kahn and Llobera, 1981a, 263-324.
Kronman, A.T. (1983) *Max Weber*, London: Arnold.
Kuhn, T.S. (1962) *The Structure of Scientific Revolutions*, Chicago: University Press.
Lawrence, Peter (1964) *Road Belong Cargo*, Manchester: University Press.
Leach, E.R. (1954) *Political Systems of Highland Burma*, London: Athlone Press (2nd. rev. ed. 1964).
Leach, E.R. (1961) *Pul Eliya*, Cambridge: University Press.
Le Goff, J. and Vidal Naquet, P. (1974) "Lévi-Strauss en Broceliande" *Critique* **325**:541-571.
Le Roy Ladurie, E. (1975) *Montaillou, village occitan de 1294 à 1324*, Paris: Gallimard.
Llewellyn, Karl, and Hoebel, E.A. (1941) *The Cheyenne Way*, Norman: University of Oklahoma.
Lloyd, G.E.R. (1979) *Magic, Reason and Experience*, Cambridge: University Press.
Macaulay, Stewart (1963) "Non-contractual relations in business" *American Sociological Review* **28**:55-66.
MacFarlane, Alan (1981) *The Justice and the Mare's Ale*, Oxford: Blackwell.
MacGaffey, W. (1970) *Custom and Government in the Lower Congo*, Berkeley: University of California.
Maine, H.S. (1861) *Ancient Law*, London: Murray.
Maine, H.S. (1871) *Village Communities in East and West*, London: Murray.
Maine, H.S. (1883) *Dissertations on Early Law and Custom*, London: Murray.
Malinowski, B. (1926) *Crime and Custom in Savage Society*, London: Kegan Paul.
Marwick, M.G. (1965) *Sorcery in its social setting*, Manchester: University Press.
Marx, E. (1972) "Some social contexts of personal violence" in *The Allocation of Responsibility*, Max Gluckman, ed., Manchester: University Press, 281-321.
Momigliano, A. (1950) "Ancient History and the Antiquarian" *Journal of the Warburg and Courtauld Institutes* **13**:285-315 (reprinted in Momigliano, *Contributo alla storia degli studi classici*, Rome: Storia e Letteratura, 1955, 67-106).
Moore, Sally F. (1978) *Law as Process*, London: Routledge and Kegan Paul.
Moore, Sally F. (1981) "Chagga 'customary' law and the property of the dead" in *Mortality and Immortality*, S.C. Humphreys and H. King, eds, London: Academic Press, 225-248.
Nicolet, C. (1976) *Le métier du citoyen*, Paris: Gallimard.
O'Brien, D.B. Cruise (1971) *The Mourides of Senegal. The Political and Economic Organisation of an Islamic Brotherhood*, Oxford: Clarendon Press.
Peel, J.D.Y. (1983) *Ijeshas and Nigerians. The Incorporation of a Yoruba Kingdom, 1890s-1970s*, Cambridge: University Press.
Ranger, T. "The Invention of Tradition in Colonial Africa" in Hobsbawm and Ranger, eds, 1983:211-262.
Renner, Karl (1904) *The Institutions of Private Law and their Social Functions* (Eng. tr. 1949 of 1929 ed.) London: Routledge and Kegan Paul.
Rudé, G. (1964) *The Crowd in History*, New York: Wiley.
Rudolph, L.I. and S.H. (1965) "Barristers and Brahmans in India: legal cultures and social change" *Comparative Studies in Society and History* **8**:24-49.
Sander, Frank and Snyder, F.E. (1979) *Alternative Methods of Dispute Settlement — a selected*

bibliography, Washington: American Bar Association.
Sharpe, J.A. (1980) "Enforcing the law in the 17th century English village" in *Crime and the Law. The social history of crime since 1800*, V.A.C. Gatrell a.o., eds, London: Europa, 97-119.
Shubert, A. (1981) "Private Initiative in Law Enforcement: Associations for the Prosecution of Felons, 1744-1856" in *Policing and Punishment in Nineteenth Century Britain*, V. Bailey, ed., London: Croom Helm, 25-41.
Smith, M.G. (1960) *Government in Zazzau*, London: Oxford University Press.
Strathern, M. (1974) "Managing information: the problems of a dispute-settler (Mount Hagen)" in *Contention and Dispute*, A.L. Epstein, ed., Canberra: Australian National University, 271-316.
Sugarman, D., ed. (1983) *Legality, Ideology and the State*, London: Academic Press.
Thompson, E.P. (1971) "The Moral Economy of the English Crowd in the 18th century" *Past and Present* **50**:76-136.
Thompson, E.P. (1972) "Rough Music! le charivari anglais" *Annales E.S.C.* **27**:285-313.
Thompson, E.P. (1975a) *Whigs and Hunters. The origin of the Black Act*, Harmondsworth: Penguin.
Thompson, E.P. (1975b) "The Crime of Anonymity" in Hay a.o., eds., 1975:255-344.
Thompson, E.P. (1979) "The Secret State" *Race and Class* **20**:219-242.
Thompson, E.P. (1981) "The Jury System: an endangered species", lecture delivered at University College London.
Tilly, C., L. and R. (1975) *The Rebellious Century 1830-1930*, Cambridge, Mass: Harvard University Press.
Tönnies, F. (1887) *Gemeinschaft und Gesellschaft* (Eng. tr. *Community and Society*, Ann Arbor: Michigan State University Press, 1957).
Turner, V.W. (1961) "Ndembu Divination: its Symbolism and Techniques" *Rhodes-Livingstone Papers* 31 (reprinted in Turner, *The Drums of Affliction*, Oxford: Clarendon Press, 1968).
Twining, W. (1973) *Karl Llewellyn and the Realist Movement*, London: Weidenfeld and Nicolson.
Vansina, J. (1978) *The Children of Woot*, Madison: University of Wisconsin.
Veall, D. (1970) *The Popular Movement for Law Reform, 1640-1660*, Oxford: Clarendon Press.
Vernant, J.-P. (1974) *Mythe et société en Grèce ancienne*, Paris: Maspero.
Viazzo, P.P. (1983) *Ethnic Change in a Walser Community in the Italian Alps*, Ph.D. thesis, University of London.
Weber, Max (1922) *Wirtschaft and Gesellschaft* (references to Eng. tr., *Economy and Society*, Berkeley: University of California, 1978).
Wesseling, H.L. (1978) "The *Annales* School and the Writing of Contemporary History" *Review* **1.3/4**:185-194.
White, Caroline (1980) *Patrons and Partisans: a study of politics in two southern Italian comuni*, Cambridge: University Press.

Ancestors: Henry Maine and the constitution of primitive society

ADAM KUPER

University of Leiden, Netherlands

Maine was the most important English figure in a generation of legal theorists who founded the comparative study of "early" social institutions. He assumed that all the Indo-Germanic speaking peoples began their development with the same social forms. Early Roman law and contemporary Hindu custom encapsulated primitive Indo-European institutions, notably the patriarchal family and the communal organisation of property rights. Maine's arguments were developed in part as a contribution to contemporary political debate, especially with reference to the Indian Empire. His work drew on the models of philology, German legal history, and English constitutional history.

ORIGINS AND EVOLUTION

DARWIN'S *The Origin of Species* appeared in 1859, Henry Maine's *Ancient Law* in 1861. Darwin and Maine shared a general concern with origins and development. They were even united under a common imprint, the publisher John Murray bringing off a series of coups. Yet Maine was not influenced by Darwin until very late in his career, and he can only very loosely be termed an evolutionist. He paid little attention to the biological arguments raging in London between the rival ethnologists and anthropologists.[1] (To the extent that he took sides he inclined to the anti-Darwinian position that the various races had separate origins). If a tentative label is helpful, he was rather a Whig constitutional historian.

The race theorists were generally medical men.[2] The writers who developed a model of "primitive society" in the second half of the nineteenth century were mostly jurists. Maine and Bachofen were professors of Roman law, as was Köhler, while Morgan, McLennan, and a number of lesser figures, were practicising lawyers. On the whole they were remote from the biologists. Nor did they merge with the classicists who were inspired by Tylor, although some of them had personal contacts with Tylor himself. Tylor's own *Researches into the Early History of Mankind and Development of Civilization* (1865) and his

History and Anthropology, 1985
Vol. 1, pp. 265-286
0275-7206/85/0102-0265 $18.50/0

Primitive Culture (1871) largely ignored the new sociological ideas, being concerned above all with matters of belief and thought. Only the French classicist, Fustel de Coulanges, married the preoccupations of a Tylor and a Maine, his *La Cité Antique* (1864) linking the evolution of belief with the development of institutions.

If Darwin was not the inspiration — more generally, if biology and geology provided little more than illustrative analogies in their work — what were the origins of the model of "primitive society" developed by these Victorian jurists? J.W. Burrow addressed the question in his influential study, *Evolution and Society*, and identified various sources. I shall briefly review the scholarly background to Maine's work, differing from Dr. Burrow only occasionally in emphasis or substance. (His recent book, *A Liberal Descent: Victorian Historians and the English Past* provides the ammunition for some revision of his earlier view of Maine.) But it is not enough to trace Maine's sources; the thrust of his argument is not conventionally academic. Maine's scholarship was bound in the service of a political theory and a reading of *Ancient Law* also requires an understanding of its polemical context. After discussing Maine's scholarly sources, therefore, I will try to place *Ancient Law* with respect to the political agenda of his day.

MAINE, ROMAN LAW, AND COMPARATIVE PHILOLOGY

Raised in conditions of shabby gentility,[3] Henry Maine went up to Cambridge in 1840 where he enjoyed a brilliant undergraduate career, marked by such Cambridge triumphs as the award of the Chancellor's medal for English verse (for a poem on the birth of the Prince of Wales), and election to the Apostles' Club. In 1844 he became Senior Classic and accepted a fellowship at Trinity Hall, a law college, where he began to specialise in Roman Law. In 1847 (a friend's father having the decisive voice) he was appointed Regius Professor of Civil Law at Cambridge, at the age of twenty-five. According to a friend, James Fitzjames Stephen, the professorship was an "ill-paid sinecure", and in 1852 Maine took a Readership in Roman Law in the Middle Temple, resigning his Cambridge chair two years later.

The testimony of students suggests that the substance of *Ancient Law* was handled by Maine in his lectures in London, and even earlier in Cambridge. Burrow accordingly identified the decade to 1853 as the crucial period in Maine's theoretical development, but commented that these years "are also among the blankest in our knowledge of his life" (1966: 140). (Lady Maine did not preserve her husband's papers, and according to a grandson she threw away his letters from famous writers after cutting off their signatures for sale.)

However, in the legal field Maine certainly derived his ideas and information largely from the German historical jurists, and his method was suggested in part by the philologists dealing with Indo-European languages. Although sometimes separated in discussion of Maine, these historical lawyers and historical linguists represented a single intellectual enterprise. Led by Savigny, it was a central force in the romantic nationalist movement in Germany in the nineteenth century.[4]

Savigny, a conservative Prussian nobleman, achieved early fame with a pamphlet published in 1814 which attacked the proposal to codify the civil law of the newly united German state. Codification was associated with French domination and generally with radical plans for rationalisation and change. Savigny put the case against codification in both theoretical and nationalist terms: in terms, indeed, that provided a theoretical foundation for a nationalist law policy. He argued that a legal system is an historical product of a nation, comparable to language, the expression of what came to be called a *Volksgeist.* It was not a proper instrument for radical change, although gradual, properly adjusted legal changes were sometimes valuable. The great example was the reception of Roman law in medieval Germany. Savigny argued that the German *doctores iuris* had made innovations which were in the spirit of the national law, allowing the *Volksgeist* to manifest itself even through Roman borrowings (an idea which Savigny may have borrowed from Jacob Grimm's distinction between *Natur und Kunstpoesie* (cf. Kantorowicz, 1937: 338). This was the central theme of his multi-volume life work, *Die Geschichte des römischen Rechts im Mittelalter*, sections of which continued to be published until 1850.

Some "Germanists" disputed the value Savigny attached to the reception of Roman law, while there were also "Romanists", notably Jhering, who developed a less nationalistic version of the argument. Jhering insisted in his *Geist des römischen Rechts* that the reception of foreign legal institutions was determined not by nationality but rather by expediency. Maine appears to have been influenced particularly by Jhering, but the differences within the school of German historical jurists were not critical to his own enterprise.

The analogy between law and language was not fortuitous. To the German romantics, language was the primary expression of the *Volksgeist*, and folktales crystallized the anonymous genius of the people. Jacob Grimm was a pupil of Savigny, and Grimm's study of German languages and folktales was also linked with his constitutional theories of the early German village communities.

Philology[5] was a field of special interest as a consequence of the discovery that the classical languages of Europe and India were related. Bopp revealed the structural similarities of declensions in Sanskrit, Greek and Latin. Jacob Grimm identified regular consonant-shifts in Proto-Indo-European (Grimm's Law), reducing to simple rules the processes involved in sound-shifts between languages as different as German, Greek, and Sanskrit. These discoveries were held to provide insights into the racial psychology and history of the German peoples.

Maine introduced the historical jurisprudence of Savigny and Jhering to Britain, but the achievements of Indo-European philology were already known, largely through the lectures of Max Müller. Max Müller had also provided striking comparisons of Sanskrit, Greek and Roman myths. Maine regularly referred back to the methods of comparative philology, but in very general terms. He was in practice indebted to the philologists only for the definition of his comparative field, the Indo-European speaking peoples.

As a comparativist, Maine was less innovative than is sometimes supposed. German historians regularly made bold comparisons in order to strengthen their inferences and Lord Acton, in his review, "German schools of history", first published in 1886, linked the work of Maine and Fustel de Coulanges with that of Humboldt, Savigny, Grimm, and Ritter, and gave them all credit for the new vitality of comparative history. "They trifled for a time with fancy, but they doubled the horizons of Europe. They admitted India to an equality with Greece, mediaeval Rome with classical ..." (Acton, 1907:346).

CONSTITUTIONAL HISTORIAN

Roman history and Indo-European philology were exotic, German specialities, but Maine's *Ancient Law* also had a great deal in common with the constitutional histories which formed one of the dominant intellectual genres in Victorian Britain. The mood of this historiography was dominantly "Whig" and progressive. Whig history did not rest with the Glorious Revolution. Varieties of whiggish constitutional history dealt also with Anglo-Saxon liberty and even foreign despotism.[6] One example of an exotic Whig history was James Mill's *History of British India* (which Macaulay called "the greatest historical work which has appeared in our language since that of Gibbon" (quoted Clive, 1973:310)). Mill, who was to be the main architect of Britain's India policy, provided a comparative review of traditional Indian society and argued that it was backward and despotic, and consequently ripe for reform. This "historical" argument neatly inverted the message of the Anglo-Saxon historians, who introduced a model of early Teutonic democracy to emphasize the historical depth of the British democratic virtues.

Although their message had to do with the peculiar purity of English liberty, the English medievalists borrowed directly from the German nationalist school. Grimm had developed an image of the democratic, communist, patriarchal *mark*-community. John Kemble, a student of Grimm, established the model in English scholarship, in his two-volume study, *The Saxons in England* (1849). (He had played an important part in the compilation of *Ancient Laws and Institutes of England*, published in 1840. Its title may have suggested to Maine the title of his own work.) This model of the *mark* inspired populist thinkers all over Europe, and also stimulated conservative racial nostalgia.[7] It served Maine as the type-case of the ancient or primitive community.

British constitutional history was a way of writing about contemporary political principles, and this remained true even in the second half of the nineteenth century, when the traditional opposition between Whig and Burkean constitutional history was increasingly blurred. If Maine is a constitutional historian in this tradition, then what constitution did he seek to explain? And from what political standpoint?

THE POLITICAL CONTEXT

When he arrived in London in the early eighteen-fifties, Maine became not only a law lecturer but also an active political journalist, and one of the founders of the *Saturday Review*. A Peelite Whig, he championed aristocratic forms of government and set himself against the extension of the suffrage and the erosion of traditional authority. He also defended the traditional form of the Indian Empire, then in a state of upheaval. "That wonderful succession of events which has brought the youngest civilization in the world to instruct and correct the oldest, which has reunited those wings of the Indo-European race which separated in the far infancy of time to work out their strangely different missions, which has avenged the miscarriages of the Crusades ..." (In W. Stokes, 1892:16.)

The future of India, perhaps the central political question of the mid-fifties, raised legal and philosophical issues of intense interest.[8] The Indian government was committed to respect indigenous law and custom by the theory of dual rule, and officials of a Burkean persuasion genuinely wished to conserve customary legal arrangements. Yet the Permanent Settlement of Bengal in 1793 had already introduced Whig principles of government, above all the principle that individual rights in land should be established and maintained by law. These were the main planks of the platform of the "anglicising" party, a coalition of evangelists, free traders, dirigiste bureaucrats and philosophical radicals, amongst whom the Utilitarians were prominent.

Jeremy Bentham had taken a keen interest in Indian affairs, and had hoped that India might provide the laboratory for his system of law. His theory of law was derived from his "calculus" of individual interests, which was designed to promote the rational pursuit of happiness. Faced, inevitably, with the problem of reconciling individual happiness and the public good, Bentham chose to rely on legislation. Imposed by a sovereign, the purpose of law was to be prevent individuals from interfering with the happiness of others. This doctrine was related to the traditional radical belief in the Social Contract, particularly to Hume's formulation of the doctrine in which both individual adherence to contracts and the attachment to a state flowed independently from a similar perception of self-interest. Working from these principles, Bentham, and his disciple John Austin, developed elaborate legal codes which were designed to promote rational individual freedom, but which remained largely theoretical. Hence the hope for an Indian experiment. Bentham had even selected his instrument. "Mill will be the living executive", Bentham said, "I shall be the dead legislative of British India".[9])

Mill obliged. His *History of British India*, published in 1817, presented the argument for reform, using the accepted vehicle of a constitutional history. Traditional India was plagued by tyranny and unreason: "despotism and priestcraft taken together, the Hindus, in mind and body, were the most enslaved portion of the human race" (Mill, 1817, vol. 2:167). The solution was a code designed on good Utilitarian principles. Fortunately there was no practical hindrance. "As I believe that India stands more in need of a code than any other country in the world, I believe also that there is no country on which that great benefit can more easily be conferred. A Code is almost the only blessing — perhaps it is the only blessing — which absolute governments are better fitted to confer on a nation than popular governments." (Cited in E. Stokes, 1959:219.)

Appointed to a senior position in the India Office, Mill was instrumental in promoting Utilitarian principles in Indian government. He was especially committed to the development of individual property rights. As Eric Stokes commented, he believed that "the marking off of individual property rights in the soil would act as a solvent of the traditional joint-ownership and communal control" (1959:69). His protegé, Macaulay, became Legal Member of the Viceroy's Council and in 1835 he designed a Penal Code on pure Benthamite principles.

The reform movement lost its impetus, however. Mill died and Macaulay's plans were shelved. In the 'fifties there was a mild revival of the reform programme, and in 1856 a law commission recommended the preparation of a code of civil law, which was to be based on simplified English law modified to suit Indian conditions. In 1857 the Sepoy Mutiny occurred, giving the debate a new urgency. In 1860 Macaulay's Penal Code was finally enacted.

Maine commented dismissively: "As to the Penal Code, nobody cares about criminal law except theorists and habitual criminals" (Feaver, 1969:102-3). Civil law, however, was a different matter entirely. He published a long series of articles in the *Saturday Review*, urging the maintenance of the dual system. His familiarity with the work of Savigny and Jhering must immediately have suggested the parallels between the Indian debate and the controversies about the reception of Roman Law in primitive German societies. Moreover, the German debate had precisely been in the context of how codification and legal reform could be reconciled with a respect for traditional law. In *Ancient Law*, drawing on these sources, he offered a solution to the apparent conflict between Indian and British legal ideas, and between Utilitarian and conservative views on Indian government. *Ancient Law* was a prospective constitutional history — at once Whig and Burkean — of the India he hoped to see.

ANCIENT LAW

The argument of *Ancient Law*[10] falls into three parts. The first (chapters 1 to 3) presents an account of the development of law. The second (chapters 4 and 5) criticises the theory of the state of nature and substitutes a model of primitive society. The third (chapters 6 to 10) offers histories of testamentary disposition, private property, contract and delict. The sources of these sections are different, and they rely on distinct modes of argument. They are therefore best treated separately in the first instance, before an attempt is made to assess the book as a whole.

Maine's account of the original forms of law was directly addressed to the orthodoxy of Bentham and Austin, who "resolve every law into a *command* of the lawgiver, an *obligation* imposed thereby on the citizen, and a *sanction* threatened in the event of disobedience . . ." This was a fairly accurate description of the conditions of "mature jurisprudence", but "it is curious that the farther we penetrate into the primitive history of thought, the farther we find ourselves from a conception of law which at all resembles a compound of the elements which Bentham determined. It is certain that, in the infancy of mankind, no sort of legislature, not even a distinct author of law, is contemplated or conceived of" (4-5). The early system might seem strange, he admitted, but it "will become more credible when we dwell more at length on the constitution of ancient society, in which every man, living during the greater part of his life under the patriarchal despotism, was practically controlled in all his actions by a regimen not of law but of caprice".[5]

The first laws were judgments delivered on the basis of divine inspiration. In time an aristocracy displaced the divinely-inspired leaders: in the west a political oligarchy, in the east a priestly caste. They took over the judicial role of the king, but did not pretend to divine inspiration. Instead the elite claimed a monopoly of knowledge of custom. "We have in fact arrived at the epoch of Customary Law. Customs or Observances now exist as a substantive aggregate, and are assumed to be precisely known to the aristocratic order or caste."(7.)

With the invention of writing the oligarchy lost its monopoly of knowledge: the customs were set down in codes. This seems a simple proposition, but Maine complicated matters by suggesting that somehow there was a moment when the system was ripe for codification. The Roman code, the Twelve Tables, "was compiled while the usage was still wholesome, and a hundred years afterwards it might have been too late". The Hindu codes, however, had been corrupted. The masses had got their hands on the law and corrupted it with irrational superstitions. (11-12.)

But how, once codified, could rational and useful changes be introduced in the law? (In progressive societies "it may be laid down that social necessities and social opinion are always more or less in advance of the law" (15).) Progressive change certainly had occurred in at least a few systems, of which the Roman was the best documented. Maine suggested that three mechanisms operated, in successive periods, to achieve legal change. These were Legal Fictions, Equity, and Legislation.

This may seem a curious trinity of instruments of reform, but once again the logic of the argument can be grasped immediately one considers its relevance to the theories of Bentham and Austin. They had given all the credit to legislation: Maine postponed its impact until relatively late in the day. They had also maligned Legal Fictions, and adopted a specific and vulnerable theory of Equity. (In Britain, "Equity" referred to the traditional right of the Chancellor to modify the law in accordance with general conceptions of justice.) Maine's historical sequence was designed to controvert them on every point.

Legal Fictions, in Bentham's view, were amongst the mystifications deployed by despots to retard progress.[11] A Legal Fiction was "a wilful falsehood, having for its object the stealing of legislative power, by and for hands which could not, or durst not, openly claim it, and but for the delusion thus produced could not exercise it". "Fiction of use to justice? Exactly as swindling is to trade."

Maine (following Savigny and Jhering)[12] took a very different view. The Legal Fictions were originally not instruments of reaction, but, on the contrary, mechanisms of progressive reform. They produced changes which the élite recognised to be necessary, while maintaining the illusion, so much cherished by the conservative majority, that nothing had really changed. They "satisfy the desire for improvement at the same time that they do not offend the superstitious disrelish for change ..." (16.) Yet this did not imply that Maine was in favour of retaining obscurantist features of the law. Bentham's view of Legal Fictions is wrong, but Legal Fictions are now no longer necessary; they have become a source of confusion and should be "pruned away"; more efficacious mechanisms of change had made them redundant.

The next mechanism of change was Equity. In Rome, Equity was administered by the Praetors, and initially it applied especially in cases which involved foreigners. Foreigners were governed by the Law of Nations, which was derived from the common customs of various Italian communities, but this law left many gaps. Borrowing the Greek notion of a Law of Nature, which should apply universally, the Roman jurists developed rules based on more abstract principles. These gradually found application in the civil law itself. A cadre of jurisconsults emerged who extended and rationalised the developing system of "Equity". Yet (like the anachronistic Equity forms in English law), the possibilities of the system were eventually played out: "... in the reign of Alexander Severus the power of growth in Roman Equity seems to be exhausted, and the succession of jurisconsults comes to a close. The remaining history of the Roman law is the history of the imperial constitutions, and, at the last, of attempts to codify what had now become the unwieldy body of Roman jurisprudence." (40.)

The view of legal history presented in the first three chapters of *Ancient Law* systematically inverts Benthamite assumptions. The Benthamite *a priori* is controverted by the creation of an "historical" sequence. The brevity of the review — forty pages in the Everyman edition — from which must be deducted many pages of mere rhetoric — suggests accurately enough the lack of documentation. There is in fact nothing in this review which could not have been gleaned from Gibbon's famous forty-fourth chapter, in which he reviews the development of Roman law. The thrust of the appeals to Roman law is beautifully caught by Maine's friend J.F. Stephen — "He was enabled to sniff at Bentham for knowing nothing about it, & writing in consequence about English law, in a merely revolutionary manner ..." (Quoted Feaver, 1969:25.)

THE STATE OF NATURE AND PRIMITIVE SOCIETY

Having sketched an anti-Benthamite myth of legal origins, Maine turned in the fourth chapter to direct philosophical attack. The ancient theory of Natural Law, from which the Romans had derived Equity, was the source of modern error. The Romans had applied Natural Law theory in a sober fashion, constrained by constant reference to the realities of Italian customary rules, and so had been spared the worst excesses of a philosophy which Maine called "the ancient counterpart to Benthamism" (p. 46). The modern French theorists, however, had abandoned the empirical and historical checks. "The theory is still that of the Roman lawyers ..., but the theory is, as it were turned upside down. It is not the Law of Nature, but the State of Nature, which is now the primary subject of contemplation." (52.) Rousseau and the French philosophers believed "that a perfect social order could be evolved from the unassisted consideration of the natural state, a social order wholly irrespective of the actual condition of the world and wholly unlike it". (52.) Anti-historical, it was in fact "the great antagonist of the Historical Method" (53). It had "helped most powerfully to bring about the gross disappointments of which the first French Revolution was fertile", and had stimulated "the vices of mental habit all but universal at the time, disdain of positive law, impatience of experience, and preference of a priori to all other reasoning". (53-4.) The only positive contribution which the Law of Nature had made in modern times was in its influence on the development of International Law (pp. 56-66).[13]

The theory of a Law of Nature and a State of Nature was to be countered by the Historical Method, by scientific procedures designed to "penetrate as far up as we could in the history of primitive societies" (70-1). This is the aim of the most famous chapter in *Ancient Law*, chapter five, entitled "Primitive Society and Ancient Law".

THE PATRIARCHAL THEORY

The basic hypothesis was simple. "The effect of the evidence derived from comparative jurisprudence is to establish that view of the primeval condition of the human race which is known as the Patriarchal Theory".

> Men are first seen distributed in perfectly insulated groups, held together by obedience to the parent. Law is the parent's word . . . society in primitive times was not what it is assumed to be at present, a collection of *individuals*. In fact, and in the view of the men who composed it, it was an *aggregation of families*. The contrast may be most forcibly expressed by saying that the unit of an ancient society was the Family, of a modern society the Individual. (74.)

Gradually family groups coalesced, but the overriding principle of social formation remained "kinship in blood".

> The history of political ideas begins, in fact, with the assumption that kinship in blood is the sole possible ground of community in political functions; nor is there any of those subversions of feeling, which we term emphatically revolutions, so startling and so complete as the change which is accomplished when some other principle — such as that, for instance, of *local contiguity* — establishes itself for the first time as the basis of common political action. It may be affirmed then of early commonwealths that their citizens considered all the groups in which they claimed membership to be founded on common lineage. What was obviously true of the Family was believed to be true first of the House, next of the Tribe, lastly of the State. (76.)

The movement from "blood" to "soil" is perfunctorily sketched. Initially waifs and strays were incorporated into flourishing family groups by means of the first and greatest of the Legal Fictions, Adoption, consecrated by shared sacrifices. "The composition of the state, uniformly assumed to be natural, was nevertheless known to be in great measure artificial" (77). Gradually, however, the members of the inner core began to discriminate against the individuals who became attached to the group through weakness. In time a majority of second-class citizens grew up, and they developed an alternative ideology of civil rights. "Their sternness in maintaining the central principle of a system under which political rights were attainable on no terms whatever except connexion in blood, real or artificial, taught their inferiors another principle, which proved to be endowed with a far greater measure of vitality. This was the principle of local *contiguity*, now recognized everywhere as the condition of community in political functions" (78).

Maine's evidence for his Patriarchal Theory depended essentially on his reading of Roman law. He made brief references to Homer and to the Old Testament, but he rested his case on the Roman notions of agnation.

The Romans distinguished a category of "agnates", relatives traced exclusively through males. "The foundation of Agnation is not the marriage of Father and Mother, but the authority of the Father" (88). Only people under the authority of the patriarch were related. "In truth, in the primitive view, Relationship is exactly limited by Patria Potestas". (88.) When the patriarch died the group faded away, but the original relationships were preserved by the mould of Agnation, and the legal emphasis on Agnation reflects the primitive arrangements. "The Powers themselves are discernable in comparatively few monuments of ancient law, but Agnatic Relationship, which implies their former existence, is discoverable almost everywhere. There are few indigenous bodies of law belonging to communities of the Indo-European stock, which do not exhibit peculiarities in the most ancient part of their structure which are clearly referable to Agnation." (88.) Any emphasis on what we would today call patrilineal principles therefore provided evidence for the original patriarchal system. Contrary evidence, however, did not weaken the model. "The Praetors early laid hold on Cognation as the *natural* form of kinship, and spared no pains in purifying their system from the older conception. Their ideas have descended to us, but still traces of Agnation are to be seen ..." (89.)

The weakness of the argument is apparent from the fact that in the same year as *Ancient Law* appeared, another professor of Roman Law, J. Bachofen, also using classical sources, demonstrated to his own satisfaction that the original condition of society was clearly "matriarchal". Maine's argument was, however, perhaps more acceptable to contemporaries since it echoed the model of ancient German societies developed by Grimm and translated to England in Kemble's *The Saxons in England*, which had appeared in 1849 and enjoyed great success. In these works the aboriginal communities were described as "great family unions ... some, in direct descent from the common ancestors ... others, more distantly connected ..., some admitted into communion by marriage, others by adoption ... but all recognising a brotherhood, a kinsmanship" (1849:56-7.) All, moreover, held property in common. The *Sippe* was not universally conceived of as an agnatic group, but this was certainly one of the main theories of the Germanists of Maine's day.

There was also a tradition in Indian scholarship which yielded a similar model of primitive communities.[14] Mill in his *History of British India* had traced an evolution from scattered family groups, to divinely-inspired authorities, to monarchy, in a passage which clearly anticipates Maine. He even wrote that:

> it was the usual arrangement in early stages of society, for the different members of a family to live together; and to possess the property in common. The father was rather the head of a

number of partners, than the sole proprietor ... The laws of inheritance among the Hindus are almost entirely founded upon this patriarchal arrangement. (Mill, 1817:146.)

And he cited Millar to the effect that among barbarians family members always enjoyed community of property.

The most profound source of the patriarchal theory is, however, more likely to have been philosophical. It served the dual purpose of providing a foil to the modern, territorial state and to the atomistic, free society of the French philosophers of a State of Nature. (Maine stressed particularly the despotic and arbitrary power of the patriarch: man was everywhere born in chains.) Modern society had emerged from its contrary — that is, if modern society is conceived of as based on individual freedom.

The movement of progressive societies has been uniform in one respect. Through all its course it has been distinguished by the gradual dissolution of family dependency and the growth of individual obligation in its place ... Nor is it difficult to see what is the tie between man and man which replaces by degrees those forms of reciprocity in rights and duties which have their origin in the Family. It is Contract. Starting, as from one terminus of history, from a condition of society in which all the relations of Persons are summed up in the relations of Family, we seem to have steadily moved towards a phase of social order in which all these relations arise from the free arrangement of individuals. (99.)

If Status is used to refer to rights derived originally from the patriarchal family, then "the movement of progressive societies has hitherto been a movement *from Status to Contract*". (100.) The free contracting individuals whom Rousseau had situated at the first stages of social development and contrasted with the victims of modern tyranny were, on the contrary, the heirs of aeons of development from an original patriarchal despotism.

THE ORIGINS OF PRIVATE PROPERTY

If primitive society was based on communal family groups, then private property as well as contract and wills were the product of an historical evolution. Chapters six to nine of *Ancient Law* address these issues.

The early family was a corporation which survived its members. "Corporations never die" (109). Succession to the patriarch's position passed by seniority amongst those subject to the same patria potestas. However, there were sometimes no obvious heirs, and contingency arrangements had to be developed. Moreover, as the powers of the patriarch were loosened, adult men were made independent. No longer subject to the patria potestas, they were by the same token excluded from property rights. Wills were introduced to allow their fond fathers to bend the rules in their favour. The Roman invention of the Will created "the institution which, next to Contract, has exercised the greatest influence in transforming human society" (114).

Turning to the evolution of private property, Maine was confronted by the difficulty that even the earliest Roman law unambiguously recognised individual rights. This fact was negated with the argument already used to dismiss the Roman emphasis on cognation: Roman jurisprudence had been transformed by the theory of Natural Law. Fortunately, "among the Hindoos, we do find a form of ownership which ought at once to rivet our attention from its exactly fitting in with the ideas which our studies in the Law of Persons would lead us to entertain respecting the original condition of property. The Village Community of India is at once an organized patriarchal society and an assemblage of co-proprietors". (153.) Maine cited a rather ambiguous passage from Elphinstone in his favour, but ignored the testimony of George Campbell, whose *Modern India*, published by John Murray in 1852, must have been known to him. Campbell admitted the existence of village communities "comprised of a number of families, claiming to be of the same brotherhood or clan", but insisted that "they do by no means 'enjoy to a great degree the community of goods', as Mills supposes. I never knew an instance in which the cultivation was carried on in common, or in which any of the private concerns of the villagers were in any way in common, and I very much doubt the existence of any such state of things" (Campbell, 1852:86-8).

On the matter of contract Maine found himself on still weaker ground. He disregarded the view of the Roman lawyers as "inconsistent with the true history of moral and legal progress ... the antiquity to which they referred was vague, shadowy, and only capable of being understood through the Present" (181) — an objection which surely applied with equal force to their views on agnation, for example. On this topic, however, he could not appeal to the Hindus. Though he had earlier claimed that Hindu law seldom "cast aside the shell in which it was originally reared" (153), there could be no doubt but that it recognised contract. The evidence presented this time concerned the introduction of Roman principles of contract to the German tribes. "It is therefore the sphere occupied in them by Contract which principally distinguishes the feudal institutions from the unadulterated usages of primitive races" (214-5).

The final chapter of the book dealt briefly with the early history of delict and crime. Crimes were initially treated as offences against an individual for which compensation was demanded by his family. In time the state replaced the family as the complainant. In this chapter the evidence was drawn largely from the Teutonic codes.

MAINE'S SCHOLARSHIP

Despite the appeals to science and to history, and notwithstanding his judicial tone, Maine's argument in *Ancient Law* is riddled with internal inconsistencies and weaknesses. The model of primitive society is buttressed by appeals to what Tylor would have termed "survivals" in early Roman law, although Roman law clearly reflects a society rooted in private property-ownership, and practising contract and testamentary disposition. On such inconvenient points Maine simply rejected his main source as contaminated, and argued from a remarkably sketchy view of the Hindu village community or the early German tribes. Appeals to the historic unity of Indo-European cultures cannot disguise a readiness to pick and choose examples on the basis of convenience alone.

According to authorities on the subject, Maine was in any case a poor Roman legal historian. His friend J.F. Stephen put the matter kindly:

> Neither Maine himself, nor I suppose, anyone else in England, knew anything whatever about Roman Law at that time, & it is remarkable and characteristic that Maine himself, though he reintroduced the study of the subject into England, never, I believe, was much of a civilian. I suppose he knew the Institutes, but I doubt if he ever knew much of the Pandects.

However, Maine found a use for Roman law and "being a man of talent and originality, coming close to Genesis, he transfigured one of the driest of subjects into all sorts of beautiful things, without knowing or caring much of its details". (Quoted Feaver, 1969:25.) Vinogradoff remarked in a lecture on Maine in 1904 that: "It is not unusual nowadays to talk in a rather supercilious manner of the lack of erudition and accuracy, of the allusiveness and vagueness of Maine's writings" (1904:2), and though he was prepared to defend Maine on some points he implicitly agreed with this view of his scholarship.

The book worked, however, as an ideological statement, an assult on radical, *a priori* social philosophy as represented especially by Bentham. If the radicals believed that government was based on a social contract entered into by individuals for the protection of property, Maine proposed to demonstrate that on the contrary the original societies were based on families, not individuals, related by status, not contract, and that in patriarchal communities man was subject to the whims of a despot. Moreover progress was rare and was brought about by an élite of lawyers.

Yet while tending to a Burkean conservatism, Maine granted the utilitarian ideas a temporary and local application. In modern, developed societies, their rationalism could be usefully applied, though with circumspection.

MAINE IN INDIA

I suggested earlier that *Ancient Law* was written more specifically with reference to the debate on the reform of law in India. Although the application is not spelt out, it is clear enough. Indian society had initially been like ancient German society: based on communal ownership and the patriarchal family, but debased by religious fanaticism, obscuranticism, and despotism. The

German societies had been civilised by the reception of Roman Law, especially Contract law, and the development of private property. The implication was that their backward Indo-European brothers could similarly be helped along by the reasoned and gradual introduction of British law.

In 1861, shortly after the publication of *Ancient Law*, Maine was appointed as Legal Member in the Viceroy's Council, effectively the head of the Indian legal system. In India he distinguished himself by a hectic legislative activity, and remained Legal Member from 1862 to 1869, longer than any other nineteenth century incumbent of the office. As his biographer remarks he "strove to make of the major theses of his *Ancient Law* a self-fulfilling prophecy" (Feaver, 1969:73), beginning with a move to increase freedom of contract. Individual land rights were also a special concern of his. (Feaver, 1969:91-8.) In speeches to the Council he cited his theories, and drew parallels between the imposition of British law in India and the reception of Roman Law by the Germans. (Cf. Feaver, 1969:87-8.) In educational policy too — like his predecessor Macaulay — he advocated the progressive introduction of European scholarship. In 1866, as Vice-Chancellor, he told the graduating class of Calcutta University that "their real affinities are with Europe and the Future, not with India and the Past". (Feaver, 1969:90.)

It is even conceivable that Maine wrote *Ancient Law* in order to become Law Member. Lord Acton, who as a young Whig MP had put Maine's name forward for the position after his book appeared, later wrote in disillusion to Mary Gladstone that Maine's nature was "to exercise power, and to find good reasons for adopted policy". (Feaver, 1969:179.) In any case, it seems clear that *Ancient Law* was consciously designed to present a policy on Indian legal reform. The policy was presented in the guise of a constitutional history: but constitutional histories were, after all, the conventional vehicles for such arguments in Maine's day. The innovation is that the constitutional history was derived (loosely) from Roman history, while the policy applied to India; but the book was written for an England in which modern constitutional issues were being debated with reference to Anglo-Saxon society.

VILLAGE COMMUNITIES IN EAST AND WEST

In 1871, shortly after he returned from India, Maine was appointed to the newly-created Chair of Jurisprudence at Oxford, but although he was to be an academic for the rest of his life he never lost his political interests and ambitions. He sought the Permanent Under-Secretaryship at the India Office and though he was not offered the position he was the first person to be appointed a life member of the Council of India. In 1878 he resigned his Oxford chair, and received offers from the Indian government and the Foreign Secretary. He accepted the position of Master of Trinity Hall, Cambridge, but later toyed with other possible government appointments until in 1887, the year before his death, he was named to the Whewell Professorship of International Law at Cambridge.

In 1871 he published his second book, *Village Communities in the East and West.* This is a slighter work than *Ancient Law,* but more methodologically self-conscious. Maine wrote of practising "comparative jurisprudence" in the manner of "comparative philology" or "comparative mythology" (following his Oxford colleague, the Professor of Sanskrit, Max Müller). "We take a number of contemporary facts, ideas, and customs, and we infer the past form of those facts, ideas, and customs not only from historical records of that past form, but from examples of it which have not yet died out of the world, and are still to be found in it". (6-7.) Once again, he yoked together Roman law and Indian ethnograpy. Only two types of knowledge were "indispensable" for the development of historical and philosophical jurisprudence in England: "knowledge of India, and knowledge of Roman law — of India, because it is the great repository of verifiable phenomena of ancient usage and ancient juridical thought — of Roman law, because, viewed in the whole course of its development, it connects these ancient usages and this ancient juridical thought with the legal ideas of our own day." (22.)

Yet Maine now drew attention especially to the German studies of early European communities, and the British studies of the Indian "village community". The Cambridge historians Stubbs, Freeman and Seeley had taken over the Germanist models of the later generation, Von Maurer and his successor Nasse.[15] Fascinated by the idea of an Aryan tradition, they regarded the Teutonic village-community as the source of British democracy. Maine found in their idea of the mark support (perhaps inspiration) for his theory of the primitive community. But, he argued, the German scholars "are obviously unaware of the way in which Eastern phenomena confirm their account of the primitive Teutonic cultivating group, and may be used to extend it . . . It has the same double aspect of a group of families united by the assumption of common kinship, and of a company of persons exercising joint ownership over land" (12).

Modern students of Indian society have pointed out that Maine's use of his sources was partial and unreliable.[16] He played down the complexities of Indian land tenure and the internal hierarchy of the village, and did not locate the village in a broader political system. As Professor Dumont commented, "he hardly ever looked at the Indian village in itself, but only as a counterpart to Teutonic, Slavonic or other institutions" (Dumont, 1966:85). Yet even the sources on India were infected by the German model. Campbell, for instance, refers to it constantly, taking it as a point of departure for many arguments.

Soon after the publication of *Village Communities,* a revisionist theory of the mark developed, which stressed private property, serfdom, the relationship of the mark to the feudal manor, the transmission of property through women, and even the ownership of property by women.[17] Nevertheless some distinguished contemporaries felt that Maine had genuinely enlarged the understanding of "Aryan" institutions.

Curious disagreement arose about the political moral of *Village Communities*. There was a radical tradition that if the original German communities were communist democracies, they provided a charter for democratization and redistribution now. J.S. Mill suggested in the *Fortnightly Review* that this was the conclusion to be drawn from Maine's work, an interpretation which upset Maine. He preferred Tylor's judgment, in the *Quarterly Review*, that "the decision of history, after a trial lasting through many ages, is being given for individual as against communistic possession of land". This, Maine wrote, was "just in the right tone". (Feaver, 1969:121-2.)

MATRIARCHY AND THE HORDE

But if the Germanists were generally committed to a vision of primitive patriarchy, other writers favoured a model of primitive matriarchy. The Swiss jurist Bachofen had put forward an argument for such a model in 1861 (the year of *Ancient Law*), based largely on a reading of Greek mythology. Maine ignored him completely, so far as I have been able to establish, and even McLennan was repelled by his vagueness and mysticism. A more formidable challenge came from J.F. McLennan and Lewis Henry Morgan, who appealed to the ethnography of contemporary "primitive people" to support their arguments. McLennan was probably inspired to formulate his thesis by a reading of *Ancient Law*, and his argument was immediately seen as alternative to Maine's. It rapidly made influential converts including, for example, Lubbock. Morgan's work was more powerful, but had less of an immediate impact in England. Both men were in direct contact with Maine, and with other leading British scholars, and although Maine delayed his answer as long as possible, he had eventually to respond to their critique.

In *Village Communities* Maine referred briefly to the claims of McLennan and Lubbock that the patria potestas in India had been preceded by a state of matriarchy, and that some of the aboriginal tribes in India showed traces of that original system. He responded that most contemporary Indian villages were based on patria potestas, and he showed his usual scepticism about inconvenient data. "Practices represented as of immemorial antiquity, and universally characteristic of the infancy of mankind have been described to me (in India) ... as having been for the first time resorted to in our own days through the mere pressure of external circumstances or moral temptations" (17).

In his *Lectures on the Early History of Institutions*, published in 1875, Maine introduced the literature in Slavic studies which had extended the Germanist model to the *mir* in Russia. He also dealt at length with the Irish Brehon law, then being translated, which he thought revealed very early Indo-European rules. He now reformulated his thesis to cover Müller's three advanced language families, the Indo-European and also the Semitic and the "Uralians" (Turks, Hungarians and Finns). "I believe I may say that there is a substantial agreement as to the correctness of these statements so long as they are confined to the Aryan, Semitic, and Uralian races ... But then a very different set of assertions from these are made concerning that large part of the human race which cannot be classed as Aryan, Semitic, or Uralian." (66.) However, the theses of McLennan, Lubbock and Morgan refer to other peoples and "do not concern us till the Kinship of the higher races can be distinctly shown to have grown out of the Kinship now known only to the lower, and even then they concern us only remotely". (67.)

In this way Maine protected the basic framework of his thesis from the critics while extending its range by incorporating evidence on the Slavs and the Irish. He even formulated a developmental sequence whose stages were identified with living communities.

> The world, in fact, contains examples of cultivating groups in every stage, from that in which they are actually bodies of kinsmen, to that in which the merest shadow of consanguinity survives and the assemblages of cultivators is held together solely by the land which they till in common. The great steps in the scale of transition seem to me to be marked by the Joint Family of the Hindoos, by the House-Community of the Southern Sclavonians, and by the true Village-Community, as it is found first in Russia and next in India. (78.)

A detailed critique of the anti-patriarchal writers appeared only in 1883, two years after both Morgan and McLennan had died, in a section of Maine's *Dissertations on Early Law and Custom* entitled "Theories of Primitive Society". It is very much a lawyer's argument: various, independent, lines of attack are developed.

Maine began by disclaiming too great a range. He had not hoped "to determine the absolute origin of human society" but "to trace the real, as opposed to the imaginary, or the arbitrarily assumed, history of the institutions of civilised men". (192.) The enquiry had been limited to the Indo-European sources, and at least for these peoples his conclusions had survived twenty years of subsequent research.

But another theory had been developed. "The other theory which is now opposed to that long called Patriarchal is the theory of the origin of society, not in the Family but in the horde ... It derives the smaller from the larger group, not the larger from the smaller. Founded, as was the Patriarchal theory, on observation, but on observation of the ideas and practices of the now savage races, it deduces all later social order from the miscellaneous, unorganised horde." (199-200.)

Maine pointed out that the picture drawn of these original groups was vague, and that Morgan and McLennan differed with one another in their view of the stages through which horde-societies passed before reaching the patriarchal stage. Their evidence for the original horde was based chiefly on the existence of contemporary "savage societies" which traced relationship for some purposes through women only. Ignorance of paternity, however, could not have lasted long. Fustel de Coulanges had wisely remarked that to the ancient "the problem of generation was very much what the problem of creation is to the moderns" (203).

For the first time, Maine enthusiastically cited Darwin. Darwin had laid great stress on sexual jealousy, and argued that it must have contributed to the early establishment of orderly mating arrangements amongst men. Promiscuous hordes were counter to man's sexual nature. Maine concluded that "sexual jealousy, indulged through power, might serve as a definition of the Patriarchal Family" (209).

Matriarchal or promiscuous institutions might occur as regression, as temporary aberrations from the patriarchal system — for example as a consequence of a local and brief shortage of women, a circumstance McLennan had posited. However, while there might be divergences from an original patriarchal state, Maine could not believe that patriarchy resulted from the convergence of systems which had originally been very different.

So far as I am aware, there is nothing in the recorded history of society to justify the belief that, during that vast chapter of its growth which is wholly unwritten, the same transformations of social constitution succeeded one another everywhere, uniformly if not simultaneously. A strong force lying deep in human nature, and never at rest, might no doubt in the long run produce an uniform result, in spite of the vast varieties accompanying the stern struggle for existence; but it is in the highest degree incredible that the action of this force would be uniform from beginning to end. (218-9.)

Confronted by the developmental history of McLennan and Morgan, Maine at last borrowed Darwinian arguments. Evolution involved diversification, not uniform development. Yet he was no evolutionist, and not much of a universalist, being ready, if pressed, to restrict his developmental history to the Indo-European peoples. Nor did he identify a general principle of change. Change was rare, required the guidance of an élite, and was apparently inspired by a single freak occurrence, the fortunate conjunction of the infant Roman legal tradition and Greek philosophy. The result is a constitutional history of past and future Indo-European civilisations in which the hero of the story is the Roman legal tradition, and the guiding élite are lawyers.

PRIMITIVE SOCIETY AND THE STATE OF NATURE

Maine's political concerns proved to be of little consequence for his subsequent reputation. His was a Whig constitutional history, which recorded the gradual and progressive but not automatic extension of liberty and welfare. It was a conservative variant of the genre, since political systems had to be guided by an élite or else they collapsed into irrationalism and despotism. (Maine's penultimate book, *Popular Government*, published in 1885, was a tract against the Reform Bill and democracy.) Yet although the political message was unambiguously delivered in each of his books, even contemporaries were prepared to ignore his views since his model could be detached from the political interpretation he gave to it: as John Stuart Mill's enthusiastic praise of *Village Communities* revealed, somewhat to Maine's chagrin.

Maine's influence among legal theorists and historians was of brief duration, his essays in legal history[18] and his extrapolations from Teutonic social structure being rapidly discredited. His subsequent reputation has been sustained largely by anthropologists and sociologists. Interest has been less and less on the legal history (though some felt this lent the theory a special authority, and eagerly borrowed the legal jargon). Maine was cited rather for his model of primitive society and for his theory of the movement from ancient to modern society — from kinship to territory, communal ownership to private ownership, family groups to individual citizens, status to contract, and despotism to liberty.

I have argued that Maine's model was an inversion of the classic models of the State of Nature, which he attacked so furiously, but whose idiom he adopted. Yet Maine introduced a new empirical emphasis, searching out examples of his ancient society in the Indian and Irish and Russian village community and the Teutonic mark. In a similar fashion, McLennan and Morgan founded their models of the original condition of human society on information about "savages". These two features gave the new models their potency. They were immediately comprehensible transformations of the traditional political myths of modern Europe into the historical idiom of the day. Yet they posited an empirical basis for their theorising, and so stimulated a generation of sociological and ethnograhic study.

The new studies led not to the abandonment of the model, but to its refinement. I have argued elsewhere (Kuper, 1982) that even "lineage theory", the dominant paradigm of modern British anthropology, is a transformation of Maine's model. This is not because Maine genuinely illuminated the constitution of real ancient or tribal societies. His model, indeed, is not of the slightest analytical value. "Lineage theory", despite its subtlety, is equally useless. The persistence of the model is due not to its explanatory power but rather to its ideological functions. At least since the development of the secular nation state, Western man has conceived of his own political arrangements with reference to an opposition between "civilised" and "primitive" society. The primitive policy, cursed or blessed, was somehow "natural", providing the ultimate contrast to modern conditions.

The persistence of the model reveals also the degree to which ethnographic discoveries are adapted to ruling theoretical presumptions. Here, too, Maine was worthy of his successors.

Notes

1. There are two excellent accounts of the debate — in Burrow, 1966:118-36 and Stocking, 1971. Broadly, the Ethnological Society propagated a monogenist view (and fostered philological interests), while the Anthropological Society was committed to the polygenist view that the different races had separate origin.
2. Medical men formed the largest single group of members of the Anthropological Society, but there were also considerable numbers of geologists and zoologists. The Ethnological Society, which broke away from it, had a similar composition.
3. Biographical information is drawn from George Feaver, *From Status to Contract: A Biography of Sir Henry Maine, 1822-1888*, which appeared in 1969. There was no typical "life and letters", W. Stokes' *Life and Speeches of Sir Henry Maine* containing only a brief memoir in addition to extracts from Maine's addresses. Burrow's *Evolution and Society* contains a long section devoted to Maine's intellectual development.
4. For Savigny's career and work see Kantorowicz, 1937. For later developments, including Jhering's contribution, see M. Smith, 1895. An assessment of Maine's debt to these writers is to be found in Vinogradoff, 1904.
5. See Pedersen, 1959, Burrow, 1967.
6. See Burrow, 1981.
7. See Burrow, 1974 and 1981.
8. My account of Indian political issues is derived from E. Stokes, *English Utilitarians and India*, 1959.
9. Stokes used this striking remark as the motto of his book.
10. *Ancient Law* was reissued unchanged many times. My citations are from the Everyman edition.
11. L. Fuller's *Legal Fictions* includes an account of Bentham and Maine's theories. The citations from Bentham are borrowed from Fuller.
12. Fuller, 1967:59-63.
13. Maine later developed this brief passage into a full-scale account of international law (Maine, 1888).
14. See Dewey, 1972.
15. See Burrow, 1981.
16. See Dewey, 1972, Dumont, 1966, Srinivas, 1975.
17. See Vinogradoff 1892 for a masterly critique of Maine in these terms. A general review of the patrilineal question in Teutonic studies can be found in Meinhard, 1975.
18. Atiyah, 1979 is a masterly recent review of the ground covered by Maine.

Bibliography

Acton, J.E.E. (1907) *Historical Essays and Studies*, London: Macmillan.

Atiyah, P.S. (1979) *The Rise and Fall of Freedom of Contract*, Oxford: Clarendon Press.

Bachofen, J. (1861) *Das Mutterrecht*, Basel: Schwabe.

Burrow, J.W. (1966) *Evolution and Society: A Study in Victorian Social Theory*, Cambridge University Press.

Burrow, J.W. (1967) "The uses of philology in Victorian England", in R. Robson (ed.), *Ideas and Institutions of Victorian Britain*, London: Bell.

Burrow, J.W. (1974) "The 'village community' and the uses of history in late nineteenth-century England", in N. McKendrick (ed.), *Historical Perspectives: Studies in English Thought and Society*, London: Europa.

Burrow, J.W. (1981) *A Liberal Descent: Victorian Historians and the English Past*, Cambridge University Press.
Campbell, G. (1852) *Modern India: A Sketch of the System of Civil Government*, London: John Murray.
Clive, J. (1973) *Macaulay: The Shaping of the Historian*, New York: Knopf.
Darwin, C. (1859) *The Origin of Species by Means of Natural Selection*, London: John Murray.
Dewey, C. (1972) "Images of the village community: a study in Anglo-Indian ideology" *Modern Asian Studies* **6**, 3:291-328.
Dumont, L. (1966) "The 'village community' from Munro to Maine" *Contributions to Indian Society* **9**:67-89.
Feaver, G. (1969) *From Status to Contract: A biography of Sir Henry Maine 1822-1888*, London: Longmans.
Fuller, L. (1967) *Legal Fictions*, Stanford University Press.
Fustel de Coulanges, N.-D. (1864) *La cité antique: étude sur le culte, le droit, les institutions de la Grèce et de Rome*, Paris: Durand.
Jhering, R. (1852-65) *Geist des römischen Rechts auf den verschiedenen Stufen seiner Entwicklung* (4 vols.), Leipzig: Breitkopf and Hartel.
Kantorowicz, H. (1937) "Savigny and the historical school of law" *The Law Quarterly Review* **53**:330-343.
Kemble, J.M. (1849) *The Saxons in England* (2 vols.), London: Longman.
Kuper, A. (1982) "Lineage Theory: a critical retrospect" *Annual Review of Anthropology* **11**:71-95.
McLennan, J.M. (1865) *Primitive Marriage*, Edinburgh: Longmans.
Maine, H. (1861) *Ancient Law, Its Connection with the Early History of Society and its Relation to Modern Ideas*, London: John Murray. (References in the text are to the Everyman edition.)
Maine, H. (1871) *Village Communities in the East and West*, London: John Murray.
Maine, H. (1875) *Lectures on the Early History of Institutions*, London: John Murray.
Maine, H. (1883) *Dissertations on Early Law and Custom*, London: John Murray.
Maine, H. (1885) *Popular Government*, London: John Murray.
Maine, H. (1888) *International Law: The Whewell Lectures*, London: John Murray.
Meinhard, H. (1975) "The patrilineal principle in early Teutonic kinship", in J. Beattie and R. Lienhardt (eds), *Studies in Social Anthropology*, Oxford: Clarendon Press.
Mill, James (1817) *The History of British India* (3 vols.), London: Baldwin.
Mill, J.S. (1871) "Mr Maine on Village Communities" *Fortnightly Review* **9**:543-56.
Morgan, L.H. (1877) *Ancient Society: Researches in the Lines of Human Progress from Savagery through Barbarism to Civilization*, New York: Holt.
Pedersen, H. (1959) *The Discovery of Language: Linguistic Science in the Nineteenth Century*, Bloomington: Indiana University Press.
Savigny, F.K. (1834-51) *Geschichte des römischen Rechts im Mittelalter* (7 vols.), Heidelberg: Mohr.
Smith, M. (1895) "Four German Jurists" *Political Science Quarterly* **10**, 4:664-92.
Srinivas, M.N. (1975) "The Indian village: myth and reality", in J. Beattie and R. Lienhardt (eds), *Studies in Social Anthropology*, Oxford: Clarendon Press.
Stocking, G. (1971) "What's in a name? The origins of the Royal Anthropological Institute (1837-71)" *Man* **6**, 3:369-90.
Stokes, E. (1959) *The English Utilitarians and India*, Oxford: Clarendon Press.
Stokes, W. (1892) *Sir Henry Maine*, London: John Murray.
Tylor, E.B. (1865) *Researches into the Early History of Mankind and the Development of Civilization*, London: John Murray.
Tylor, E.B. (1871) *Primitive Culture* (2 vols.), London: John Murray.
Vinogradoff, P. (1892) *Villainage in England*, Oxford: Clarendon Press.
Vinogradoff, P. (1904) *The Teaching of Sir Henry Maine*, London: Frowde.

Law and Local Knowledge

Disputes, their conduct and their settlement in the village communities of eastern Brittany in the ninth century

WENDY DAVIES

Department of History, University College London

There were formal and informal means for the settlement of disputes within the village communities of ninth-century eastern Brittany, although both depended essentially on local knowledge of local history and on confidence in the good faith of those with the knowledge. Reference was not made to written law, nor sets of customs, nor principles; the answer to all problems was seen to lie in the past, and all problems were assumed to have an answer. Where the procedure was formal and the meeting presided over by some official, presidents do not appear to have determined the outcome; judgment was made and due settlement assessed by panels of 'suitable' local men. Peasant communities sometimes became involved in the disputes of high politics, through the property interests of more substantial landowners. In these cases the means of arriving at a judgment and the procedure of expressing it often differed: though local knowledge might be cited, cases were usually heard by the ruler, who then both judged and determined the due settlement. Sometimes this appears to have been done for obvious political purposes.

THE RECORDS THAT survive from Europe in the early middle ages include a rich and significant corpus of law codes, but relatively few accounts of cases. Where such accounts do survive in any numbers, as they do in Italy and Spain, the sporadic and incidental nature of their recording and collection produces considerable disparities in time and place, and this makes systematic analysis of practice exceptionally difficult. Medieval historians, therefore, are more accustomed to treat law as text than as process and to treat the prescriptive and quasi-descriptive clauses of the codes as sufficient indication of practice, discussion frequently concentrating on the descriptive potential of different types of text. Some areas, however, do produce records which allow insight into practice, and there exists a collection of charters from east Brittany which is not only unusually rich in detail of persons and place but also unusually large in quantity for a limited area and period. These

History and Anthropology, 1985
Vol. 1, pp. 289-312
0275-7206/85/0102-0289 $18.50/0

charters include records of disputes, amongst a range of property transactions, and the size and character of the collection permits consideration of the occasions of dispute and the process of making them public, as well as the procedures adopted to bring about settlement and the range of persons who became involved. Since the problems are of small scale, since most of the protagonists are peasant farmers and since many of the disputes are conducted within the limits of a single village and its associated territory, we have an opportunity to consider aspects of life and relationships at village level in a period when most available documentation deals with the activities of emperors, kings and major clerics. This paper is consequently about village communities in ninth-century Brittany and the way that they handled their problems in public.[1]

Before engaging with these, two preliminary comments are essential to explain both the context and the limits of the investigation: these concern the available sources and the wider political context. To begin with the primary source material: in the year 832 AD a monastery was founded at Redon, at the confluence of the rivers Oust and Vilaine, 65 km south west of Rennes, the present capital of Brittany. Though the land for it was donated by a local magnate, the foundation was made with the patronage and involvement of the Frankish emperor Louis and his representative in and for Brittany, Nominoe. The monastery was the beneficiary of many small grants of property in eastern Brittany during the succeeding decades, and these properties came to Redon together with records of the gifts and other pertinent documentation. In the eleventh century many of the documents were compiled into a cartulary, and it is this, the *Cartulaire de Redon*, which is the principal source of our present knowledge.[2] (Though collection of the records occurred after a period of political dislocation partly occasioned by the Vikings, it is clear that the monastery retained control of many of the properties throughout the later medieval and early modern periods.[3]) A high proportion of the charters in the cartulary relates to the grants made to Redon in the decades shortly after its foundation; since those grants involved handing over extant documentation the cartulary includes material from at least a generation previous to 832 and records of other transactions too, i.e. the disputes, sales, loans, mortgages, leases and gifts which had touched the lands before they were absorbed by Redon. The range of business recorded is therefore far greater than might be expected from a monastic cartulary and the number of documents referring to small-scale transactions by private individuals is quite exceptional for northern Europe and unusual throughout Europe in the centuries previous to the record-making revolution of the twelfth century.

There are 283 charters in the cartulary from the years *c.* 800-925; a further 55 were not included in the collection but are known from early modern transcripts;[4] about three-quarters of this total refer to the years 830-880. The properties with which they deal lie within a polygon which stretches to 100 km at its furthest limits, but by far the greater proportion of them lies within a circle of 40 km diameter, whose base rests in the south at Redon itself. The charters not only record the actual transactions but also normally name all interested parties in and witnesses to them, and include considerable detail about units of property and tenure and the personnel associated with them. Now, it is clear that the proprietary interests of a major landlord rather than the endeavours of some would-be disinterested observer determined the circumstances of collection, that much crucial information must be lost and cannot be recovered, and that records of dispute settlement procedure will tend to focus on property disputes and not others; nevertheless, the density of information supplied by this corpus for a limited area for two generations in the ninth century is so extraordinary that it is worthy of very serious consideration. Though we must not forget the limitations imposed by the nature of the source material, it remains possible to comment in some depth on relationships at village level.[5]

Secondly, the wider world and politics: during the eighth century an unusually large state had been created by the Carolingian rulers of the Franks who, though often returning to a Lorraine base and its neighbourhood, were crowned as emperors in Rome on Christmas Day 800. The state included lands which comprise much of modern France, Germany, Italy, Switzerland, Austria and north-east Spain, but its integrity as a single political unit was always unstable and was not sustained for more than two generations. After the death of the Emperor Louis, in 840, a series of partitions produced successor states with increasingly separate political identities. West Frankia, comprising much of modern France, was ruled by Charles the Bald as king until 877, and as emperor also for his final two years. Throughout this time the extension of governmental activity was considerable and included innovation in administration and some standardisation of judicial procedure.[6]

The political status of Brittany throughout this period of change for western and central Europe was a fluctuating matter and was sometimes decidedly anomalous. From at least the sixth century the Franks had sought political control of it and had sometimes, at least partially, achieved this. But only under the Carolingians do we hear of any effective over-running of the whole peninsula: a series of expeditions in the late eighth and early ninth centuries ended with two that were led by the Emperor in person and occasioned the introduction of some Carolingian institutions in at least eastern Brittany. Moreover, a Breton, Nominoe, was appointed by the Emperor Louis round about 830 as his representative, with responsibility for all Brittany. After a decade Nominoe was in revolt against Charles the Bald, as successor to Louis in West Frankia; though relations between Bretons and Franks changed several times during the next forty years, it is clear that someone remained responsible for Brittany as a single unit and that this responsibility was transmitted hereditarily; at times this operated as independent kingship.[7] For the period during which there is the greatest charter cover, therefore, Brittany had a principal ruler (whom I shall refer to as the *princeps*[8]); this ruler was initially under Carolingian authority but after 840 was either unwillingly subject or in practice not subject at all. At times, therefore, and particularly in the period *c.* 865-74, Brittany was effectively an independent state.

The fundamental question of the relationship between government and localities is clearly complicated in this case by the comparatively recent introduction and probably imperfect application of Carolingian institutions to Brittany and also by the fluctuating political status of the area itself. Moreover, it is obvious that this was a period of major change for Brittany and for the eastern areas influenced by Redon: before the end of the century the monastery succeeded in establishing itself as a landlord of exceptional power and wide interests, quite probably on a scale not encountered in the locality before; and the Carolingian conquest clearly in some senses stimulated the unification of Brittany, for we have no indication of its existence as a single political unit before this period. The evidence of disputes, their publicising and their settlement is not necessarily typical, therefore, of other centuries in the middle ages or of other areas at the same time. Nevertheless, although the material is particular to a particular situation, the processes it records share many characteristics with those of other medieval societies.

VILLAGES

The area covered by the Redon charter material and worked from the ninth-century villages does not have a single geographical personality. Coastal parts, sometimes to an extent of 20-25 km inland, are low-lying and perforated by pools, lakes and water courses. Near the mouth of the Loire saltpans characterised the landscape and the economy in the ninth century as they do now. The river Vilaine runs south and west to the coast, and with its principal tributary the Oust, running south east, provides the major waterway of the area, which is cut by a pair of parallel ridges (the Landes de Lanvaux) running from east to west, six to seven km apart and 20 to 30 km back from the coast. Beyond this lies the area most intensively treated in the charters: an undulating landscape of mixed farming practices and many settlements stretches from the ridges of Lanvaux to the forests of central Brittany 25 km to the north (Forêts de Lanouée and Paimpont). This is a land that appears to have been worked, and well worked, from at least the Roman period until the present; arable farming seems always to have constituted a substantial part of the agrarian economy, with pastoral husbandry an important supplement. In the ninth century properties were small but packed together, their bounds much disputed, emphasising the intensity of the exploitation. There is little to suggest that the people of this area worked other than as farmers, though it is

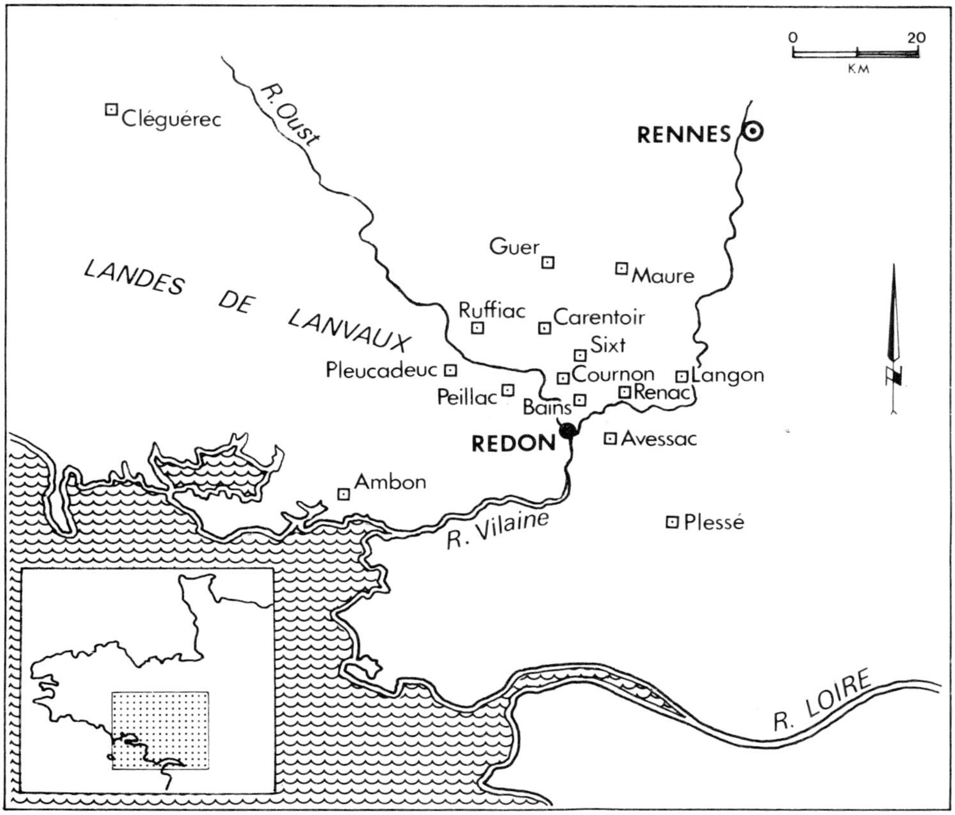

clear that in coastal and riverine parts some were engaged in the production of salt and in commercial activities. Redon itself must have functioned as a market centre and port.[9]

It is clear that agrarian society of this region in the ninth century organised itself in village-based units, known as *plebes* in Latin (and as some comparable-sounding word in the vernacular, since the Latin term was borrowed to give Breton *plou*, which still survives in modern place-names like Pleucadeuc, Pluherlin and Ploërmel). The basic meaning of *plebs* is simply 'the common people' but in the ninth century in this part of France it was used to refer to the primary unit of civil association between people, as also to the land inhabited by the group. Men referred to themselves, therefore, as belonging to this or that *plebs*; transactions might be formally notified to the men of the *plebs*; lands lay in this or that *plebs*; and often there is mention of the church of the *plebs* too. The territories were quite small — usually in the order of six to ten km in diameter — and frequently formed the basis of later ecclesiastical parishes and modern communes, though there has in many cases been some subsequent subdivision. In at least a social sense, and probably also in a spatial sense, the church was focal to the *plebs*: transactions might take place and disputes might be heard in it or before it; roads led to it and it was cited as a point of reference; mention of houses near it suggests some nucleation of settlement in its neighbourhood.[10] But however great the nucleation at the focus of the *plebs*, it is equally clear that there were other settlements within it: a scatter of hamlets is often implied and sometimes explicitly indicated, as are also the occasional seigneurial residence and small monastery.

Each *plebs* appears to have had its own regulator of public relationships, known as the machtiern. This man (and on one occasion a woman) presided over transactions of sale, loan and gift and sometimes stood as guarantor for such transactions. When members of the community had a grievance they might take it to the machtiern for resolution, who would thereupon order an investigation and who might himself preside over any formal hearing that ensued. In some cases there are suggestions that he had powers over vacant properties within the *plebs* and in others that he might expect both the loyalty and a proportion of the surplus of men of the *plebs*. There was undoubtedly a proprietary element in his exercise of these functions, although it would be misleading to present his activities as purely self-interested. In practice one machtiern often served for several *plebes*, and had relations who served for neighbouring communities, and he and his family often had personal properties in some of them; transmission of his 'office' was most frequently hereditary; indeed, no alternative means of succession are suggested in the material, and there are no indications of methods (if any) of appointment. He was therefore a local, powerful man whose personal and family interests might well stretch over several village communities: the greatest distance over which a single machtiern had interests is more than 30 km but half of that distance, spanning two or three *plebes*, is much more common.[11]

There were other men in the village community with specialized roles: occasionally we hear of a man called a *mair*, who was certainly used as a mediator in one case of dispute but whose function may have been primarily that of seigneurial agent and rent-collector.[12] The evidence is insufficient to comment more decisively on this case but that on the role of the Christian clergy is much clearer. Two, three or four priests seem to have served each church, being resident in the *plebs* and owning property in it. Some clearly had hereditary interests in their office and/or their property, and a few may have belonged to machtiernly families.[13] They played a major part in public business, not only as witnesses and guarantors but also — in effect — as moneylenders. Priests had sufficient liquid capital not merely to be more involved in purchasing property than others but also to make cash loans on the security of the loanee's property. The geographical range of a priest's interests, however, was much more limited than that of the machtiern for it was usually restricted to his own *plebs*. Some might travel to neighbouring villages to act as witnesses but that is as far as they went.[14]

Other named individuals are not distinguished by function and we can do no more than assume that the names which recur as the witnesses and guarantors of transactions were the respected and respectable, the leaders of these peasant farming communities. Most of those directly involved in property transactions seem to have been independent — though small — proprietors, for they are clearly distinguished from the servile dependents who were often alienated together with the lands they worked. Since the serfs (*manentes, coloni, mancipii, homines*) are hardly ever cited as witnesses to the transactions of which they formed a part (and apparently in no other cases) it would appear that it was the peasant proprietors that formed the body of witnesses. One aspect of their appearance is worthy of comment: of those names which occur repeatedly in the lists of witnesses, three-quarters only ever appear in transactions pertaining to one *plebs*; the remainder appear in neighbouring *plebes* but only rarely do people travel farther away — even to the increasingly dominant monastery of Redon, the beneficiary of so many transactions. This therefore seems to have been a society of highly localised interests and very limited mobility, with only the machtierns and their families habitually moving between village communities, at once a part of village society and beyond it. There existed an aristocracy — of a few counts and wealthy landowners[15] — which had wider interests, but their interests were so wide that they scarcely impinged as individuals on these communities, although we do know of one case in which the *princeps* himself (Salomon) used a machtiern to report to the *plebenses*. These are, then, peasant communities, with small-scale interests and very limited horizons.

DISPUTES AND THEIR SETTLEMENT

The ninth-century disputes of which we have evidence in this society number about forty, and nearly three-quarters of them date from the generation *c.* 840-70. They are very largely concerned with property rights and the commonest occasions of dispute are firstly — as might be expected — appropriation of land, stock or income from the monastery of Redon and, secondly, conflict over the allocation of property rights, especially between the members of a family. Hence, in the first category, we find the abbot of Redon accusing a priest of holding on to land which the priest's uncle had given to the monastery; accusing a peasant of stealing the monastery's pigs and cattle and beating up its men; accusing a machtiern of constructing a boundary bank on Redon's property; and so on (*CR* lvi, xxxii, ccxlvii). Almost as common are cases of the second category, in which, for example, two men claim that their cousin had no right to land that he had given to the abbot and that the gift was therefore invalid; or two brothers quarrel with another brother over a share-out of family property previously agreed; or a peasant maintains that he has sold rather less of his land than the purchaser subsequently uses; or another peasant maintains that land given to his local priest was not free to be bestowed on whomever the priest might think fit (*CR* clxii, cxcii, cxxxix, cxliv). Occasionally, however, there is evidence of other types of dispute which, although involving some property element, include non-proprietary aspects in the cause of offence. For instance, the abbot moved in one of the cases cited above not merely because of the theft of stock but also because of physical assault on his dependent serfs, and he moved again because of threats of burning in addition to theft (*CR* xxxii, cv). Very rarely there is notice of killing and of the action subsequently taken: grants were made to the abbot and to the *princeps* as a consequence of deaths — to the *princeps* as agreed compensation for killing his vassal and to the abbot for killing his serf (and in this latter case the amount was clearly more than the value of the property lost so that there is an element of penalty as well as of compensation); the abbot was also granted property as a consequence of an assault made on a priest (instead of the offender losing his right hand as initially judged; *CR* cvii, clxiii, ccii).[16] We cannot comment on the total range of disputes aired in these villages at this period, nor on the relative proportions of different types, but the evidence is sufficient to show that property disputes were not the sole source of conflict.

The procedure by which a grievance was made public — a necessary precondition to achieving a satisfactory settlement — is not always clear. In about a third of the recorded cases a direct request for intervention was made to political leaders — most frequently to the *princeps*, but also to machtierns, counts and even local village elders (*principes plebis*).[8] Occasionally, problems appear to have been aired for the first time in court: in these cases the charters state that the abbot came to a public court, before an appropriate official, and made his accusation, but we have no means of knowing if previous attempts at settlement had been made. In about half of the cases the first that we hear is that one man accused or questioned or made demands of another, in a context that clearly was not formal. Here we have a sense of a private grumble gradually being made known to more and more people, until the community at large knows that the two men are in dispute, before any formal action is taken. This process is explicit in one case that took place in Ruffiac in the 860s: a man called Uuordoital complained that the priest Maenuueten had improperly given away a parcel of land which he, Uuordoital, had previously given the priest for the use of himself and Ruffiac church. Hearing about this, Maenuueten started to gather his evidence — written documentation and witnesses of the gift — preparatory to raising a formal case. Seeing that Maenuueten was doing this, and not wishing to lose his friendship, Uuordoital sent him a message suggesting that if he were to pay a further four silver shillings Uuordoital would confirm the gift, together with free powers of alienation. Maenuueten did so and harmony was restored (*CR* cxliv). It is perfectly clear from this and from many other cases that formal proceedings were often not taken and that many disputes — though a matter of public knowledge and concern — were settled out of court (see below, p. 302).

When complaints were made to political leaders the action taken seems to have depended on the political level at which the complaint was made. When local leaders or machtierns were approached, the invariable outcome was an investigation and, if necessary, a ruling by local elders on the rights and wrongs of the case. When the *princeps* was approached he might do one of several things: he might refer the case to a local court; he might send representatives to the locality to collect information from local elders; he might demand that the accused appear at his own court to answer the accusation, first allowing him an opportunity to gather evidence (*CR* lxi, cv, cvi, cxci, ccxlvii, cclxi). His response appears to have been determined by the status of the persons accused: at the simplest level, peasant problems were referred back to their communities but machtiern offences were dealt with by the *princeps* himself. When the machtiern Ratfred and his brothers acquired eight shares of land in Bains and four and a half in Sixt by threatening Redon with burning, Salomon demanded that Ratfred appear in his court and explain why; on discovering that the explanation of monks and machtiern were inconsistent, he insisted that the disputed property be put into his own hands, and gave Ratfred ten days to assemble his case and present it at another of Salomon's courts (*CR* cv). When the abbot went to the *princeps* Nominoe and accused a peasant and his family of refusing to acknowledge the obligations of a parcel of land, Nominoe sent two representatives to hold a court in the locality. Six local men then testified as to the associations of the disputed parcel and a settlement was arranged (*CR* lxi). But when two priests from a minor monastery near Redon went to Nominoe to request the income from tolls taken at Balrit (presumably a subject of dispute in the locality), the *princeps* sent a representative to the neighbourhood to enquire of the elders of the *plebes* of Peillac, Bains, Renac and Sixt (which lay near the confluence of the rivers Oust and Vilaine) who had a right to these tolls (*CR* cvi).

Cases which were not resolved by the *princeps* or settled at an early stage were taken to court. Our information about the precise manner in which proceedings were conducted is very limited and there is no reason to suppose that the few cases of which there is detailed evidence are typical, given the variations between them. Here is one example:

> ... Couellic and Brithael, cousins of Lalocan, came to accuse the monks of Redon about their inheritance, which Lalocan had given the monks. Lalocan had given his inheritance, i.e. the villa called Trebhinoi in the *plebs* called Sei (Plessé), to St Saviour's and the monks of Redon. The cousins therefore came before Hoiarnscoit, who controlled that *plebs*, and asked him with many prayers to do justice to them over the case of Redon and Lalocan. They testified that the inheritance was more theirs than Lalocan's. Afterwards he summoned Lalocan with the monks,

leading men and elders of that *plebs* and other *plebes*, whose names were: Maencomin the priest, Uuetenuuoion the priest, Catuuotal, Uuetenoc the priest, Catloiant, Rihouuen, Uuarnher ... [and six more names]. They all came with Lalocan before Hoiarnscoit in the villa called Sarant, and testified that he had more right than the cousins because in earlier times their family had divided the inheritance between them, and the villa in question had fallen to the share of Lalocan's ancestor. They [the cousins] were proved wrong, and after Lalocan had proved them wrong with his witnesses he again handed over his inheritance, as he had done before, to the monks who were in that court, Tribodus and Riuuere. ... This was done before these witnesses [13 names] on the seventh of the Ides of December, on Friday, in the fifteenth year of the reign of King Charles and the third year of Erispoe governing Brittany (after his father's death), Courantgen being bishop in Vannes and Conuuoion abbot in Redon (*CR* clxii).

Other cases diverge in several respects, but some general observations can usefully be made. A court might take place at a machtiern's residence (*lis*), in front of or inside a church, in a village or small town (*vicus*), or on the disputed land. A machtiern, or a group of machtierns, or a representative of the *princeps*, or some combination of these, presided. The recording of the names of judges and elders presumably indicates the presence of an official scribe or notary. It would appear that accuser and accused usually spoke for themselves and that investigation was made of the judges' suitability to judge before any judgment was made. Judgment was usually given and formally noted.

How was judgment made and by whom? It was occasionally made by the *princeps*, presiding in his own court; much more commonly it was made by a panel of local people, members of the village community who sat in a local court. For example, Abbot Conuuoion accused one Merchrit in a public hearing before several machtierns of forcefully holding on to property previously donated to Redon; no truth was found in Merchrit's statements, and he then "returned the land which he unjustly held, in accordance with the judgment of the *scabini* who were present, whose names were: Hitin, Framuual, Uuolechaec and Drihican" (*CR* clxxx). The judges were sometimes known by the distinctively Carolingian term *scabini* and at others by the more general *iudices* (judges) and *boni viri* (good men), and their number per case varied from three to fourteen. It is clear that their work involved responsibility for establishing the good faith of witnesses: in the 830s, twelve *franci* testified on oath in a property case, and the *scabini* then judged that these *franci* were worthy (*digni*) to testify and swear (*CR* cxxiv). Their testimony then determined the outcome of the case.[17] In a further case the *scabini* also had some part in vetting the good faith of oath-helpers: at Langon in 802 an accused man was required by six of them to establish his innocence by swearing by the saints to the truth of his position together with twelve others, who had to be 'suitable' (*CR* cxci). We do not know how the *scabini* were chosen although selection of them must have hinged on reputation, as did the suitability of those who might be called upon to give evidence.

Repeated reference to the notion of 'suitability' suggests that procedure depended very closely on the acceptance of a sufficient number of qualified men in the community to act as judges and witnesses and get the business done. For, both informally, when the *princeps* or an interested party sought local information, and formally, in court, it was the testimony of *nobiles* and *seniores* (leaders and elders) which was taken, a testimony that in all recorded cases was decisive (*CR* cvi, cxcv, cclxi; clxii, ccv). In a case about ownership between two laymen in the 890s heard in front of the church of Bains, the record actually specifies that, when all parties and their supporters had gathered together "suitable men (*idonei*) were chosen, proved in their conduct and character, who would not be seduced into giving false testimony by any bribe to do injustice, but who would know what was right and true" (*CR* cclxxi). These were duly selected and they then swore about the appurtenances of the disputed parcels of land, and this determined the outcome. There is no statement of essential qualifications beyond this, although the notion that witnesses should be 'suitable' is not uncommonly instanced in early medieval charters and canonical material, and some legal texts from other areas and other periods explicitly prohibited those convicted of certain offences from giving evidence.[18] However, though these Breton 'suitable' men might be clear of offence they certainly were not personally outside dispute: legal functionaries sometimes brought cases themselves. There are a few further indications in the charters of the status and character of those regarded as suitable: judges and suitable witnesses seem to have been propertied, since several occur on other occasions as donors and vendors, and as sureties for the sales, loans and settlements of other parties. There are no cases of serfs nor, apparently, of females performing these functions. The same men were called upon to act as witness and judge and surety over a period of several years: hence Tiarnan, who was *scabinus* at Langon *c.* 832-40, donor at Cournon *c.* 847 and surety used by Branoc in a sale at Renac *c.* 846 (*CR* cxxiv, cviii, liii); Catlouuen, who was *scabinus* at Langon in 802 and then oath-helper in the oath required by the *scabini* in the same case (*CR* cxci); Houuori, who was named as surety for a sale in Ruffiac in 821 and later appeared as *scabinus* in the court considering a dispute about that sale (*CR* cxlvi, cxlvii); Burg and Antrauual, who were among the *franci* who testified at Langon between 832 and 840 and were *scabini* in a different case at Langon between 834 and 838 (*CR* cxxiv, cxcii). All those who appeared more than once in this capacity did so with reference to small areas — either one *plebs* only or two/three in the case of Langon, Cournon and Renac.[19] Judges and witnesses, then, seem to have been free, male, village men with a property qualification, and there appears to have been a relatively small body of village notables available to perform such roles at any one time; it did not include clerics.

The actual means of finding judgment in the disputes where a settlement could not be reached without it was preponderantly by the use of these suitable local men, whether acting as *scabini* or special witnesses. A pronouncement of right or wrong was not the inevitable outcome: occasionally, as in the 802 case at Langon cited above, it was decided that the problem might be resolved if one of the protagonists could gather enough supporters of sufficient status prepared to swear to the truth of his claim. When a layman of Sixt was accused about property rights some fifty or sixty years later, the elders of the community required him to swear to the truth of his statement, with three others, on the holy altar (*CR* xlvi).[20] Judgment, however, is evidenced much more frequently than oath-helping, and it is clear that it was made in different ways at different political levels.

At village level community members and not any appropriate officer took responsibility for determining right, even if someone controlled the machinery through which this was done; machtierns did not judge and pass sentence even where they presided over the hearing of cases. How did these elders arrive at their judgments? Those formally required to make a decision, whether known as *scabini* or not, appear to have done so in three related ways: they heard and assessed 'evidence' produced by either party, the evidence consisting of documents about, sureties for, and witnesses of former transactions concerning the disputed property; alternatively the judges heard the (sometimes sworn) testimony of worthy local men on the nature of past practice, the understanding being that these were impartial witnesses. Or, thirdly, they themselves stated, from their own experience, who they believed to be the owner of the land or who had the greater rights. Their personal knowledge of local custom was therefore often sufficient for them to arrive at a decision, without the necessity of enrolling a panel with more detailed local knowledge. Hence, when the two men proceeded against the abbot of Redon on the grounds that their cousin had given him a parcel of land to which he had no right, the machtiern made enquiries of the local elders (*CR* clxii). Knowledge of previous events in the locality — effectively a knowledge of local family history — is therefore fundamental to the process of resolution, and there is no admission in this material of the possibility of other standards of right nor of the possibility of both claimants having equal rights. The answer to all problems was seen to lie in the past; and all problems were assumed to have an answer.

At a higher political level the process was different, although the methods used to arrive at judgments also sometimes had recourse to this local machinery. In cases of aggression by machtierns, heard by the *princeps* in his own court, it was customary for the *princeps* to preside, make a judgment and pass sentence himself. Here, the ruler had clearly established the power to exercise personal jurisdiction over the lesser aristocracy, who were therefore outside the customary judicial procedures. He arrived at his judgment by hearing statements, and sometimes evidence, from both sides, as in the Ratfred case cited above, and sometimes by making his own investigations in the locality, as in the case of the machtiern Greduuocon and the serfs of Bains (*CR* cclxi). The usual outcome was an order for the restitution of the disputed property, and in one case Salomon laid down a penalty of 5000 *solidi* in the event of contravention of the judgment — an enormous sum (*CR* ccxlvii; cf. xxi, cv, cclviii). The tyrannous Alfrit, accused by two successive abbots of constructing a boundary across Redon's property in Cléguérec and appropriating a small monastery there for himself, confessed that he had no right to do this when questioned by Salomon. The ruler then went to the disputed lands and personally walked the boundaries, proclaiming his sanction against further contravention.

Machinery for the enforcement of judgments was as minimal as political considerations might lead one to expect. In most cases there is reference to none, but there is one practice — the use of sureties — which indicates some institutionalisation of machinery, while the actions of rulers indicate that they might take personal responsibility in political cases. There is also a hint in a fragmentary charter that machtierns would investigate mortgage transactions in which the terms of redemption had not been met (*CR* cclxv). More usually, however, sureties were named at the time of making the arrangement, whose duty was to see to the implementation of the terms. In transactions where there are no suggestions of dispute, this appears to have been normal practice where money changed hands, but sureties were also very frequently named when property was handed over as a result of dispute settlement at village level. (Machtierns were *not* required to produce sureties.) Hence, where a tenant's payments had lapsed, sureties might be named for the future payment of render; if the terms of settlement of disputed ownership were that A owned but B became his tenant, sureties might again be given for the payment of render; in ownership cases resolved by one party resigning all interest, sureties might be named as a guarantee of withdrawal of claim, sometimes to the extent that neither the loser nor his offspring would ever bring a further case (cf. *CR* lxi, lxxxviii, cxviii).[21] It is clear that in practice most of these sureties agreed to cover the loser's financial obligations, guaranteeing the victor that he would not lose income. In other cases, it would appear that the sureties were members of the loser's family; effectively they were agreeing to a resignation of their interest too. One case is very clear on the multiple functions of sureties, though, in the nature of the case, it is unlikely that this was anything other than exceptional: the cleric who assaulted a priest and avoided losing his right hand by making a grant in compensation to Redon named three sureties as security for the grant and then those three with a further three as security that he would do no wrong to Redon's men and property in future. The charter then goes on to specify the action they were to take in the event of the latter: if they thought he was about to do anything they were to try and prevent it and warn the abbot; and if he did anything, they were to give his worth to the abbot and pursue him to death. These sureties had both a financial and a physical obligation, and apparently an obligation to engage in a feud against the malefactor (*CR* ccii). Such varieties of suretyship appear to have been the principal method of enforcing the terms of judgments; they again depend on local contacts and the mutual interdependence of the network of local relationships.

In informal cases the procedure for arriving at a settlement was obviously different, although there were many similar elements. It was usually effected by a meeting of the parties, or occasionally their representatives, and a solution being found; sureties might then be given by one party and promises of future good behaviour made. The solution itself varied: money might change hands, or the agreed owner might lease the disputed property to the loser, or the opinion of some respected local person might be sought and boundaries consequently reestablished with the disputed plot divided. Only rarely is the means of arriving at this solution detailed, but it is interesting to note that when the abbot was accused of wrongly holding land in Augan, he sent three of his most experienced monks to the locality to enquire of the respected men of the *plebs* the truth of the matter. Since the outcome was the lease of a second property by the abbey to the accuser, we may suppose that the abbot took note of the local wisdom in determining his future course of action (*CR* cxxvii). When another man accused the abbot about a dam on the River Vilaine near Avessac, the men of Bains and Avessac collected on the river bank which formed their common boundary and maintained that the man was telling lies — whereupon he confessed (*CR* cxcv). Alternatively, there are two occasions on which mediators were used: round about 820 a man asked the machtiern in Pleucadeuc to give him his father's hermitage: the machtiern used the local *mair* and his own chaplain as mediators before conceding the grant. Fifty years later, the abbot of Redon sent three mediators to question another man about his right to properties near the coast; on the advice of the mediators he paid the man 60 *solidi* and then made him a tenant (*CR* cclxvii, ccxlii).

In some senses a distinction between local gatherings such as the Avessac case and local 'courts' is a false one, for they were all public assemblies in which the business of the community was conducted. Nevertheless, from the terminology used, it appears that contemporaries did see a distinction and did regard some public occasions as having a special status. The Carolingian terms *mallus* and *placitum* ('court' and 'session') are used for most of the formal occasions and expressions like *cum lege, in lege, secundum legem et veritatem et rationem* and *in ratione* are used to distinguish their proceedings from those of the more or less amicably produced settlements out of court.[22] We can only guess at the visible difference between the two types of occasion, for courts might take place at locations also used by the less formally described gatherings and local men, of law-worthy status, often played a part in determining the outcome of both. Some distinction there may have been, however, in the status of the presiding chairman, for in most of the court cases machtierns or representatives of the *princeps* sat in the chair. It would not be unreasonable to argue — from the proportion of such cases — that this must always have been so. Another distinction may lie in the fact that judgment was almost always given and formally noted. The overwhelming impression is that procedure was more formal in the court cases, even if the crucial role of local knowledge in achieving a settlement was effectively the same as in the informal local gatherings. Presumably someone chaired the informal gatherings — or did he? We have *no* indications of this. The further implication, of course, is that formal proceedings were at times an aspect of state apparatus — sometimes explicitly an aspect of Carolingian regularisation and at others of Breton politicisation — whereas the informal gatherings were not.[23]

POLITICS

Any attempt to assess the way that political influence worked at village level is hindered by the nature of the available sources. It is nevertheless possible to make some suggestions, on the basis of the frequency of citation of certain names in association with their known property interests. Although there is less information about dispute settlement at a high political level, the operation of political influence in these cases is easier to assess. There is no evidence in this material of the intervention in disputes of the highest level of ruler, the Carolingian emperor or king, but, as we have seen, there are clear indications of the role of the Breton ruler, whether acting as the agent of the Carolingians or independently. Firstly, it is evident, although nowhere explicitly formulated, that the ruler acted as a court of appeal for those with grievances which could not be settled at county or village level. These were nearly always disputes involving machtierns, though not invariably so; the other cases were raised by the abbot and it is plausible if not probable that these disputes involved major landowners, aristocracy rather than peasantry (*CR* lxi, ccxlii). Secondly, it is clear that although the ruler allowed the accused an opportunity to speak and produce evidence in his own support — witness the ten days which Salomon allowed the machtiern Ratfred to prepare his defence; and although he often went to some pains to collect local opinion on problems — as Nominoe did when he sent his envoy to gather opinion from the elders of four *plebes* in the case of the tolls of Balrit — nevertheless in making the judgment he adopted a procedure which diverged from local practice. Since he himself presided, judged and passed sentence, he used political power in an obvious manner in order to control the aristocracy.

No similar practice is apparent at the lower political level of the machtiern. He might receive a complaint, he might preside over the proceedings which sought to resolve the problem, but he neither judged nor prescribed the necessary compensatory action or penalty. If machtierns used the political power which they undoubtedly exercised over small groups of villages then they must have done so indirectly in cases of dispute. Nor could they be used by the ruler as an automatic channel for his own influence in the localities, since they represented entrenched local families of long standing, and much about them was independent.[24] The person of the president, therefore, was only significant in formally conducted cases at the highest level, since presidents do not appear to have determined the outcome at the lower levels.

Within the village community, there are a few indications of the distribution of power. In nearly half of all cases the initiative in making a dispute public was taken by ordinary laymen, whose range of recorded property interests suggests that they were peasants rather than significant landowners — they only appear in one *plebs*, with small parcels of land. Sometimes their grievance was against the abbot of Redon, sometimes against other laymen. Though there is a slight tendency for the number of cases against Redon to decrease from *c.* 860, when the monastery was presumably making its power felt, it would appear that members of the peasant community in the ninth century were not inhibited from claiming against the abbot: two brothers were able to go to their machtiern and complain that their cousin had no power to grant their land to the monastery, and Uurbudic was able to challenge the abbot over control of his inheritance (*CR* clxii, cxcv). Further, though the abbot did frequently win such cases, and those raised by himself, there are occasions when he did not. Though the language of the records is nearly always such as to suggest that the monastery was the victor (why else would the record be preserved?), the content of some of them suggests otherwise: when the abbot accused a man of appropriating land near the coast at Plaz, in 869, it is curious to find that he ended up by giving the man a not inconsiderable sum of 60 *solidi* for the property *and* installing him as a tenant (*CR* ccxlii).[25] Of cases where the abbot was not involved, a high proportion were intra-family problems and it is not possible to comment on the relative power and status of the contenders. Of the remainder, it is worth noting that one layman succeeded in forcing his local priest to hand over an additional sum of money for a past sale; another seems to have successfully proceeded against his local machtiern, who — using mediators — ceded the man's father's hermitage to him; and another brought a successful case over ownership, but nevertheless made the loser a small payment of three *solidi*, 'for peace' (*CR* cxliv, cclxvii, cclxxi). The reasons for these successes remain hidden if they are other than the immediate explanation — the drive to maintain harmony in a small community whose members were in the last resort dependent on each other.

The close network of inter-relationships (and even of functions) in these communities is explicitly stated when we find that members of the panel of judges, *scabini* et al., also acted on the side of one of the contenders.[26] So, when the six *scabini* at Langon in 802 judged that Anau should clear himself of a charge of appropriation with an oath and twelve oath-helpers, three of them served as his oath-helpers; and when six local elders testified *c.* 840 that Puz belonged to the Urblon inheritance, two (or three) of them then stood as sureties for the payment of render from the property; and when four *scabini* judged that Merchrit had no claim on the properties of Rethuuobri in Guer, at about the same time, two of them then stood as sureties that Merchrit would make no further claim (*CR* cxci, lxi, clxxx). The same intertwining of interests is evident in other contexts: when an agreement to pay rent by four men in Peillac was renewed in 867, sureties were given for its future payment, and three of these were three of the men liable: of the four men — a), b), c), d) — a) gave b) and d); b) gave a), d) and another (x); c) gave x) and two others (y and z); and d) gave z) (*CR* xcvi). Obligations and responsibilities must have been extremely difficult to separate, and it does not necessarily follow that a man who performed two functions acted with wickedness, partiality or cynical self-interest. In the end it is impossible for us to perceive the reasons for local alignments — sometimes family members provided support but this too did not necessarily happen for as often brothers or cousins or children were in conflict.

The only interest whose operation can clearly be identified is that of the abbey of Redon itself, though it is evident that the abbey's interest was not totally predominant. Independence of Redon *was* possible, for Uurbudic who testified on behalf of Redon near Avessac between 836 and 842 also brought a case (unsuccessfully) against Redon *c.* 840 (*CR* lxi, cxcv). Laymen who brought cases against Redon did not always lose, though notably those who won tended to have more than one unit of property, i.e. they were more than minimally propertied. The effect of Redon's victories was usually to institute a new rent-paying relationship; the absence of reference to subsequent problems over these properties — there are no cases at village level where questions were re-opened — suggests that the rent was thereafter paid and the dispute ended, but one cannot argue too strongly from negative evidence. At the higher political level Redon had sometimes repeatedly complained to the *princeps*, or successive *principes*, about machtierns' depredations: such repetition must imply Redon's initial failure and imply further that when Redon did fail, it continued until an effective judgment was made in its favour. Persistence brought victory.

In non-Redon cases any attempt at assessment of interest is confused by the fact that information about them is preserved because the disputed property and associated documentation subsequently (and independently) was transferred to Redon. All we can say is that apparently the resolution of these cases was interest free and apparently groups of local men attempted to produce amicable settlements by re-allocating realisable resources, or if that failed, they genuinely attempted to establish truth by calling upon evidence (normally oral — documents were only cited in a quarter of cases[27]) and local knowledge. Charter xcii suggests that the judgment in cclxxi was correct for although it was not cited in the latter case it substantiates the main burden of the argument which won the decision.

DISCUSSION

The Redon charter material has a unique character and permits exceptional insight into the dealings of a group of co-terminous village communities in ninth-century Europe. It is notable that disputes were settled both informally and formally — by village gatherings outside court and in court, and also by recourse to the ruler. The latter has an element of both the formal and the informal, procedure being less standardised and political interest being much more overtly expressed. Many cases were settled out of court, informally, a compromise being reached and most interested parties conceding a little. Judgment, if necessary, was made by the ruler, when he was involved in the case by either party, and more usually by local people. At village level, formal and informal, the means of arriving at a decision and at a settlement depended essentially on local knowledge and on good faith about the character of those who possessed it; this also entered into some of the ruler's judgments, although he wielded political weight in accordance with the status of the accused. In political cases procedure therefore diverged from the norm. In that judges and testifiers had to be of suitable reputation, and in that village interests were clearly immensely entangled, we must suppose that particular influences operated within village communities; but we cannot perceive *how* they operated. A knowledge of local history emerges as the most consistent means by which problems were solved, and reference to neither local nor 'national' principle plays much part in the process. There is only one case which could even remotely be construed as involving principle — whether a son inherit his father's hermitage, cultivated from the waste (*CR* cclxvii) — and this principle is inevitably tied to property, and was in fact resolved by mediators mediating between the conflicting property interests. It can scarcely be overlooked that a corpus of material which is so rich in reference to disputes and the process of their settlement is strikingly lacking in reference to law and lawyers. Though contemporaries might refer to going to court as going 'to law', professional lawyers do not appear to have been involved in the solution of these cases — at any level, from *princeps* to village — and principles of law are never stated or mentioned. On the other hand broad principles — on the level of killing requiring compensation and marriage requiring negotiated payments between the families involved — must have been acknowledged.[28] The impression given is that rules for the regulation of social relations were not *perceived* as being common to areas beyond the single *plebs* and not committed to writing. This may be an impression moulded by some peculiar bias of the records but it is notable that no collection of written legislation survives from early medieval Brittany. Only the 63 (67) clauses of the 'Excerpta de libris Romanorum et Francorum' remain and these clauses were almost certainly compiled (at some point between the fifth and eighth centuries) from a range of written sources of varying cultural provenance.[29] Now it may be that the absence of reference to law and lawyers is entirely occasioned by the nature of the source material and that in reality both were significant. My view is that this was not so, for it would be extraordinary in a corpus so rich in detail if no incidental reference to them survived. We must therefore consider the possibility that these communities operated without professional lawyers and written law. The lack of law books contrasts with the large corpus of early medieval law tracts from Ireland and rather later law-books from medieval Wales and the lack of lawyers with the number of high status, highly trained, highly professional lawyers which characterize the insular societies.[30] This may partly be explained by the recent emergence of Brittany as a single state and by the absence of any other notable political units previous to the ninth century — it is exceptionally rare to find reference to a king, even of part of the peninsula, and such references tend to come in foreign sources.[31] Brittany, for all its common background with western Europe and Britain, was politicised late; until hit by the Carolingian onslaught it may really have been a land of small, independent, inward-looking, self-sufficient communities, communities that were more self-contained, with narrower horizons than their Irish and Welsh counterparts.[32] The combination of the absence of state responsibility for the law *and* the introverted nature of village communities perhaps explains the contrast.

The problems and procedures of these communities will sound familiar to anyone who is accustomed to the village records of medieval Europe. What is curious in this case is that procedures make so little reference to principle, either as formal lawcodes or collections of customs. Perhaps surprisingly, a simple, non-professional approach to resolving the property disputes of small-scale peasant communities appears to have worked. We have no evidence of cases for which it proved inadequate, and we must presume that it was workable because communities were small and discrete — people had little contact with other *plebenses* and therefore little chance to encounter principles that were contrary. It means that there was apparently no problem in applying fixed rules to real cases; in mediating between the centre and a range of localities; in manipulating the rules to allow for a variety of legitimate interpretations. Where Carolingian institutions are evidenced there is little to suggest that these had occasioned any real change in local procedure.[33] The contrast with Wales and Ireland can hardly be explained by the mere fact of limited politicisation in Brittany, for both insular areas were politically undeveloped. The contrast therefore presumably implies some difference in the inter-relationship between state, village and aristocracy. Size, economic and social self-sufficiency, internal cohesion, communications, must all be critical variables; hence, not only does this ninth-century material permit insight into dispute settlement procedures within rural communities but it also suggests insights into political processes in a period of fundamental change. Moreover, the contrast between village and aristocratic machinery for settling disputes emphasises the distinction between non-political and political cases. The combination of contrasts ultimately serves to throw light upon the very creation of political power at a formative stage. In much of Europe the manipulation of judicial institutions by all levels of the aristocracy was fundamental to the exercise of political power throughout the central middle ages and the opportunity to perceive the early stages of that development is therefore of considerable interest and importance.

Notes

1. I am indebted, for much helpful discussion on the particular subject of this paper and on dispute settlement in medieval Europe in general, to the friends and colleagues who meet regularly at my house in Bucknell to study early medieval charters; our own collection of papers, *Dispute settlement in early Medieval Europe*, ed. W. Davies and P. Fouracre, will shortly be sent to press. I am also especially grateful to Tom Davis, Jinty Nelson, Morfydd Owen and Chris Wickham for their detailed comments on drafts of this paper.
2. *CR*, with references to charters as numbered in the edition; the manuscript is at present under the care of the archbishop of Rennes. The published edition is an extremely and inconsistently inaccurate transcript. The charters of the diocese of Vannes have been helpfully re-edited by M. Tonnerre (Tonnerre 1978) but this is not easily available.
3. Cf. Jausions 1864; de Corson 1880-6:II.164-218; Morice 1742-6: III.961.
4. These are printed in an Appendix to *CR*: 353-402.
5. There are other relevant sources from the area but they are too varied and discursive to permit systematic analysis. They have, nevertheless, to be taken into account. They are principally 'De Gestis Sanctorum Rotonensium'; *Annales de Saint-Bertin*, other sets of Frankish annals and the series of letters about the Breton church (principally *MGH Epistolarum* VI: 619-22, 639-40, 646-9), inasmuch as they involve the rulers who were patrons and protectors of Redon, include material that is generally but not specifically relevant.
6. This is a very superficial survey of a long series of well-documented developments. There is a vast modern literature on the Carolingians; there are brief surveys of many of the issues in Fichtenau 1957, Halphen 1947, and more recently James 1982. More detailed consideration can be found in Braunfels 1965-8, Lot and Halphen 1909. Guillotel 1975-6 and Werner 1980:210 are especially pertinent to the issues discussed here. Modern discussion concentrates on Charlemagne and it is therefore difficult to acquire a balanced overview of events after 814.
7. The best modern discussion of these developments, though it is extremely questionable in its interpretation, remains La Borderie 1898; Durtelle de Saint-Sauveur 1935 is more easily accessible. I have considered the political status of Brittany briefly in Davies 1981.
8. He is most consistently termed *princeps* in this material, but also *dux* and *rex* (especially in the 860s and 870s). The Latin terminology of political authority is clearly not precise, however; *princeps* (*plebis*) is also used of machtierns and village leaders, while *comes* is used of counts with wide territorial responsibilities — counties — but also sometimes of machtierns and village leaders. Both the words *princeps* and *comes* therefore seem to have been used to signify political leadership at a number of levels.
9. Dr. Grenville Astill and I are conducting a survey of landscape and land use over the past two thousand years; publication of the results will be in progress over the next five years,

especially in *Archéologie en Bretagne.* For ninth-century land use, I am preparing a book on the villages of east Brittany, which will deal with it. Flatrès (1971) has argued for distinctively Frankish and Breton patterns of land use in the Loire and Oust/Vilaine regions respectively.

10. I have briefly discussed this in Davies 1981:93; for fuller discussion see La Borderie 1898: 142-4 and Planiol 1981:II. 60f. *Ecclesiae plebis* were not exclusive to France; see Castagnetti 1979: 16-30 on the ecclesiastical nature of the *plebs* in eighth- and ninth-century Italy.
11. See Davies 1981: 93-9; La Borderie 1898: 142-64; Planiol 1981: II. 63-96; Sheringham 1981.
12. See Planiol 1981: ll.149-52; *CR* cclxvii, ccli, xlii, cxi, cxvi, App. xvii. Cf. Welsh *maer*, collector of dues, agent of a king; *Armes Prydein*, ll.18, 21, etc.; there is a useful discussion of the occurrence of the Welsh term in Jones 1972:373-80. Cf. also the Carolingian *maior*, steward of an estate; 'Capitulare de Villis', cc. 10, 26, 60 etc. and Ganshof 1968:38; cf. the several *maiores* cited in mid-ninth-century contexts, Ganshof 1975:s.v. *maior.*
13. If Hinuualart the Ruffiac priest of *CR* lxii (866) is Hinuualart the Ruffiac donor of *CR* lxv (866), he was related to the Ruffiac machtiern Iarnhitin.
14. See Davies 1983.
15. Brittany was divided into seven or eight distinct counties at least at times during the ninth century, including the two, most Frankish influenced, eastern counties of Rennes and Nantes. The Breton *princeps* tended to keep the latter under his own personal control; the counts of the remainder appear to have been directly answerable to the *princeps*, although transmission of the countship was often hereditary. See Davies 1981:92; Planiol 1981.II:48f.; La Borderie 1898:137-41. The occasional occurrence in the Redon cartulary of persons with property interests spanning several *plebes*, who had agents to carry out their business, suggests in addition the existence of a landowning aristocracy; cf. *CR* cix.
16. In the last case it is not clear if the grant was made to the abbot as priest's lord or to the abbot as the person with powers of (private or delegated) jurisdiction over offences committed in the neighbourhood.
17. The term *franci* may signify Frankish rather than Breton people, but this seems unlikely in view of the fact that most of them have Breton names; it more probably refers to their status as law-worthy freemen, whatever their cultural associations; cf. Ganshof 1968:76; Werner 1980:213.
18. For charters see Davies 1982:277-8. The pre-ninth-century Breton legal compilation known as 'Excerpta de libris Romanorum et Francorum' suggests remedies for those not qualified to testify on their own behalf, cc. A4, 28, 43 etc. (Bieler 1963); see further below n.29 and Fleuriot 1971:626f. Legislation from seventh-century Spain banned murderers, thieves, perjurors and other evil-doers from giving testimony (*Leges Visigothorum* II.iv.l) and late ninth-century charters from northern Spain continued to refer to the requirement; cf. a Cuxa charter of 874 where the judge directed witnesses *absque ullo crimine* to be produced (Marca 1688:796-7). Charlemagne also proclaimed measures providing for the examination of witnesses before testimony was given and prohibition of any found dishonest or without local knowledge, e.g. 'Capitulare missorum' of Thionville, 805, c.11 (*MGH Legum* II.i:124).
19. All formal cases of which we have evidence were heard at different locations in the ninth century. Since there was no overlap in personnel between Ruffiac, Guer, Maure (Anast) and Renac within the same decade, nor Ruffiac, and Sixt in another decade, it appears that a different panel operated for each *plebs*. (These places are within 15-17 km of each other.) Though the locations for meetings vary, the same individuals appeared in formal capacity in Langon and Renac (and they owned property in Cournon and Ambon — the latter some distance away). This area, which is close to Redon, appears to have had a panel acting for several *plebes*; it is notable that these are the *plebes* given to Redon by the Emperor Louis and it therefore seems possible that these men operated with reference to the seigneurial jurisdiction of Redon. See further Davies in Davies and Fouracre 1986.
20. Oath-helping was one of the standard modes of proof in early medieval European court procedures. In most circumstances the oath-helpers were gathered by the accused and swore to his good reputation, reliability and honesty, and not to any particular points of

fact. See 'Formulae Salicae Lindenbrogianae' (*c.* 800) c.21, 'Capitulare legi Ribuariae additum' (803) c.4, 'Capitulare Karoli Magni de latronibus' (804) c.3, Ganshof 1968:86-7; for oath-helping in non-European contexts see Gellner 1969:104-25. These Breton cases appear to be variants of the usual practice since the records state that the oath-helpers were required to swear to fact rather than reputation; they therefore functioned more like partial sworn witnesses.

21. Fleuriot 1971:650-1; I have discussed the question of suretyship in a forthcoming paper (Davies 1985).
22. *CR* lxi, cxxiv, cxxix, cxxxix, clxxx, cxcii, cclxxi; xxix, cxlvii, cv, cxxiv, lxi.
23. This is only certain when the *missus principis* appeared; machtierns were used by the ruler at times but it is not clear that they were his appointees; in my view they were persons of independent authority and the procedures they regulated were of local, non-state, pre-ninth-century origin. See Fleuriot 1971:622-3; Davies 1981.
24. The position of the machtiern is controversial; see above n.23. Salomon appears to have been especially successful in establishing contact with, and control over, machtierns; witness his success in disciplining them, cited frequently in this paper. The presence of the ruler's representative *and* machtierns in the chair in some cases may provide us with an opportunity to see the visible coalescence of two systems — the Frankish, under the count or his envoy, and the Breton, under the machtiern.
25. Cf. *CR* xlvii, ? lxi, cxxvii. All suggest victory against the abbot.
26. See above, p. 299.
27. The question of forged documents is only of limited significance since the value of documentation was itself limited; not only were documents cited in a small proportion of cases but when they *were* cited oral evidence was also taken. It is in fact possible that the record of the grant in *CR* cxlviii was emended by Redon, in its own interest.
28. See *CR* cvii, clxiii for compensation for killing and ccxxxvi for *enepuuert*, 'morning gift'.
29. Published in two versions in Bieler 1963:136-59 — where it is misleadingly headed 'Canones Wallici'; it has been plausibly but inconclusively argued by Professor Fleuriot that it belongs to the sixth century (Fleuriot 1971); Thomas Charles-Edwards argued very persuasively at a conference in Oxford in January 1981 that it was a handy digest of answers for common problems, compiled from extant sources.
30. For Irish law see Binchy 1978 and his many papers on particular aspects, of which Binchy 1943 remains a good introduction to the nature of early Irish law. The Welsh texts in Owen 1841 are gradually being replaced by modern editions: Wiliam 1960, Williams and Powell 1942, and Wade-Evans 1909; there is useful introductory material on the nature of Welsh law in *WHR* 1963, Owen 1976, and Jenkins 1981.
31. *Chronicle of Fredegar* c.78.
32. The southern Welsh law books instance the use of non-professional judges, however, and I have argued for the importance of 'self-regulating communities', without professionals and without state machinery, in eighth- and ninth-century south-east Wales (Davies 1978a, 1978b).
33. Cf. the comments of Nelson 1977:64-5, but n.b. those of Werner 1980:224 on the requirement that Carolingian *comites* and *missi* should know the law when administering their regions.

Abbreviations

CR	*Cartulaire de Redon*, ed. A. de Courson, Paris, 1863.
MGH	*Monumenta Germaniae Historica*
WHR	*Welsh History Review*, special volume.

Bibliography

Annales de Saint-Bertin, ed. F. Grat, J. Vielliard and S. Clémencet (1964) Paris: Klincksieck.

Armes Prydein, ed. I. Williams, trans. R. Bromwich (1972) Dublin: Institute for Advanced Studies.

Bieler, L., ed. (1963) *The Irish Penitentials*, pp. 136-59, Dublin: Institute for Advanced Studies.

Binchy, D.A. (1943) "The linguistic and historical value of the Irish law tracts" *Proceedings of the British Academy* **29**:195-227.

Binchy, D.A., ed. (1978) *Corpus Iuris Hibernici*, six vols., Dublin: Institute for Advanced Studies.

Braunfels, W., ed. (1965-8) *Karl der Grosse. Lebenswerk und Nachleben*, five vols., Düsseldorf: Schwann.

'Capitulare de Villis' see *MGH Legum* Sectio II, pp. 82-91.

'Capitulare Karoli Magni de latronibus' see *MGH Legum* Sectio II, pp. 180-1.

'Capitulare legi Ribuariae additum' see *MGH Legum* Sectio II, pp. 117-18.

Castagnetti, A. (1979) *L'Organizzazione del Territorio Rurale nel Medioevo*, Turin: Giappichelli.

Charles-Edwards, T.M., a.o., eds. (1985) *Mach ac Ynad. Law and its enforcement in the Middle Ages*, Cardiff: University of Wales.

Chronicle of Fredegar (1960) *The Fourth book of the Chronicle of Fredegar*, ed. and trans. J.M. Wallace-Hadrill, London: Nelson.

Davies, W. (1978a) *An Early Welsh Microcosm*, London: Royal Historical Society.

Davies, W. (1978b) "Land and Power in early medieval Wales" *Past and Present* **81**:3-23.

Davies, W. (1981) "On the distribution of political power in Brittany in the mid-ninth century" in *Charles the Bald: Court and Kingdom*, ed. M. Gibson and J. Nelson, British Archaeological Reports, International Series, CI, pp. 87-107.

Davies, W. (1982) "The Latin charter-tradition in western Britain, Brittany and Ireland" in *Ireland in Early Mediaeval Europe*, ed. D. Whitelock, R. McKitterick, D. Dumville, Cambridge: University Press, pp. 258-80.

Davies, W. (1983) "The role of the priest in the local community in east Brittany in the ninth century" *Études Celtiques* **20**:177-96.

Davies, W. (1985) "Suretyship in the *Cartulaire de Redon*" in T.M. Charles-Edwards, D. Walters, M.E. Owen, eds., 1985.

Davies, W., and Fouracre, P., eds (1986), *Dispute Settlement in Early Mediaeval Europe*, Cambridge: University Press.

de Corson, G. (1880-6) *Pouillé Historique de l'archevêché de Rennes*, six vols., Paris: Fougeray.

'De Gestis Sanctorum Rotonensium' (1738) in L. d'Achery, *Acta Sanctorum Ordinis S. Benedicti*, ed. J. Mabillon, saec. IV pt. 2, pp. 202-31, Venice: Colet and Bottinelli.

Durtelle de Saint-Sauveur, E. (1935) *Histoire de Bretagne des origines à nos jours*, two vols., Rennes: Plihon.

Fichtenau, H. (1957) *The Carolingian Empire* (trans. P. Munz from *Das Karolingische Imperium*, Zürich, 1949), Oxford: Clarendon Press.

Flatrès, P. (1971) "Les anciennes structures rurales de Bretagne d'après le Cartulaire de Redon" *Études Rurales* **41**: 87-93.

Fleuriot, L. (1971) "Un fragment en Latin de très anciennes lois bretonnes armoricaines du vi^e siècle" *Annales de Bretagne* **78**:601-60.

'Formulae Salicae Lindenbrogianae' see *MGH Legum* Sectio V, pp. 265-84.

Ganshof, F.-L. (1968) *Frankish Institutions under Charlemagne*, trans. B. and M. Lyon, Providence: Brown University Press.

Ganshof, F.-L. (1975) *Le Polyptyque de l'Abbaye de Saint-Bertin (844-859)* Paris: Klincksieck.

Gellner, E. (1969) *Saints of the Atlas*, London: Weidenfeld.

Guillotel, H. (1975-6) "L'action de Charles le Chauve vis-à-vis de la Bretagne de 843 à 851" *Mémoires de la Société d' Histoire et d'Archéologie de Bretagne* **53**:5-32.

Halphen, L. (1947) *Charlemagne et l'Empire Carolingien*, Paris: Michel.

James, E. (1982) *The Origins of France*, London: Macmillan.

Jausions, Abbé (1864) *Histoire de la Ville et de l'Abbaye de Redon*, Redon: Thourel.

Jenkins, D. (1981) "The medieval Welsh idea of law" *Legal History Review*, **49**:323-48.

Jones, G.R.J. (1972) "Post-Roman Wales" in *The Agrarian History of England and Wales* I pt. 2,

ed. H.P.R. Finberg, Cambridge: University Press, pp. 281-382.
La Borderie, A. Le Moyne de (1898) *Histoire de Bretagne* II, Rennes: Plihon and Hervé.
Leges Visigothorum, ed. K. Zeumer (*MGH Legum* Sectio I.1), Hanover, 1902.
Lot, F. and Halphen, L. (1909) *Le Règne de Charles le Chauve*, Paris: Champion.
Marca, P. de (1688) *Marca Hispanica sive Limes Hispanicus*, Paris: F. Muguet.
MGH Epistolarum VI, *Epistolae Karolini Aevi* IV, ed. E. Dümmler, E. Perels *et al.*, Berlin, 1925.
MGH Legum Sectio I, see *Leges Visigothorum*.
MGH Legum Sectio II, *Capitularia Regum Francorum* I, ed. A. Boretius, Hanover, 1883.
MGH Legum Sectio V, *Formulae Merowingici et Karolini Aevi*, ed. K. Zeumer, Hanover, 1886.
Morice, H. (1742-6) *Mémoires pour servir de preuves à l'histoire ecclésiastique et civile de Bretagne*, three vols., Paris: C. Osmont.
Nelson, J. (1977) "On the limits of the Carolingian renaissance" *Studies in Church History*, XIV, ed. D. Baker, pp. 51-69.
Owen, A., ed. (1841) *Ancient Laws and Institutes of Wales*, London: Record Commission.
Owen, M.E. (1976) "Functional Prose" in *A Guide to Welsh Literature*, I, ed. A.O.H. Jarman and G.R. Hughes, Swansea: Christopher Davies, pp. 248-76.
Planiol, M. (1981) *Histoire des Institutions de la Bretagne*, three vols., Mayenne: Association pour la publication du manuscrit de M. Planiol.
Sheringham, J.G.T. (1981) "Les machtierns" *Mémoires de la Société d'Histoire et d'Archéologie de Bretagne* **58**:61-72.
Tonnerre, N-Y. (1978) "Le diocèse de Vannes au IXe siècle d'après le cartulaire de Redon", Thèse de troisième cycle, University of Paris X.
Wade-Evans, A.W. (1909) *Welsh Medieval Law*, Oxford: Clarendon Press.
Werner, K.F. (1980) "*Missus-Marchio-Comes*" in *Francia*, Beiheft IX (Histoire Comparée de l'Administration IV-XVIII siècles), Munich, pp. 191-239.
Wiliam, A.R., ed. (1960), *Llyfr Iorwerth*, Cardiff: University of Wales.
Williams, S.J. and Powell, J.E., eds. (1942) *Cyfreithiau Hywel Dda yn ôl Llyfr Blegywryd*, Cardiff: University of Wales.

Social relations on stage: Witnesses in Classical Athens

SALLY HUMPHREYS

Department of Anthropology, University College London

The study of witness testimony raises questions which are fundamental for the student of other cultures, whether past or contemporary. What are the standards expected of a reliable informant and how is reliability to be recognised? How is reliable knowledge about the past established?

The aim of this paper is to analyse the use of witnesses in classical Athenian lawcourts both for its epistemological implications — what does it tell us about Athenian ideas of 'expert witnesses', of reliability, of truthfulness and bias — and for the information it gives us about Athenian society and court practice. What kind of men did Athenian litigants select to act as witnesses for them, and what effect did they hope their witnesses' testimonies would have on the jury?

If we start out from the assumption of modern courts that witnesses are called to 'establish the facts of the case' we shall misunderstand the Athenian data. What witnesses actually testified often was not very important: their testimonies might be insignificant, irrelevant or repetitive. To understand their role it is necessary to see them as minor characters in a drama, whose presence provides the backdrop against which the litigant wishes his own actions and character to be seen. Respectable witnesses — officials, members of the 'professions', reputable politicians — establish his own respectability. The support of neighbours, associates and kin shows that those who know the milieu in which the dispute arose are on the litigant's side. Denigration of the opponent's witnesses, kin and associates presents him as a vicious and unreliable character. In the construction of a character-portrait in court, witnesses had an important role to play.

SURPRISINGLY LITTLE WORK has been done on the comparative study of witnesses and witness testimony in different societies. The pervasive doctrine of modern Anglo-American legal theory, that witnesses are called 'to establish the facts', has created an impression even among anthropologists and historians that the functions and activities of witnesses do not vary much from one culture to another. When lawyers have studied witness testimony in past societies their questions have been shaped by the Anglo-American law of evidence: they establish who is debarred from testifying, either by social status or by relationship to the litigants, and discuss rules of relevance and of hearsay, perjury procedure, and ways of compelling witnesses to testify (cf.

History and Anthropology, 1985
Vol. 1, pp. 313-369
0275-7206/85/0102-0313 $18.50/0

e.g. Bonner, 1905). Students of the evolution of law have pointed out that in some early legal systems witnesses act as 'oath-helpers' whose support for the litigant is more active and committed than that of the modern witness (cf. below, n. 33), and students of Communist legal systems have noted that these take a broader view of the defendant's character, record and standing in the community than that presented to the Anglo-American jury (e.g. Feifer, 1964; cf. however, Shapland, 1981). But I know of no general study which relates the act of bearing witness in court to the two central issues which it raises: how is a particular account of past events legitimated as a valid representation of 'the facts', and how is the complex web of interactions which make up social experience related to the selective representations of the person and of actions which are offered in court?

The first of these two themes — testifying as the construction of socially accepted knowledge — leads directly to enquiries into the bases of authority and the social factors influencing perception, questions which our own culture has until recently been very unwilling to face (cf. Kuhn, 1962; Chalmers, 1976). It is not enough merely to note that in many cultures women, children, the mentally sick or members of "inferior races"[1] have been debarred from testifying, that members of certain occupations may have a privileged status as 'expert witnesses', or that in some cases those with especially close ties to defendants in criminal cases cannot be compelled to testify against them. Such categories are far too crude for a sociological analysis of the cognitive processes involved in selecting, preparing and evaluating testimony given by witnesses. Even in daily life we are all constantly involved in assessing the reliability of what we are told, taking into account not only the informant's access to relevant information but also his or her character, qualifications, possible biases and general standing in the community. Historians and anthropologists should be particularly aware of this, since assessment of the reliability of sources and informants is fundamental to their research (cf. Lewis, G.C., 1852, 185-97; 1849, 21-43; Malinowski, 1913, ch. 1, part 2). Some legal codes explicitly specify that witnesses must be of a certain jural status or social standing (cf. the paper by Wendy Davies in this volume); it would be extremely naive to assume that, in modern legal systems which set no such formal limits to the capacity to testify, except those related to undeveloped or impaired mental powers, judges and jurors are not influenced by their perception of the social class, sex, age and probable politico-cultural orientation of witnesses.

In the view of modern Anglo-American legal textbooks (e.g. Mauet, 1980, p. 98) the typical witness is the 'occurrence witness', a stranger who just happened to be present when a car accident or similar incident took place. Witnesses who are to appear in court are selected partly on the basis of impartiality; it is quite possible that kin, friends and neighbours may be questioned during the preparation of a case but not called as witnesses (cf.

Twining, 1983). The fact that most witnesses in Athenian lawsuits are overtly partisan has surprised modern commentators, but in comparative perspective this is far from unusual. Among the Tiv of Nigeria, no one will act as witness for a man with whom he has no social relationship because this would be an act of aggressive mischief-making (cf. Kurczewski and Frieske, 1978, p. 182). When a stranger is needed as a witness, a relationship is created by paying him to testify (Bohannan, 1957, pp. 39-40). Witnesses reluctant to testify against those with whom they are closely associated may be compelled by the court to testify on oath — which gives them an acceptable excuse for speaking out.[2] In small village communities any expression of opinion concerning a dispute involves taking up a position about how it should be settled; no sharp distinction can be drawn between testifying, mediating and judging. The formal hearing of a dispute essentially dramatises power relations between opposing groups within the society, although it also allows the demonstration or withdrawal of support to be expressed in the impersonal terms of an argument about justice (cf. Gulliver, 1963; Brown, 1975; Moore, 1977). It is understood by all that the significance of what is said depends on the speaker's status and relationship with the contending parties.[3]

An ideal lawcourt would have perfect knowledge of all the circumstances of the disputes brought to it, and perfect impartiality. But these two ideals stand in opposition to each other — not merely for practical, operational reasons but because the notion of impartiality implies a detachment from the immediate social process. Institutionalised arrangements for impartial judging[4] have to rely on 'outside' (objectivist) rather than 'inside' knowledge; the court sets itself and its judgment outside the temporal process of social life (cf. Bourdieu, 1977, pp. 3-9; Gernet, 1956); it selects only a limited segment of that process for its attention.[5] It is faced with the problem of obtaining information: whose responsibility is it to do this, and what powers are they to be given? As soon as the court is in any way detached from the ongoing social process of the community, these become crucial questions. At some point there must be communication between the inside knowledge of the local community and the outsider's perspective adopted by the court. Our own culture has elaborated a fantasy world round this point of interaction: the amateur detective immerses himself or herself, like an anthropological 'participant observer' in the local community and discovers the truth which the plodding policeman's routine methods of investigation would have missed. The detective story was invented in China, where it was the duty of the judge (appointed to a district in which he was a stranger) to find his way through the labyrinth of local relationships (Van Gulik, 1956; cf. Cohen, 1968, pp. 461-3, 466-8, 502-3 for modern parallels). Continental courts, where police investigators work under a 'juge d'instruction', and continental detective stories (Simenon, Freeling) remain closer to the Chinese pattern.

Legal process can be thought of as having three elements: gathering information, the re-presentation of that information, and passing judgment on it. Different aspects of the process are emphasised in different systems. In Athenian courts the collection of information was left to litigants, and at least after 378/7, when the use of written witness testimonies became compulsory, witnesses could not be cross-questioned.[6] Judgment was expressed only by the jury's vote; the presiding magistrate did not sum up the case. The process in court therefore consisted of two contrasting representations of the litigants' behaviour and rights. The work of investigation is rarely emphasised;[7] litigants wished to give the impression that they were stating truths obvious to all. The function of witnesses, I shall argue, is to bring the inside knowledge of the local community into the court process. A similar employment of witnesses can be observed in the local courts of communist Russia and China (cf. especially Feifer, 1964); as in ancient Greece, the court is presented with stereotypes rather than the complex web of real-life interactions, but there is the same attempt to show what kind of person the litigant is by locating him or her in a social milieu whose consensus of opinion is — supposedly — represented by the witnesses (cf. below, p. 355).

I have argued elsewhere (Humphreys, 1983c) that the legal process in ancient Athens evolved between c.750 and 450 B.C. from the kind of small community moot which anthropologists have described and which is depicted in Homer's description of the trial scene on the shield of Achilles (*Iliad* 18:497-509)[8] to trial before a mass jury of 200 or more in a city court. Awareness that the transfer from local community to urban court meant a loss of knowledge even if it increased impartiality was shown at various points in the process of evolution by the creation of supplementary institutions: the boards of local judges (*dikastai kata dēmous*)) to deal with minor cases, and the public arbitrators who had to hear most types of suit before the disputants (if dissatisfied with the arbitrator's verdict) took their case to court. Specialist speech-writers used their skills in presenting juries with a favourable picture of the litigant's character, past behaviour and social milieu. The purpose of the present paper is to show how the selection and presentation of witnesses was designed to recreate in court the social context from which the litigant had been detached.

THE EVIDENCE

Before considering what we know about witnesses in Athenian courts, it is necessary to say something about the texts of lawcourt speeches from which this knowledge is derived, and the processes which influenced their circulation and transmission. It has at times in the past been argued that all the witness testimonies in extant speeches are forgeries, 'restored' in the text by pedantic editors (cf. especially Westermann, 1850). On this view it was necessary to assume either that witness testimonies and texts of laws were not included in the original published versions of speeches, or else that they were later omitted by copyists; in either case, it was assumed that speeches were published and read only as specimens of the art of rhetoric, narrowly defined as skill in prose composition. There are, it is true, examples of speeches in which most scholars consider the extant witness testimonies and documents to be forged: Demosthenes 18 *De Corona* and Aeschines 1 *Timarchus*[9]. There are also many speeches which lack witness testimonies. In at least some of the speeches put into circulation before 378/7 this will be due to the fact that witnesses could give their testimony orally until that date (thereafter, they appeared in court to affirm a written testimony: Calhoun, 1919a; Harrison, 1971, 139). However, there is no reason to assume that none of the extant witness testimonies are genuine. Epigraphic evidence has been slowly building up over the years to confirm the historicity of persons and details mentioned only in witness testimonies[10]; and in any case the argument that speeches either lacked *ab initio*, or soon lost, their witness testimonies because readers were only interested in 'rhetoric' stems from a much over-simplified view of a complex process of transmission in which a variety of interests and motives were involved.

The use of mass juries of 200 or more to try legal cases was very much extended in Athens after 461 B.C. (Humphreys, 1983c). Even though appearance before a court of law was always restricted to those who had sufficient property for litigation to be worth while[11], this change meant that men who had not hitherto had much experience of addressing large audiences had to do so in the courts. In the assembly, too, increasing attention was being paid at this period to the way in which opposing views were argued rather than the status and achievements of their proponents (Connor, 1971; Lanza, 1979, pp. 37-49). Teachers of the art of argument came forward to offer their services both to the politically ambitious and to litigants. Antiphon, the earliest of these experts whose speeches have survived, does not seem to have taken money for his services but gave advice to friends both on political matters and on litigation (Thucydides 8.68); he published, probably in the 440s-430s[12], sets of four speeches (*Tetralogies*) in which both sides of an imaginary case were argued, and he wrote speeches for others to deliver in court — a practice which was already becoming established by the end of the fifth century.

It might be considered surprising that no profession of advocacy developed. An Athenian litigant was permitted to share his allotted speaking time with one or more supporting speakers (*synēgoroi*). In a few cases known to us the *synēgoros* carried the main burden of presenting the case: Demosthenes[13] or some other client did so for the ex-slave banker Phormio in Demosthenes 36, Apollodorus son of Pasion of Acharnai for his wife's brother and daughter's husband, Theomnestus, in [Demosthenes] 59 *Neaira* 16 ff.; Demosthenes may also have spoken for his cousin Demon in the Zenothemis case (D.32). The absence of personal ties between litigant and *synēgoros* in the first example is rather unusual; more commonly, as in the two latter instances, *synēgoroi* play an extensive part in the presentation of a case only when they can represent themselves as kin or long-standing friends[14]. But normally *synēgoroi* only appeared briefly to praise the litigant's character. It seems likely that the emergence in Athens in the later fifth century of quasi-professional prosecutors (sycophants) who made a living by bringing charges in cases where 'anyone who wished' could prosecute, and got a reward if the defendant was convicted, made Athenians suspicious of those who spoke in the courts for money (cf. Plato *Laws* 937e-938c). Instead of becoming advocates, experts in presenting legal cases became *logographoi*, who composed or helped to compose speeches to be delivered in court by litigants or by their supporters.

As Dover has pointed out in his study of Lysias (1968)[15] what an expert speech-writer did for his client could vary widely, from outlining a few key points to composing an entire speech for the litigant to learn by heart. It is important to bear in mind that the client expected advice on all aspects of his case: what laws to cite, what witnesses to call and what their testimony should say (cf. Aeschines I *Timarchus* 45, 67); what arguments the opponent was likely to use (cf. Dorjahn, 1935); how to divide the presentation of the case between the first and second speeches allowed to the litigant, and between the litigant and his supporters. Rhetorical handbooks have little to say on these practical points because it was difficult to generalise about them, and handbooks therefore give a misleading impression of the speech-writer's functions. An adviser who merely supplied the litigant with suitable examples from a selection of stock proemia and exordia would not have been worth much.[16]

Occasionally a speech-writer would indulge in a virtuoso display of specialised knowledge: for example, in Lysias 10 *Against Theomnestus* 15-19 a number of early laws are cited and their archaic terms explained (cf. also Demosthenes 23 *Aristocrates* 22-62). It might sometimes be necessary to make clear (or unclear) to the jury a complicated financial transaction or genealogy, or to argue an abstruse point of law: Isaeus 11 *Hagnias* illustrates all three points. But in most cases the litigants did not wish to sound too clever. The speech-writer had to practice the *ars celandi artem*, to use his skill and ingenuity on the task of presenting the speaker as the honest, innocent, sympathetic victim of villainy and intrigue (cf. Dover, 1974, pp. 25-8; Carter, 1982).

The speeches which have reached us had to survive three crucial tests. In the first place either speech-writer or speaker had to consider it worthwhile to begin to circulate copies of the speech in Athens. Secondly, a bookseller had to consider the speech interesting enough to export to Alexandria. Thirdly, it had to find its way into a collection of speeches attributed to one of a small number of famous orators.[17] The motives of those responsible for having copies made, and of readers, were different at each stage; understanding of the process has been impeded by telescoping all three stages together and assuming that the whole process was uniformly dominated by 'interest in rhetoric'. The common view is that speeches were put into circulation by speech-writers as a means of attracting further clients, and that they remained in circulation because they were used as rhetorical models. Exceptions to this rule are recognised only in the case of certain speeches which admittedly also aroused 'political' interest, such as Demosthenes' *De Corona.*

It is, however, impossible to draw a sharp line between 'political' and 'non-political' speeches. For the man with political ambitions such as Apollodorus son of Pasion of Acharnai, author of speeches 45[18]-46, 49-50, 52-3, and 59 in the Demosthenic corpus, any occasion for public speaking was a political opportunity. Apollodorus, who was clearly both conceited and insensitive to the opinions of others, may have considered his speeches rhetorical masterpieces; but he certainly also wanted as many Athenians as possible to hear his side of any dispute in which he was involved. The cases for which his speeches were composed show a mixture of 'political' and 'private' elements which is characteristic of the Athenian courts. [Demosthenes] 50 *Polycles* comes from a private suit for damages but is concerned with Apollodorus' zealous performance of the public role of trierarch. [Demosthenes] 59 *Neaira* (in which Apollodorus acted as *synēgoros* for his wife's brother and son-in-law Theomnestus: *APF* 11672.X) was written for a 'public' charge (graphē)[19] concerning civic status; the accusation was motivated by Apollodorus' desire to get revenge for his own trial after his one moment of political importance, when he acted as fall-guy for Demosthenes' proposal to spend the theatre fund (*theōrikon*) on military purposes; but the main theme of the speech was the sex-life of the prostitute Neaira. One of the earliest speeches preserved, Antiphon 6 *Choreutes* (419/8) was written for a member of the Council of 500 who had been accused of homicide — a 'private' suit in Attic law — in order to prevent him from charging a public official with corruption.

The two latter examples illustrate another point relevant to the motives of those who published speeches: in Athenian courts one case often led to another. The laws prohibiting reopening of issues already settled in court were ineffective (Harrison, 1971, pp. 119-20, 190-9); witnesses might be sued for perjury either as a way of preparing the ground for reopening a case (*ibid.*, pp. 192-7) or — so speakers allege — merely from a desire for revenge; 'private' cases were often brought as part of a complex of political manoeuvres. Furthermore, a man who had won his case might still have difficulty in exacting restitution or reparation from his adversary. It is only reasonable to assume that speeches were often initially put into circulation because the speakers viewed them as part of an ongoing conflict.

'Publication' in the ancient world was not necessarily aimed at a large audience. Before the invention of printing there were no economies of scale to be considered[20]. Dover (1968, p. 170) defines the reading public for speeches as "the partisan, the floating voter, the would-be politician and the connoisseur." The interest of the two latter types of reader would keep a speech in circulation for longer than those of the former two. But even politicians and connoisseurs of the art of speaking, in the Greek world of the 4th-3rd centuries B.C., did not think of oratorical expertise in narrowly scholastic terms. What the would-be politician wanted to learn was 'how to manage public affairs' and 'how to win cases'. He had to be familiar with the technicalities of court procedure and the art of drafting testimonies acceptable to reluctant witnesses (Aeschines I *Timarchus* 45, 67; Harrison, 1971, p. 144; below, p. 337) as well as with the niceties of prose rhythm. Connoisseurs must have relished the conversational tone of Demosthenes' private speeches (e.g. 36 *Phormio* 52-62), the dramatic outburst of the reported speech of Diogiton's daughter in Lysias 32 *Diogiton* 12-17 and the rueful description of his folly by Hyperides' client in Hyperides 3 *Athenogenes* 1-12 at least as much as the more stilted eloquence of Isocrates. Court speeches were — in the company of dramatic texts and mimes, with which they had much in common (Humphreys, 1983a, pp. 7-9; Dover, 1968, pp. 185-6) — the light reading of the period: real-life stories hot from the popular press (cf. Wilamowitz, 1923b). Familiarity with Attic law was widespread, owing to the jury system; Athenian readers could appreciate better than we can a speech-writer's skilful concealment of the weaknesses in his client's case, selective quotation of laws or adroit deployment of witnesses (cf. Wolff, 1969).

Many of the speeches launched into circulation in Athens will have attracted only limited, local and ephemeral interest. The wider reading public outside Athens preferred — or was thought to prefer — works by orators whose names were well known. But even within these limits the export trade reached amazing proportions. The library of Alexandria contained 425 speeches attributed to Lysias alone, of which 233 were still regarded as genuine by the critics of the Augustan period[21] (Dover, 1968, pp. 15, 21). Such a massive production was not the result of the occasional publication of speeches by professional speech-writers for purposes of advertisement, but of widespread general interest in courtroom dramas. It was only in the later Hellenistic and Roman periods, when the legal system was very different and other forms of light literature had developed, that interest became more narrowly stylistic.

The variability of the interests involved in the transmission of speeches also affected the form in which they survived. In some cases the author may have decided from the beginning only to publish part of a speech (Dover, 1968, p. 160)[22]. At the opposite end of the spectrum, some speeches are only known to us from fragments selected by Dionysius of Halicarnassus in the 1st century B.C. to illustrate points of style. The history of the documents included in speeches — witness testimonies, quotations of laws[23] and other citations — has been, as indicated above, the subject of controversy. But in my view there is every reason to suppose that contemporary readers were — and were expected to be — interested in knowing what witnesses had attested. It was only later, when speeches were copied for readers no longer familiar with Athenian prosopography or law, that copyists tended to omit such material.

COURT PRACTICE[24]

In the classical period, from which our evidence comes, all court cases were tried by juries of 200 or more members. Before reaching court the litigants would have had to present their cases either to one of the city's annual magistrates or to one of the public arbitrators (men in their sixtieth year). The magistrate's function was merely to determine whether the plea lay within the competence of the court over which he presided[25]; the arbitrator, if he could not persuade the parties to compromise, had to pass judgment, but his verdict could be rejected (Gernet, 1939). After 378/7, written pleas and texts of witness testimonies and other documents produced at these preliminary hearings were, at least in the case of hearings by arbitrators, sealed and passed to the officers of the court in which the trial was to be held[26] (Calhoun, 1919a). Each witness had to appear in court at the trial and formally confirm his acceptance of the testimony drafted for him — or else take an oath disclaiming knowledge of the facts concerned (Harrison, 1971, pp. 143-4, and n.55 below). If a witness was going to be absent from the city at the time of trial he could testify formally in the presence of other witnesses who appeared in court on his behalf. A witness who failed to appear could be sued for damages by the litigant, but there was no effective way to compel a reluctant witness to testify[27].

Each speaker was entitled to make two speeches, for which an allotted time was allowed, and a third speech in the *timēma* (in which the penalty to be paid by the defendant was assessed) if there was one (cf. Harrison, 1971, pp. 80ff., 152-162). Witness testimonies and citations of laws were not included in the time-allowance; the court's water-clock was stopped while they were read. However, supporting speakers (*synēgoroi*) shared the litigant's time-allowance. He could divide it as he wished between himself and his supporters[28]. *Synēgoroi* often served more or less as character witnesses but, unlike witnesses, were not exposed to the risk of perjury charges (Aeschines 2 *Embassy* 170). They could speak in the *timēma* as well as, or instead of, contributing to the presentation of the case.

At least after written testimony was made compulsory in 378/7, witnesses could not be cross-questioned. It seems likely that this rule was introduced to simplify the trial of perjury charges against witnesses, which were common: seven extant speeches derive from perjury cases[29]. It was the litigant's responsibility to summon his witnesses, and he could sue them for non-appearance if they failed to present themselves in court after being formally summoned. In court, a witness could refuse to accept the testimony drafted for him, but only by taking an oath disclaiming all knowledge of the facts in question, which in many cases was liable to make him look foolish and perhaps lay him open to a subsequent perjury charge. In practice this tactic seems to have been most commonly used as a way of discrediting the adversary or his witnesses by trying to make them testify against their own case[30]. Most witnesses were friends or kinsmen of the litigant whose willingness to support him and consent to the testimony as drafted had already been established.

WITNESSES AS SUPPORTERS: ATTIC LAW AND ITS SOCIAL CONTEXT

The fact that witnesses in Athenian lawsuits appear as supporters of the litigant rather than offering independent corroboration of his account of the facts of the case[31] has often been noticed, but has usually been treated as a survival of the use in earlier periods of 'oath-helpers' who supported the litigant by taking an oath attesting to his version of the facts of the case. This practice is attested in the Law of Gortyn in Crete, c.450 (Kohler and Ziebarth, 1912, p. 36, no. 6.; pp. 82f.) but parallels from small medieval communities or from the Cretan countryside are not relevant to the courts of classical Athens, with jurors drawn from an urban population which is likely to have included 10-15,000 adult male citizens[32]. Oath-helping and the use of friends and kin as witnesses and supporting speakers in Athenian courts should in my opinion be viewed as two alternative ways of formalising the influence of interested members of the community in dispute settlement, which by now is ethnographically well documented (Gulliver, 1963; cf. Brown, 1975); there is no reason to suppose that oath-helpers had ever been used in Athens[33]. In fact we find oath-helping formalised in codes which dictate to courts how they are to reach decisions. Attic laws were concerned, in the procedural sphere, with the distribution of cases to different courts, with specifying who was entitled to accuse, and with the specification in some cases of penalties, rather than with defining what constituted decisive proof. The evolution of law in Athens followed its own path; the key factors in explaining the role of witnesses as supporters in Athenian courts are the non-technical approach of Athenian juries and the rarity and marginality, even in the fourth century, of the use of written documents as evidence.

In the last thirty years of the fifth century — not long after the generalisation of trial by jury — many Athenians had hurriedly uprooted themselves from their villages and moved into the walled area between Athens and Piraeus to escape the dangers of Spartan invasion. The sources of wealth changed; land, during the war, lost much of its value, while riches could be made from political office at home or in the subject cities, from attacking wealthy men in the courts, from financing urban trade or from owning urban property and slave workshops. The restraining effects of local community opinion in village or urban neighbourhood were lessened by the general sense of social upheaval and uncertainty, which had been exacerbated by the experience of the plague of 430-429 (Thucydides 2.53). The jury-courts were faced with an increasing flood of business. Jurors were paid; Aristophanes in the *Wasps* portrays the typical juror as elderly, in need of ready cash and somewhat boorish,[34] and it is likely enough that the older refugees from the countryside would have taken up jury service as an easy source of cash payments (cf. Humphreys, 1978, pp. 71, 147). Hence many of the jurors of the Peloponnesian war period, when the profession of speech-writing was developing and the pattern of presentation of cases to juries was crystallising, were men who had experience of life in a stable village community in which judgments on the behaviour of neighbours were based on detailed knowledge of the social context (cf. Moore, 1977). In an Athenian court jurors got no instruction in law. The presiding magistrate did not sum up the arguments made by the two parties or give authoritative rulings on legal issues. Litigants quoted laws selectively and incompletely, subject to no control except the production of counter-quotations by the opposing side. The move to the city did not therefore introduce jurors to a new and different type of legal culture. What it did was to complement the ideas of equity and morality formed in the social milieu of the village (or pre-war city neighbourhood) with the experience of two urban institutions: the assembly and the theatre. Both put the audience in the position of judge; both made extensive use of competitions in argument. The assembly however had a greater tendency to depersonalise the issue under discussion; although, to judge from Thucydides' report of the debate over the Sicilian expedition, references to the *ethos* of competing speakers were not excluded, the assembly had to decide between alternative future policies for a collectivity, the city. The theatre on the other hand represented the past actions (or in the case of comedy actions in a fictional present) of individuals. In the theatre therefore action inevitably became, as Aristotle said, 'coloured' by ethos or 'moral style' (cf. Jones, 1962, p. 37).

The litigant in court also had to give an account of his past actions, and to represent them as proceeding from an *ethos* which the jury would find sympathetic. His witnesses had an important role to play in showing what kind of man he was. One of the characters in Euripides' *Phoenix* (fr. 812 Nauck^2) says:

> I've already been chosen to judge many disputes and have heard witnesses competing against each other with opposing accounts of the same event. And like any wise man I work out the truth by looking at a man's nature and the life he leads ... I never question[35] a man who likes bad company. I reckon you can tell what a man's like by the company he keeps.

The theory — though perhaps not the practice — in modern western courts is that what matters about a witness is not who he is but what he says. As we shall see, this theory does not apply to Athenian courts, where the content of witness testimonies is often unimportant or irrelevant. For example, the father-in-law of the egregious Apollodorus, Deinias son of Theomnestus of Athmonon (*A.P.F.* 11672.X), appeared as witness for Apollodorus when he was suing Deinias' nephew (ZS) Stephanus for perjury ([Demosthenes] 45.55). Deinias' testimony said only that he had married his daughter to Apollodorus according to law, and that he had not been present when Apollodorus released his father's ex-slave Phormio from alleged debts, nor had he heard of such a release being given. As factual testimony this counted for little; but it was significant that Deinias was prepared to support his son-in-law against another member of his own family[36]. In [Demosthenes] 43 *Macartatus* and Demosthenes 57 *Eubulides* the litigants produce numerous witnesses to testify to the same facts (not always relevant) again and again. What matters to them is to show that they are solidly supported by a large body of kin. The aim of every litigant was to represent himself as surrounded by a substantial group of respectable and law-abiding kin, friends and associates, and conversely to accuse his opponent of relying on the dubious services of professional *rhetores*, bribed witnesses and disreputable drinking companions.

The choice of witnesses was also, as I have said, conditioned by the limited use made of written documents as evidence (cf. Pringsheim, 1955). Official procedures for registering and authenticating written documents did not exist. In cases where a business contract, marriage settlement or will was felt to be potentially controversial the parties concerned might indeed put its provisions in writing and deposit the document with a trusted third party. But the document would have to be written and deposited in the presence of witnesses prepared to appear in court and testify to its validity; it was not sufficient merely to have a contract signed by witnesses.

In [D.] 35 *Lacritus* 10-14 the speaker successively presents (1) the text of a loan contract concluding with the names of three witnesses, (2) the testimony of the man with whom the contract was deposited, and (3) the testimony of the three witnesses to the contract and two other persons that they were present when the loan was made and knew that the contract had been deposited with the previous witness. Written wills were made in the presence of the testator's kin and often other witnesses as well. (Harrison, 1968, 153-4; cf. Thompson, 1981; Humphreys, 1983a, pp. 84f.).

Even where transactions with the state are in question, documents are not produced[37]. Since the actual text of witness testimonies is not preserved in any of these cases we cannot be absolutely certain that documents were not mentioned, but in only one case is the witness a secretary with specific responsibilities for record-keeping: here, in [Demosthenes] 58 *Theocrines* 8-9, cf. 26, the secretary to the supervisors of the port (*epimelētai tou emporiou*) witnesses that he received a denunciation, and other witnesses testify that they saw it posted outside the supervisors' office; the port supervisors also testify. No reference is made to the preservation of a copy of the denunciation in the records of the office. In general, when testimony is required on transactions with the state in past years it is the man who held office in the relevant year who is called; there is no request to men currently in office to consult the records for past years and testify to what they find, or reference to the production of certified copies of records.

In [D.] 59 *Neaira* 40 and perhaps also in Isocr. 17 *Trap.* 12 and 14 ex-*polemarchoi* witness concerning cases brought before them; in Lysias 17 *Dēm. adik.* 8-9 the archons of the previous year and the *nautodikai* of the current year witness to the speaker's attempts to claim land owed to him; in Aeschines 2 *Embassy* 84-5 and Andocides 1 *Myst.* 46 men who had been members of the presiding board of *prytaneis* in the assembly give testimony concerning events which had taken place under their presidency. Officials responsible for various aspects of taxation are called to testify to amounts demanded, collected or paid out in Lys. 31 *Philo* 16, Isocr. 17 *Trap.* 40-41, [D.] 47 *Euerg.* 22-24, [D.] 50 *Polycles* 10 and perhaps also D.27 *Aphobus i* 46, but no reference is made to the production of written records. In [D.] 42 *Phaen.* 16 officials perhaps testify to the date on which the speaker had handed in a property declaration, but again there is no suggestion that written evidence was produced[38].

THE CHOICE OF WITNESSES

The marginal status of written documentation meant that witnesses were recruited in Athens well before any question of legal proceedings arose. For any transaction which might conceivably give rise to a legal dispute in the future, an Athenian had to provide himself with witnesses who could be relied upon to support him if the need arose. Kinsmen, fellow-members of deme and phratry, and neighbours were often essential for establishing family relationships, legitimacy and ownership of property; but even outside these fields it was natural to turn to kin and close associates. Even in the new types of urban business transaction which were developing in the late fifth and fourth centuries, such as banking and loans for sea trade, contacts remained personal. A man had to trust to his own assessment of the reliability of a lender or borrower; one did business with friends, or with friends of friends. For example, in [Demosthenes] 35 *Lacritus* 6-7, Aristocles of Sphettos says that he lent money for a trading voyage on the basis of an introduction by a pair of brothers, his fellow-demesmen and friends (*epitēdeioi*), with whom he regularly associated. Admittedly, to be supported only by close kin as witnesses could be a weakness; the opponent would suggest that they were lying out of family loyalty. Witnesses who looked independent were desirable — but they were not always available. In the following analysis I shall proceed, roughly speaking, from more independent to less independent categories of witness as I think an Athenian jury would assess them, discussing first city officials and members of 'respectable' professions (doctors, teachers, bankers); then business associates, who often had their own motives for publicising transactions in which they had been involved; then witnesses chosen because they were present when particular events took place — bystanders, fellow-voyagers and fellow-soldiers, witnesses from abroad; then the use of well-known politicians and of the opponent's enemies as witnesses; then the outer circle of the litigant's associates — neighbours, fellow-members of cult groups, fellow-clansmen — and finally those identified as kin and friends.

OFFICIALS

An Athenian magistrate had to pass scrutiny before entering an office and submit to a strict process of accounting at the end of his period of tenure (Pierart, 1971); the need for impartiality in public roles was in some instances stressed in oaths taken before assuming office. The fact that one of the guarantors and private arbitrators who testifies had held office as *thesmothetes* and that the father of another had been elected eponymous *archon* is cited, apparently as an indication of respectability, in [Demosthenes] 59 *Neaira* 65. It is perhaps in the use of office-holders as witnesses that Athenian courts came closest to the modern idea that the witness has a civic duty to tell the court what he knows.

Court officials testify to earlier indictments in [D.] 58 *Theocr.* 8-9 (cf. 26) and 32, and in [D.] 25 *Aristog. i* 58 (if genuine); in [D.] 47 *Euerg.* 27 and 41-44 magistrates and members of the Council of 500 testify to previous condemnations of Theophemus, whose brother and brother-in-law the speaker was suing for perjury as witnesses for Theophemus in a previous suit. In Andocides 1 *Myst.* 112 the council's herald testifies to events which took place in a meeting of the council held at the Eleusinion. Members of the Areopagus council (who held office for life) testified for Dinarchus (1 *Dem.* 51-2) that he had not been denounced by the Areopagus, and for Demosthenes (18 *Crown* 134) that when his opponent Aeschines was elected to plead a case against the Delians at Delphi the Areopagus rejected him and substituted Hyperides. In Lysias 22 *Corn-dealers* 8-9 one of the archons witnessed to instructions which he had given to corn-merchants; in Lysias 16 *Mantitheus* 13 Orthobulus, commander of the cavalry squadron of the speaker's tribe, testified that he had called up the speaker to serve in the cavalry and that he had asked to serve on foot as a hoplite instead, which was considered more dangerous.

It is likely enough that in some of these cases the magistrates and ex-magistrates who testified were also personal friends or acquaintances of the litigant, and in some cases this is explicitly stated. In Demosthenes 51, *On the Trierarchic Crown*, the general Cephisodotus, a family friend, acted as supporting speaker (*synēgoros*) for Demosthenes while at the same time functioning *de facto* as an official witnessing to the events of the campaign in which he had commanded (cf. *A.P.F.* 3597, XXII B). In an exceptional instance which is rather revealing, the speaker of Isocrates 18 *Callimachus* (§ 8) calls Rhinon and his colleagues in the government of Ten which had briefly ruled Athens in 403 after the tyranny of the Thirty oligarchs, together with members of the council, to testify that he had not been responsible for the confiscation of his opponent's property. Those who had held office under this oligarchic regime had a very dubious reputation, and the speaker was probably heavily compromised already by association with them; Patrocles, the man who had held the religious office of king-archon at the time, was his friend (*epitēdeios*) and probably one of the witnesses. But some idea of the authority of office-holders as witnesses seems to survive even in this case.

THE 'PROFESSIONS' AND THE WORLD OF BUSINESS RELATIONS

There were certain other occupational groups at Athens whose members, although not necessarily holding official positions[39], relied for their success on having a reputation for honesty, and were therefore unlikely to compromise themselves by perjury in court. Doctors are the most notable example. They are also, in a sense, expert witnesses; they do not give technical medical reports, but their assessment of the seriousness of a wound is considered more authoritative than that of laymen.

The speaker of D. 54 *Conon* calls a doctor to witness to his critical condition after being beaten up by his opponents (§§ 10, 12) and points out that although they claim he started the fight, they have not found a doctor to testify for them (§ 36). In [D.] 40 *Boeot. ii* 32-3 we are told that the speaker's half-brother Boeotus had accused him before the Areopagus of having wounded him, and he was only saved by Euthydicus the doctor who testified that Boeotus had asked him to fake a convincing head wound. Euthydicus may have repeated this testimony — which highlighted his own honesty — in § 33[40]. Demosthenes in his suit against Onetor called a doctor, Pasiphon, to testify that when he had attended Onetor's sister in an illness Aphobus, supposedly divorced from her, was present at her bedside (D. 30. 34). A doctor's word was not however always accepted as sufficient in itself. In [D.] 47 *Euerg.* 67 the speaker reports that he summoned a doctor to examine a freedwoman who had been attacked on his premises and summoned other witnesses to testify to what the doctor said. The only doctor on whom suspicions are cast in the extant speeches is Execestus, who came with Aeschines' brother to swear that Aeschines was too ill to go on an embassy to Philip of Macedon in 346 (D.19 *Emb.* 124).

It is noteworthy that in three out of these five cases the doctor's name is given in the text of the speech, perhaps suggesting that these men were already well known to the general public.[41]

Whether teachers enjoyed a similar reputation among the general public is more difficult to say, but it certainly would not improve a teacher's chances of attracting pupils if he appeared in court in obviously suspect company. Demosthenes' teachers witnessed for him that his guardian Aphobus had failed to pay them (27.46), a fact which it was in their interest to publicise; and in Isaeus 9 *Astyphilus* 28 the speaker's teachers testified that he had been educated together with his matrilateral half-brother Astyphilus, whose estate he was claiming.

Another profession in which success depended heavily on maintaining a reputation for honesty was banking (Isocrates 17 *Trapeziticus* 2). Bankers had to keep careful records of their transactions. Apollodorus, as a banker's son, recorded in his trierarchy "not only my expenses, but where the money was paid out, and what we were doing at the time, and the price and in what currency it was paid and what the exchange rate was" ([Demosthenes] 50 *Polycles* 30).

In his suit against the general Timotheus for money borrowed from the bank of his father Pasion, Apollodorus called Phormio, the manager of the bank, to testify ([D.] 49 *Tim.* 18, 33, 43) and referred to the bank's records and to Pasion's oral statement concerning money owed to him, made to his two sons in his last illness (§§ 42-3). In [D.] 34 *Ag. Phorm.*, a bottomry-loan contract is deposited with the banker, Cittus, who may have appeared in court to witness to this (§§ 6-7). The banker Blepaeus probably acted as witness in [D.] 40 *Boeot. ii* 52, and the witness who testified to a purchase of gold coin in Isocr. 17 *Trap.* 40-41 was presumably a banker or money-changer.

There were, however, some problems involved in calling bankers as witnesses. In the first place, they were often involved in litigation themselves; bank clients might need others to testify for them to their transactions with the bank, as is probably the case in Isocrates 17 *Trapeziticus* 40-41, or the bank might need to draw on supplementary witnesses to substantiate its own case (*ibid.*, § 38). In [Demosthenes] 52 *Callippus* Apollodorus called not only Phormio but also two witnesses who had vouched for the identity of the recipient of a payment, and others (presumably clients of the bank) who had been present when it was made (§§ 7, 18-19). Furthermore, banks were largely staffed by slaves, who could only give evidence under torture[42], and bank-owners would scarcely be willing to hand over valuable slaves to be tortured to provide evidence for a client's case (cf. Isocrates 17 *Trap.* 11-17).

Witness testimonies concerning monetary transactions occur in many types of case, not only in suits arising out of the quasi-professional world of banking and business deals[43]. Lessees of land testify for their landlords in Lysias 7 *Sacred Olive* 9-10 that the estate contained no sacred olive trees, and in Lysias 17 *Demos. adik.* 8-9 (cf. § 5) that the land was not liable to confiscation as part of Erasistratus' property, having been awarded by a court to the speaker's father. In such cases the tenant shared the landlord's interest in proving that the property was free from liabilities; such common interests can normally be perceived where witnesses testify to business transactions which are not directly involved in litigation.

In Is. 11 *Hagn.* 40-43 lessees of properties belonging to Theopompus' brother Stratocles may have corroborated Theopompus' statement of the extent of his wealth. Several witnesses testify to having bought land or other items from litigants. The speaker of Is. 6 *Philoct.*, accusing his opponents of having persuaded the elderly Euctemon to convert 'visible' into 'invisible' property so that they could more easily gain control of it, produces witnesses who have bought land, and perhaps also livestock, and slave craftsmen, from Euctemon (§§ 33-4); Aeschines, to show that his opponent Timarchus had squandered away his inheritance, produces two witnesses who had bought land from him, a third witness who had purchased a house resold by one of these two, and a fellow-demesman who had borrowed money from Timarchus' father and repaid part of the loan to Timarchus (Aesch. 1 *Tim.* 98-100). Demosthenes, while detailing the sums of which his guardians had defrauded him, brings witnesses to testify that they had purchased ivory from both his father and his guardians (D. 27 *Aph. i* 30-33).

In [Demosthenes] 40 *Boeotus ii* 58, the speaker says that his opponents have produced testimony that he sold or mortgaged to one of their witnesses, Crito, a one-third share in the house which he is claiming as due to him in lieu of his mother's dowry. His arguments are interesting. First he claims that Crito is too profligate to be able to buy a house — thereby implying also that he is just the type of irresponsible young man who would bear false witness for a companion. Secondly, he says this is not a witness testimony but a counter-claim in law: "As you all know, witnesses are people who have no interest in the matter under dispute, while interested parties appear as opponents". This is somewhat tendentious; everyone must have been aware that witnesses frequently had an interest of some kind (cf. Bonner, 1905, p. 29). It was true, however, that a procedure existed by which Crito could have put in a counter-claim for his share of the property[44]. Finally, the speaker stresses the fact that only one further witness to the transaction has been produced, an age-mate (*hēlikiōtēs*) of the plaintiff who has already brought suspicion on himself by claiming knowledge of a naming ceremony held for the plaintiff when he was ten days old (§ 59).

A number of witnesses testify either to loans made in the past which have been repaid, or to debts still outstanding. A creditor who was prepared to bear witness that he had been repaid would obviously be believed; he would only have made difficulties for himself if he had been lying.

Satisfied creditors testify in Is. 2 *Menecles* 34 (cf. §§ 9, 29) that the speaker's adoptive father repaid a debt, and in Lycurgus 1 *Leocr.* 24 that the opponent's debts had been paid by his elder sister's husband while he was in Megara. The witnesses in [D.] 40 *Boeot. ii* 52 — a banker, Blepaeus, and a fellow-demesman, Lysistratus of Thorikos, who had lent money for funeral expenses (cf. Finley, 1952, pp. 83-7) — will also have testified that they had been repaid[45]. However, Apollodorus son of Pasion failed to get testimony from the steward of Philip the shipowner that Pasion had repaid a debt to Philip on behalf of Apollodorus' opponent Timotheus. The steward, Antiphanes of Lamptrai, failed to appear when the case came up before the public arbitrator ([D.] 49 *Tim.* 18-20)[46]; he and his employer may have been reluctant to offend Timotheus, a powerful general, especially if selling supplies to the fleet was part of their business.

Other creditors of Timotheus, who presumably had not yet been repaid, were quite ready to testify for Apollodorus on the same occasion that the general had been borrowing from them without giving security ([D.] 49.61)[47]. Apollodorus' own creditors may have testified on his behalf to the loans they had made him while serving as trierarch ([D.] 50 *Polycl.* 13, 56?) and on another occasion ([D.] 53 *Nicostr.* 18, cf. 13). In two of these cases Apollodorus had mortgaged land, i.e. had 'sold' property on the understanding that he could repurchase it by repaying the debt (Finley, 1952); his creditors were personal friends.

Those who had borrowed money and repaid it were also happy to publicise the fact. The speaker of D. 37 *Pant.* (§ 54) calls ex-creditors and ex-debtors as character witnesses. In Demosthenes' suit against his guardian, Aphobus, Moeriades testified that he had borrowed money from Aphobus and repaid it (D.27.27-8)[48].

The witnesses in [D.] 33 *Apat.*, [D.] 35 *Lacr.* and D.37 *Pant.* were involved in more complex business transactions. In [D.] 35.23 the witness had lent money against the security of property which had already — unknown to him — been mortgaged to the speaker. Possibly the latter offered to him, in return for his testimony, support in his own proceedings against the debtor. In [D.] 33 the speaker had lent money for a trading voyage and had been repaid, as his witnesses testify (§§ 8, 12), but had been drawn into a subsequent dispute involving his ex-debtor. In D.37 Pantainetus had borrowed money from the speaker, putting up his mining works and slaves as security (§ 4), and had subsequently borrowed money from others in order to repay the first loan; witnesses testified that the speaker and another man who shared in the loan with him had transferred the workshop to the second set of creditors and had been freed from all liability towards Pantainetus (§§ 13, 17). Witnesses were also called to testify that the workshop had subsequently changed hands again (§ 31).

The relationship of employer to employee rarely forms the subject of witness testimonies[49], since most employees were slaves, but there are two examples. In [Demosthenes] 53 *Nicostratus* 21 men who had hired slave harvesters from the speaker's opponent, Arethusius, testified that he acted as the slaves' owner, and in Demosthenes 57 *Eubulides* 44-5 a family which had employed the speaker's mother as a wet-nurse testified on his behalf that she was a free citizen. Cases such as this last, in which one citizen appears almost in the relation of patron to another, are rare; though it should be noted that resident aliens and freedmen had to be supported in court by citizen patrons in some circumstances[50].

There are a few cases in which 'clients' provide aid in legal cases for patrons. In Demosthenes 27 *Aphobus i* 19-22 it is just possible that the freedman manager of the workshop Demosthenes had inherited testified for him. In [Demosthenes] 49 *Timotheus* 43 we learn that Timotheus had sent Phrasierides of Anaphlystos, who had been granted citizenship on his proposal and enrolled in his deme (D. 23 *Aristocrates* 202; *A.P.F.* 14976) to copy bank records which Timotheus needed for his defence against Apollodorus. In this case Apollodorus got Phrasierides to witness on his own behalf that he had been given full facilities, a testimony which had little strict bearing on the case but which, like the testimonies of Timotheus' creditors in § 61, was probably designed to give the jury the impression that all Timotheus' supporters were deserting him and aiding his opponent.

Rich men who were generous with gifts and loans to the impecunious expected to be repaid by help in court when needed. In Lysias 19 *Aristophanes* 59 those who had been given, or lent, money by the speaker's father for dowries, funeral expenses or ransoms testify to his generosity, and in Demosthenes 19 *Embassy* 169-70 (cf. 166-8) prisoners-of-war to whom Demosthenes had lent money support him. The speaker of Lysias 16 *Mantitheus* was supported by witnesses from his deme to whom he had given money to help them equip themselves for campaign (§ 14).

BYSTANDERS

As has already been indicated, in small-scale societies disinterested bystanders are hardly to be found; the impartial witness is not one who has no ties with the litigants, but one who has ties with both parties of approximately equal weight. Though fourth-century Athens was no village, members of the litigating class would probably be able to find an acquaintance or two in most urban gatherings. The fact that a witness is presented as a bystander does not necessarily imply that he was a total stranger.

Since, as we have seen, it was a normal precaution for an Athenian to provide himself with witnesses while going about his lawful business on many different occasions, it was the man who wished to present himself as the victim of unprovoked and unexpected aggression who called on 'bystanders' to act as witnesses. This is the case in Lysias 3 *Simon* 14 and 20, Demosthenes 54 *Conon* 9, and probably also in [Demosthenes] 53 *Nicostratus* 17-18 and Isocrates 18 *Callimachus* 8[51].

In Demosthenes 54 the speaker, Ariston, claimed to have been seriously wounded by his opponent, Conon, in a fight in the agora one evening. Conon, for his part, maintained that the incident had been an insignificant scuffle between young men — his son, Ariston, and others — in which he himself had not taken part. Ariston introduced his own witnesses in § 9. The exact words of their testimony are not preserved, nor are their full names. It is clear, however, that one was a well-known member of a distinguished family, Niceratus III son of Nicias II of Kydantidai (*A.P.F.* 10808). His great-grandfather Nicias I had been a respected general in the Peloponnesian war, his paternal grandfather Niceratus II had been killed by the Thirty Tyrants, his maternal grandfather Thrasybulus of Steiria was another noted democrat of the late fifth century. Niceratus III, born in 389/8 (D.M. Lewis, 1955, p. 30), was at the time of this case in his mid-forties, suffered from weak health and had served as trierarch and treasurer of military funds; he was later to figure as one of the elder statesmen associated with the conservative reforms of Lycurgus. Demosthenes (21 *Meidias* 165) calls him *ho agapētos*, 'dear old Niceratus'. He was an ideal example of the respectable witness and was hardly picked out of the crowd at random; he must almost certainly have been known at least by sight, if not personally, to Ariston and his companion[52].

Ariston gives only the first names of his witnesses, so the other three cannot be identified with confidence. Lysistratus might be the son of Polyeuctus of Bate, councillor in 341/0 and member of a rich and distinguished priestly family (*A.P.F.* 4549); if so, he was another respectable supporter, somewhat younger than Niceratus — but the name is common and the identification highly conjectural. The other two, Paseas and Diodorus, are unidentifiable.

In §§ 31-2 the speaker contrasts his own witnesses with those of his opponent. Conon, he tells the jury),

> put in a false testimony in the name of men whose reputation even you, I think, will recognise when you hear them: "Diotimus son of Diotimus of Icaria, Archebiades son of Demoteles of Halai, Chaeretius son of Chaerimenes of Pithos testify that they were going away from a dinner-party together with Conon and met Ariston and Conon's son fighting in the agora, and that Conon did not strike Ariston" — as if you would immediately believe that, and not reason out

the truth, namely that, in the first place, Lysistratus, Paseas, Niceratus and Diodorus, who have explicitly testified that they saw me being beaten by Conon and being ill-treated in all these other ways, being strangers to me who arrived on the scene purely by accident, would not have been willing to bear false witness, and so would not have testified as they did unless they had actually seen that I had suffered these things. . . .

The testimony which Ariston quotes had not yet been heard by the jury (Conon, as defendant, had not yet spoken) but was known to Ariston from the preliminary hearing of the case by one of the public arbitrators. We should not assume without question that he is quoting the testimony either of Conon's or of his own witnesses verbatim (cf. Mensching, 1963). He carefully includes the detail that Conon's witnesses were leaving a dinner-party (*deipnon*), which fits in which his own earlier assertion that they had been drinking (§ 7); apart from this, he tells us only that Conon's witnesses explicitly testified that Conon took no part in the fight — a damaging testimony which he had to weaken as far as he could. The fact that he called his own witnesses at an earlier point in the speech (§ 9) strongly suggests that their testimony did not formally contradict that of Conon's witnesses; if Niceratus and the others had explicitly stated that they saw Conon strike Ariston (as he claims in his summary of their testimony in § 31), one would expect him to have called them to testify immediately after his quotation of Conon's witness statement. Instead, he vaguely insinuates that Conon's witnesses are notoriously disreputable, without however being able to cite any specific incidents to their discredit. We know that Archebiades (*A.P.F.* 819) came of a wealthy trierarchic family and had a nephew (BS) who held the office of polemarch c. 330, so Archebiades is likely to have been in his forties at the time of this speech[53]. Probably Conon's witnesses were just as well-to-do and reputable as those of the speaker; the latter's witnesses included Demosthenes' enemy Meidias (§ 10; *A.P.F.* 9719), and it is easy to imagine what Demosthenes would have said against him had he been writing his speech for the other side — though to an unprejudiced eye Meidias was respectable enough.

A similar attack on the opponent's witnesses occurs in Isaeus 3 *Pyrrhus* 23, where the speaker says of the witnesses to a formal deposition (*ekmartyria*, Harrison 1971, pp. 146-7) made by an absent witness, Pyretiades, which he had subsequently repudiated, that they were "none of his intimate associates (*oikeioi*), but Dionysius of Erchia and Aristolochus of Aithalidai. With these two men they say they took the deposition in the city — these men, for such an important deposition! Men whom no one else would trust on any matter whatsoever." Here the implication is that the deposition was forged and the witnesses bribed; but note that again the speaker produces no specific evidence of their unreliability.

The speaker of [D.] 47 *Euerg.* also had to face attacks on the credibility of his witnesses (§ 39). He had gone to the house of Theophemos, one of his opponents, with a slave from the office of the port supervisors (*epimelētai tou emporiou*)[54], to collect trireme gear for which he was responsible. When Theophemos refused to allow them to enter, the speaker sent the slave to collect passers-by to testify to his refusal (§ 36), and they testify in §§ 38-40 to this and to the fight which took place when he tried to enter the house.

In [D.] 58 *Theocr.* 9, 26 the speaker presents his witnesses as if they were picked at random, but actually he can have had no difficulty in calling on persons known to him; the witnesses merely testify that a denunciation had been posted in front of the office of the port supervisors.

The witness presented as bystander or passer-by, then, was often subject to suspicion, either because this description could be used to conceal personal ties with the litigant or because it was felt that witnesses who lacked personal ties were likely to be testifying for payment or out of an irresponsible pleasure in making trouble.

FELLOW-VOYAGERS AND FELLOW-SOLDIERS

Other witnesses were thrown together with the litigant by chance, but remained associated with him for long enough to develop a closer relationship. Owing to the celebrated case between Demosthenes and Aeschines over the embassy to Philip of Macedon in 346 B.C., those who served as fellow-ambassadors figure prominently in the data. Boards of ambassadors were partly self-recruiting — those nominated could themselves suggest additional names — and might therefore be divided into cliques even before setting out.

Aeschines calls fellow-ambassadors to testify for him about Demosthenes' behaviour, and his own in 2 *Embassy* 19, 46, 55, 107 and 127; the ambassador Dercylus son of Autocles of Hagnous also testified for him (to events which had taken place in Athens) in 2.155.

Demosthenes probably called a fellow-ambassador in D.19 *Emb.* 163-5, to bear witness to the time taken over journeys, and challenged his fellow-ambassadors in 19.175-6 to give testimony against Aeschines or take an oath disclaiming knowledge[55]. In 19.129-30 he calls fellow-ambassadors of Aeschines to testify about another embassy in which he himself did not take part. None of these ambassadors gave testimony on controversial matters except for Dercylus son of Autocles of Hagnous — named by Demosthenes in 19.175 as an ally set by him to watch Aeschines' movements — who testified in Aesch. 2. 154f. that he had heard Aristophanes of Olynthus relating that Demosthenes had tried to bribe him. The main purpose of summoning fellow-ambassadors to testify was apparently to show the jury where the sympathies of the board of ambassadors predominantly lay — which was, on this criterion, with Aeschines. Note that two of his witnesses, the ambassador Iatrocles and Aglaocreon of Tenedus, representing Athens' allies, are said to have shared his tent (Aesch. 2. 126).

In a less controversial situation Eunomus, who had gone to Sicily on an embassy in 393 with Aristophanes son of Nicophemus, witnessed for the speaker of Lysias 19 *Aristoph.* (§ 23) that Aristophanes had borrowed money on this occasion.

Those whose suits concerned events which had happened on campaign naturally had to call on fellow-soldiers or on trireme crews and their commanders, the trierarchs. Isaeus 4 *Nicostratus* concerns the estate of a mercenary soldier who died on campaign. The speaker delivered the second speech in the case on behalf of Hagnon and Hagnotheus, who claimed that they ought to inherit as next-of-kin; the other side produced a will in favour of Chariades, who had been with the deceased on campaign, witnessed by fellow-soldiers. Hagnon and Hagnotheus had brought forward other soldiers to testify that the dead man, Nicostratus, and Chariades were not friends or members of the same unit (*taxis*) and did not mess together (§ 18), and that Chariades and his supporters did not conduct Nicostratus' funeral (§§ 19-20). They claimed that Chariades' witnesses were friends of his own and not friends of Nicostratus (§ 23). Astyphilus son of Euthycrates of Araphen (*A.P.F.* 7252) died on campaign in Mytilene;[56] fellow-soldiers brought his bones home and aided his kin in making arrangements for burial, and probably testified to this in Isaeus 9 *Astyphilus* 4. Those who testified in Demosthenes 57 *Eubulides* 18-19, in 346-5, that the speaker's father had been taken prisoner in the Peloponnesian War, can hardly have included fellow-soldiers, but might have included their sons.

Fellow-soldiers were often also called as character witnesses. The speaker of Lysias 20 *Polystratus*, defending his father on a charge of helping the oligarchic government in 411, calls witnesses to testify to his own and his brothers' conduct on campaign (§§ 24-29); some of these witnesses may have been ransomed by him (§ 24). The speaker of Lysias 16 *Mantitheus*, calling witnesses to testify to his bravery in war, states explicitly that he fought boldly in order to get a reputation which would help him if he found himself in danger in the lawcourts (cf. Adkins, 1960, 201-8). Conversely, the speaker of Demosthenes 54 *Conon* calls fellow-soldiers and perhaps officers to testify that when his opponent's sons had camped near him on guard duty two years earlier they had behaved in such a disorderly and aggressive manner that he and his messmates had reported them to the general, after which the two parties had come to blows (§§ 3-6).

Trierarchs, being members of the wealthy class, were quite often called upon to bear witness to events which took place during their period of service. Demosthenes' ally Euthycles called trierarchs as witnesses in Demosthenes 23 *Aristocrates* 168 to Charidemus' attacks on Athenian forces in Perinthus and the Thracian Chersonese; Demosthenes' witnesses "who were in the Hellespont" in D.19 *Embassy* 162 may also have been trierarchs, though alternatively they may have been traders. Apollodorus son of Pasion called fellow-trierarchs to witness to his attempts to get his successor Polycles to take over his ship ([Demosthenes] 50, 33-42; cf. [Demosthenes] 47 *Euergus* 77-8); he also called the officers and some of the crew of his own ships (§§ 10, 24-31, 37). In Lysias 21 *Bribery*, the concluding part of a defence in which the speaker dilated on his character and services to the city, a fellow-trierarch who had served with him at the battle of Arginusae gave evidence that the speaker had rescued his trireme (§§ 9-10). In [Demosthenes] 47 *Euergus* 48 fellow-trierarchs are called to testify that they, like the speaker, had seized property from men who had failed to hand over trireme gear: a clear example of the way in which members of the upper class call on their peers for testimony which has little direct bearing on the case, but indicates solidarity with the litigant and legitimises his behaviour.

When disputes arose as a result of trading voyages, ships' captains, crew and fellow-passengers might be called as witnesses, as in Demosthenes 34 *Against Phormio* 9-10 and 37, [Demosthenes] 35 *Lacritus* 20 and 34, Lysias frag. XL.8 Gernet (1926) and probably in Demosthenes 32 *Zenothemis* 13 and 19[57]. In a more unusual case, the Lesbian speaker of Antiphon 5 *Herodes* was accused of having murdered an Athenian fellow-passenger on a voyage round Lesbos; the witnesses who testified for him in §§ 22 and 24 must have been fellow-passengers, and those who testified in §§ 20, 28 may also have been on the vessel. The prosecution tortured a witness who had been a fellow-passenger and had explicitly corroborated the defendant's story (§ 42)[58]. All these witnesses are likely to have been Lesbians rather than Athenians; those called by the defendant had to travel to Athens to support him and may have been personal friends. Alternatively, they may have been motivated by opposition to the Athenian empire; the victim was an Athenian colonist (cleruch) settled on Lesbian land.

This may be an appropriate place to collect together other evidence for the use of witnesses from abroad in Athenian courts.

The speaker of [D.] 40 *Boeot. ii* apparently calls Mytileneans in §§ 36-7 to rebut his half-brother's assertion that he had used money owed to their father when recruiting mercenaries in Mytilene. Their father was *persona grata* in that city and the witnesses are described to the jury as "your friends", i.e. pro-Athenian. The orator Lycurgus called witnesses from Rhodes, probably traders, to describe the scene when his opponent Leocrates arrived there with the news of the Greek defeat at the battle of Chaeronea (Lyc. 1 *Leocr.* 19-20). The speaker of Hyperides 3 *Athenog.* called Troezenian witnesses to testify that his opponent Athenogenes, an Egyptian resident in Athens, had been made a citizen of Troezen (§§ 31-33). Witnesses from Plataea and Thebes testified for the speaker of Lys. 23 *Plat.* that his opponent (who claimed to be a Plataean citizen) was not known in Plataea and had been living in Thebes, a city for which the Plataeans felt deep enmity (§§ 5-8, 15; some of the Plataean witnesses may have lived in Athens). Foreigners were also, from time to time, drawn into Athenian political disputes. Aeschines in his speech *On the False Embassy* (2.86) calls on representatives of Athens' allies, and on Phocian and Boeotian ambassadors (2.143). Demosthenes calls Olynthians to testify that Philip of Macedon had given grants of Olynthian land to Aeschines and Philocrates for their role in negotiating peace between him and Athens (D.19 *Emb.* 145-6); being grateful to Demosthenes for his championship of their city and bitterly hostile to Philip, these will have been eager witnesses.

POLITICIANS *(RHĒTORES)*

As has already been indicated, it is impossible to make a sharp distinction in Athens between 'political' and non-political cases, and similarly it is somewhat arbitrary to distinguish between calling 'politicians' as witnesses and calling on friends. Nevertheless, Athenians were aware of a distinction between those who regularly spoke in courts and in the assembly and those who did not (Dover, 1974, pp. 25-8), and litigants who called on the services of experienced speakers, *rhētores*, had to balance the advantages of their skills and the fact that they were well known to the jury against the risk that the opponent would accuse them of insincerity, inconsistency (cf. Demosthenes 51 *Trierarchic Crown* 16) and self-interest.

Such accusations are directed particularly against supporting speakers (*synēgoroi*), since ordinary witnessing gave no scope to rhetorical talents; but witnesses and *synēgoroi* supplied similar kinds of support. Aeschines remarks that he might have asked the general Phocion to act as *synēgoros* but prefers to call him as witness so that he will be liable to perjury charges if he deviates from the truth (2 *Embassy* 170); the statement is disingenuous, since Phocion might not have been willing to identify himself with Aeschines to the point of acting as *synēgoros*, but illustrates the functional similarity of the two roles. The speech of the general Cephisodotus in support of Demosthenes' claim to the trierarchic crown (Demosthenes 51.1), and those of his opponents' supporters (*ibid.* 16) presumably took the form of testimony about their activities on campaign. The speaker of Isaeus 3 *Pyrrhus* says that Diophantus of Sphettus, a well-known politician (*P.A.* 4438[59]), both defended the opponent, Xenocles, on a perjury charge and was taken by him as a witness when he tried to take possession of disputed property (§ 22). Hyperides in two speeches (2 *Lycophron* 10, 19-20, 3 *Euxenippus* 11-13) makes the point that because the speaker's friends are skilful orators his opponent will complain and warn the jury against listening to them, even though he too calls on politicians to act as his *synēgoroi.* The speaker of Demosthenes 48 *Olympiodorus* accuses his opponent of collecting *rhētores* to speak against him (§ 36). Hyperides 3 *Eux.* 11-13 mentions the custom of asking one's tribe to provide ten *synēgoroi* to support one's defence in court (cf. below, p. 345); we have another example in Andocides' defence against the charge of profaning the Eleusinian Mysteries (1.150). This speech also provides an instance in which we can measure more precisely than usual the significance of a politician's appearance in court as a supporter; one of Andocides' other *synēgoroi* (*ibid.*) was Anytus, who in the same year acted as one of the accusers of Socrates[60]. His support for Andocides was intended to symbolise Andocides' complete dissociation from the milieu of Alcibiades and his friends, who had been responsible for the profanation of the Mysteries and for whose misdeeds Socrates was in effect being brought to trial.

In most cases we do not know enough about the details of Athenian political life to understand the precise implications of support by well-known public figures; we can catch only a faint whiff of the aura of importance, respectability or glamour imparted by the appearance of Moerocles (Ampolo, 1981) as *synēgoros* for the speaker of [Demosthenes] 58 *Theocrines* (§§ 53-4), by the testimony of Demosthenes and others for Apollodorus in [Demosthenes] 59 *Neaira* 123, of Glaucon of Cholargos ('*andri kai mala chrēstōi*', 'a very worthy man') for Aeschines in 1 *Timarchus* 62-65, or the possible testimony of Demos son of Pyrilampes — a colourful character who owned peacocks and was a personal friend of the Persian king, *A.P.F.* 8792.VIII[61] — for the speaker of

Lysias 19 *Aristophanes* (§ 27).

Sometimes the enhancement of prestige was mutual; I suspect that the men who witnessed for Apollodorus that they had known Neaira as a prostitute, who included the *rhētor* Philostratus son of Dionysius of Kolone (*A.P.F.* 14734: [D.] 59.23), the statesman Eubulus of Probalinthus ([D.] 59.48), an ex-*thesmothetes* and the son of an archon (*ibid.* 71)[62], got a certain kick and even kudos out of making it publicly known that they had — long ago — had connections with such a notorious lady. Aeschines had a more difficult time, naturally, in persuading witnesses in 346 to substantiate his case that Timarchus had had a career as a male prostitute in his youth. He had witnesses who knew that Timarchus had lived in the house of Misgolas (Aeschines 1.50) and with their testimonies in hand was able to persuade Misgolas — a man of 54 (*A.P.F.* 14625 II) who was quite possibly still unmarried and making no secret of his sexual preferences[63] — to subscribe to a tactfully worded testimony (§§ 45-50[64]). Phaedrus son of Callias of Sphettos (*A.P.F.* 139647), general in 347/6, testified that he took part in a procession at the city festival of Dionysus with Misgolas and Timarchus (§§ 43, 50), a fairly harmless testimony; and Philemon, an actor, testified that he had bribed Timarchus to accuse Philotades of Kydathenaion of not being a citizen (§ 115). Aeschines also proffered an insulting challenge to the politician Hegesandrus of Sunium (*A.P.F.* 6351) to testify that he had slept with Timarchus (§67); since Hegesandrus and his brother were among Timarchus' supporters (§71), Aeschines did not expect him to testify but was merely trying to prejudice the jury against him[65].

As can be seen, politicians who appear as witnesses are not necessarily asked to testify on strictly political business, though a few instances of this can be found.

Aeschines in his speech *On the False Embassy* hoped to get Amyntor of Erchia to testify against Demosthenes that the latter had tried to get him to propose peace with Philip (§§ 67-8); in the same speech (84-5) he called Aleximachus of Pelex and those who had served on the presiding committee of *proedroi* in the assembly with Demosthenes to witness that Demosthenes had tried to prevent a decree proposed by Aleximachus from being put to the vote; he also called various Athenians officially concerned in relations between Athens and Phocis to testify to the roles they had played (§ 134)[66]. Demosthenes in the same case (19 *Embassy* 31-2) summoned a witness to testify that he (the witness) had proposed a motion in the Council implicitly censuring the members of the embassy to Philip. Finally, Aristomachus son of Critodemus of Alopeke (*A.P.F.* 1969) testified c.340 for the speaker of [D.] 58 *Theocr.* that the latter's opponent Theocrines had received 1½ minas (about 150 days' wages) in the witness's house about three years earlier "for the decree which Antimedon was proposing on behalf of the Tenedians" (§ 35). Aristomachus was also one of those who testified for Apollodorus in the Neaira case ([D.] 59.25); he seems to have had a taste for notoriety.

Authoritative figures from political life were sought after as witnesses for all kinds of transactions. The banker Pasion, whose position as an extremely rich ex-slave who had been granted citizenship was inevitably precarious, deposited his will with Cephalion of Aphidna (*A.P.F.* 8410) whose son, the well-known politician Cephisophon, testified to this on behalf of Phormio when Pasion's son Apollodorus tried to dispute the will ([Demosthenes] 45 *Stephanus i* 19). Pasion had used another prominent politician, Agyrrhius, as mediator earlier in a banking dispute[67] (Isocrates 17 *Trapeziticus* 31-2); his profession gave him contacts in the highest circles. The speaker of [Demosthenes] 42 and his adversary Phaenippus made an agreement to delay filing property statements in the presence of Polyeuctus of Crioa, another well-known public figure (*A.P.F.* 13772), and other witnesses, who testified to this in court (§§ 11, 16). Xenocles, opponent of the speaker of Isaeus 3 *Pyrrhus*, took well-known men as witnesses when trying to take possession of disputed property (§ 22).

THE OPPONENT'S 'ENEMIES'

One obvious way to score over an opponent was to persuade his close associates or supporters to testify against him.[68] Aeschines' challenge to Hegesandrus (1 *Timarchus* 67) and the substantially innocuous and irrelevant testimony extracted from Timotheus' client Phrasierides by Apollodorus ([Demosthenes] 49.43) have already been mentioned. The author of [Demosthenes] 25 *Aristogiton i*, a speech which is likely to be a rhetorical exercise or pamphlet even if fourth-century (Treves, 1936; cf. Sealey, 1967) offers as witnesses, (1) a man who had buried the opponent's father and had been unable to recover his expenses from the son, (2) the arbitrator responsible for the case which the opponent's half-brother had brought against him for trying to sell his half-sister into slavery, (3) the patron (*prostatēs*) of Zobia, a freedwoman prostitute who had helped the opponent when he had escaped from prison and whom he had later denounced for failing to pay the resident alien's tax (the officials responsible, the *pōlētai*, also appear as witnesses) and (4) a man whose nose the opponent had bitten off while in prison (§§ 54-58, 62)[69]. It is also stated that witnesses in an earlier speech in the same case had testified that Aristogiton had sexually attacked his mother and had deserted his father when the latter was in prison (§§ 54-5).

In another suspect speech, Demosthenes is represented as having forced Aphobus' brother Aesius in a previous suit to give a testimony against Aphobus which he is now disclaiming ([D] 29 *Aph. iii* 15-18, cf. 23, 55)[70]. These probably fictional examples throw into high relief the aim of many more realistic and reliable testimonies, to portray the opponent as a man whose behaviour was such that he had gone through life making enemies rather than friends. Seeking out the opponent's enemies was a routine tactic for the speechwriter (cf. Dorjahn, 1935).

The commonest type of enemy is one who has previously been involved in a lawsuit against the opponent. In D.36 *Phorm.* 21 those who had been sued by Apollodorus for debts to his father's bank testified that his claim that the bank accounts had been destroyed was false, and in §§ 53, 56 witnesses testify that Apollodorus was constantly bringing lawsuits. The speaker of [D.] 58 similarly accused his opponent Theocrines of being a sycophant, promising to bring witnesses including the orators Hyperides and Demosthenes to testify that he took bribes for his activities (§ 35; but cf. § 4). He accused Demosthenes of having bribed Theocrines to drop a charge (*graphê*) against him (§§ 42-3) and in consequence breaking his promise to support the speaker in his suit; he called Micon of Cholleidai[71] and officials to witness that Theocrines had denounced Micon for taking corn to a port other than Athens and had been bribed to drop the charge (§§ 9, 26); and he introduced Cephisodorus to testify that Theocrines' father had illegitimately tried to claim his slave-girl as free (§ 19). Further examples of witnesses who had been concerned in lawsuits of various kinds against the speaker's opponent can be found in Isocr. 18 *Callim.* 52-54: Aesch. 1 *Tim.* 115, Lyc. 1 *Leocr.* 19-20, Lys. 23 *Pancl.* 3-4 and (?) 13-14, D.39 *Boeot.i* 19, and [D.] 53 *Nicostr.* 20. In [D.] 47 *Euerg.* 32 and [D.] 50 *Polycl.* 68 witnesses testify to disputes with the opponent over trierarchic obligations[72]; in Lys. fr. XXXVIII G. §§ 4-5, [D.] 42 Phaen. 29, [D.] 53 *Nicostr.* 20 and probably D.41 *Spud.* 11, to conflicts over debts. In Lys. 13. 66 witnesses testify that they had convicted the opponent, Agoratus, on adultery charges (cf. Lys. fr. XXXVIII G. § 5).

Other conflicts had not reached the courts. In [Demosthenes] 59 *Neaira* Phrastor of Aegilia (§§ 50-54) and Theagenes of the *genos* Koironidai (who had held office as king-archon: §§ 72-84) testified, with some signs of embarrassment[73], that they had successively married Neaira's illegitimate daughter Phano, accepting the assurances of the defendant that she was his legitimate child. The speaker of Isaeus 8 *Ciron* (§ 46) says he will call a witness to prove that his opponent's main supporter, Diocles, had been caught in adultery. The speaker of Isaeus 5 called witnesses to testify to the miserliness of his opponent Dicaeogenes (§§ 35-38). In Lysias 31 *Philo* the plaintiff calls witnesses to testify that they had been robbed by the defendant during the rule of the Thirty Tyrants, when he was living at Oropos and raiding across the border (§§ 18-19, cf. 14). The witnesses who testified to the misdeeds of Eratosthenes in the same period and said that they had heard him admit to being an 'ephor' under the Thirty (Lysias 12. 43-47, cf. 61) probably also had personal grudges, and the same is likely to be true of some of the witnesses who testified against Agoratus (Lysias 13. 23-28, 67-8, 79, 81). The speaker of [Demosthenes] 47 *Euergus* describes his witnesses as those 'wronged' (*ēdikē-menoi*) by his opponents (§ 82).[74]

In other cases the hostility of witnesses arose out of more intimate ties. In Lysias 23 *Pancleon* one of the speaker's witnesses claims that the opponent is not, as he alleges, a Plataean, but the witness's slave (§§ 7-8). Even after a slave had been freed his former master might testify against him or his descendants; if a freedman became too successful, his position could give rise to resentment. In Lysias 13. 64 the ex-owners of the father of the defendant, Agoratus, testify to his slave origin and in Demosthenes 36 *Phormio* 45-48 the ex-owners of Apollodorus' father Pasion did the same; since Apollodorus was a particularly arrogant, graceless and ostentatious *nouveau riche* citizen, their hostility is scarcely surprising. Similar resentments may have motivated the witnesses who made statements for Demosthenes (19 *Embassy* 200) about the early upbringing and menial occupations of Aeschines.

Kin also could feel resentment, either as a result of disputes over property or merely from jealousy of others' success. In Isaeus 8 *Ciron* 40-42 the speaker says that he will call the victims, 'or if they are afraid to speak, others who know the facts'[75], to testify that his opponent's supporter Diocles imprisoned the husband of one of his sisters and had the husband of a second sister murdered, subsequently defrauding her son of his property.

In [D.] 48 *Olymp.* 34-5 witnesses who had initially put in a successful claim for the estate of Comon, which had subsequently been awarded to the speaker's opponent, testified that the speaker had duly handed property over to them (a testimony of little relevance serving mainly to suggest that the speaker had the support of his kindred). In [D.] 42 *Phaen.* 23 the witnesses who testified that the defendant Phaenippus had inherited two large estates, one from his father and one from his mother's father, may well have been resentful kin. In Is. 7 *Apoll.* 31-2 witnesses testify that the opponent and her sister had sold up the property of their deceased brother and divided the proceeds, instead of posthumously adopting a son to him to 'continue his oikos', and in §§ 23-25 witnesses testify that the son of this sister, Thrasybulus son of Aeschines of Lousia, did not wish to put in a claim against the speaker for the estate of his mother's cousin (MFBS) — a testimony implying that the opponent, who stood in the same relation to *d.c.* as Thrasybulus, had equally little right to claim[76]. Very probably the division had left the families of the two sisters on bad terms.

NEIGHBOURS, CULT ASSOCIATES AND CLANSMEN

From enmity to friendship is a short step; a man's personal network of associates included both enemies and friends. With most of them association was due to circumstance rather than choice, even though choice could partly determine alignments and alliances within ascribed groupings: villages, city neighbourhoods, cult groups and the patriclans which mingled elements of co-residence, shared cult and kinship in their organisation — tribes, trittyes, demes and phratries. Interest in maintaining good relations and potential sources of conflict and friction mingled in all these relationships.

Neighbours It is taken for granted that neighbours know all about each other's affairs (cf. Lysias 7 *Olive tree* 18-19, 29). In [Demosthenes] 55 *Callicles* the speaker's neighbour was suing him for damages allegedly caused by his having diverted a rain-gully so that it inundated the plaintiff's land. The speaker claims that this suit was part of a campaign of harrassment aimed at getting him to cede or sell his land to the plaintiff's family; a cousin had contested his title, and the plaintiff and his brother had previously brought other suits (§§ 1-2). The parents of the two parties were on good terms (§ 23); relations apparently became bad after their fathers died. It is not impossible that there was some kind of kinship between the two parties and some dispute about inheritance underlying the whole quarrel. Neighbours of both parties testify on the speaker's behalf in §§ 12-15, 21 and 27; but his opponent no doubt had his local supporters too. In [Demosthenes] 47 *Euergus* the speaker was supported by neighbours who bore witness that they had seen his opponents taking property from his house and had protested at the seizure of his son, whom the opponents had taken to be a slave; they had come to Piraeus to inform the speaker of all this (§§ 60-62). A stonemason who had been working on a funerary monument near the speaker's house — again, probably, a local man — seems to have testified about a second seizure of property (§§ 65-6). In Isaeus 3 *Pyrrhus* 12-15 Pyrrhus' neighbours bore witness for the speaker, who was claiming his estate, that the woman alleged by the opponent to have been Pyrrhus' wife had behaved like a prostitute — noisy parties, male visitors at all hours (these are presumably city neighbours).

The speaker of Lysias 17 *Dem. Adik.* brought neighbours to testify that he had been trying unsuccessfully to get possession of property in Kikynna (in the plain east of Hymettus?) awarded to his father by a court judgment (§ 8-9). In Lycurgus 1 *Leocrates* 22-3 "those who know", who testify that the husband of the elder sister of the defendant, Leocrates, bought his house when he had gone to Megara, were probably also neighbours; neighbours also witnessed in §§ 19-20 that Leocrates left Athens after the defeat at Chaeronea. In D.31 *Onetor ii* 4 the witnesses who testified that Onetor had put up notices (*horoi*) on his house stating that it stood as security for a dowry of 2000 drachmai, and had subsequently removed them, were again probably neighbours; so probably were the witnesses who stated on Demosthenes' behalf in D.30 *Onetor i* 26-30 that Aphobus had continued to farm and harvest crops from land supposedly ceded to Onetor as surety for dowry repayments. Similarly, it will probably have been neighbours who testified for Apollodorus in [D.] 53 *Nicostratus* 19-20 that the slave Cerdon belonged to the household of Arethusius, from whom Apollodorus was claiming damages, and who testified in §§ 16-18 of the same speech to the damage caused by the opponents to Apollodorus' property.

Cult associates (thiasotai and gennetai) *Thiasoi* were groups founded solely for performance of cult and membership was voluntary. However, no element of conversion was involved (Nock, 1933) and one does not have the impression that the choice of one cult or another usually carried much significance in terms of the worshipper's conception of his or her identity; a *thiasos* would overlap in membership with the other groupings discussed in this section and would not form a significantly different reference group.

In Isaeus 9 *Astyphilus* 30 members of a *thiasos* of Heracles testify that the speaker's father had introduced his stepson, Astyphilus, to it; the speaker was no doubt a member himself, and the purport of the testimony was to show that his father and his step-brother, whose estate he hoped to inherit, were on close terms (cf. Isaeus 8 *Ciron* 15-17).

A *genos* was both a cult association and a clan, a subdivision of a phratry. Not all phratry members were members of a *genos* (*gennētai*), but *genos* membership automatically conferred phratry membership (Andrewes, 1961). Only legitimate children of members were eligible for admission and therefore *genos* members may be called as witnesses where legitimacy is in question. In

[Demosthenes] 59 *Neaira* 61 (cf. 56-60) Apollodorus called members of the *genos* Brytidai to testify that they had refused to accept the daughter of Phrastor of Aegilia by Neaira as legitimate; when Phrastor objected, they had challenged him to take an oath and he had withdrawn his claim.[77] Similarly, members of the *genos* Kerykes gave evidence for Andocides (1 *Mysteries* 126-7) that Callias III son of Hipponicus of Alopeke had presented to them as legitimate a child which he was known previously to have repudiated. Objections were raised, but Callias took an oath that the child was legitimate and was allowed to register it. Callias was a controversial figure, belonging to a very rich family which had held the leading position in the *genos*, the office of Torchbearer in the Eleusinian Mysteries, for at least three generations; he failed to pass the office on to his son, and was said to have dissipated much of the family fortune (*A.P.F.* 7826, VIII); he can hardly have been universally popular in the *genos*.[78]

Genos witnesses may also have been called to testify that the speaker of Demosthenes 57 *Eubulides* was selected "among those of noble birth" (*en tois eugenestatois*, § 46) as one of those from whom the priest of Heracles in the deme Halimous was to be selected by lot.

Phratry Since *genos*, phratry and deme were all recruited by patrifiliation a man's fellow-*phratores* always included kin. If he lived in the place where the phratry had its cult centre, they also included neighbours and allies and rivals in local politics — as was the case for those who resided in the deme to which they belonged. The testimony of *genos* and phratry members was particularly important in questions of marriage, legitimate filiation and adoption because phratry rituals were carried out at marriage (*gamēlia*) and soon after the birth of children (*meion*), and because the formal introduction of a boy to his father's phratry (*koureion*) took place two years before the admission to the deme by which citizenship was officially conferred (Labarbe, 1953). In the phratry Demotionidai (*I.G.* ii^2 1237) each candidate had to be supported by three witnesses from his introducer's sub-section of the phratry (*thiasos*) who took an oath attesting his legitimacy and could be subjected to cross-questioning (l.74) — an interesting variation from practice in the city courts.

Phratores testified to the introduction of boys to their phratries in D.39 *Boeot. i* 4-5 (cf. 20), *P. Oxy.* 2538 col. iii. 1. 23-28 (cf. Thompson, 1968) and Isaeus 12 *Euphil.* 3, 8. In Isaeus 6 *Philoct.* 26 *phratores* testified to the elderly Euctemon's unsuccessful attempt to introduce a freedwoman's child to his phratry (§§ 22-24), and possibly to the boy's subsequent admission[79]. In the same speech, §§ 10-11, Euctemon's *phratores* attested that he had had only one wife, and five children. In Isaeus 3 *Pyrrh.* 76 *phratores* of the speaker's uncle (MB), Pyrrhus, testified that he did not sacrifice *gamēlia* in the phratry for his alleged marriage to the mother of Phile, the counter-claimant to his estate, nor present Phile to the phratry as his daughter. The speaker's deceased brother Endius had been adopted into Pyrrhus's phratry, which no doubt helped him to find allies there. In Isaeus 8 *Ciron* 18-20 *phratores* of the speaker testified to the celebration of *gamēlia* for the marriage of his mother, and to the introduction of the speaker and his brother.[80] In

Isaeus 2 *Menecles* 16 *phratores* and *orgeōnes* (members of a sub-group within the phratry with privileges like those of a *genos*) testify to an adoption; so do *phratores* and *genos* members in Is. 7 *Apoll.* 13-17. *Phratores* in Is. 9 *Astyph.* 33 testify that the opponent, Cleon, had been adopted out of their phratry into another (cf. *ibid.* § 8); and in [D.] 44 *Leoch.* 44 *phrateres* testify concerning a series of adoptions and associated manoeuvres.

In D.57 *Eub.* 19 the speaker's *phrateres* testified that his father had never been accused of lacking the qualifications for citizenship; in § 23 they testified again to his father's membership of the phratry and of the citizen body; in § 43 his kin and family friends (*oikeioi*) in the phratry testified that his father had sacrificed *gamēlia* for his mother when he married her; in § 46 *phrateres* bore witness to his own introduction to the phratry, and perhaps also testified that he had been a candidate for the priesthood of Heracles (cf. above, p. 342); in § 40 the *phrateres* of his mother's family testified that she was of citizen parentage. The speaker was a rich and locally influential man; his mobilisation of supporting witnesses in his appeal against his deme's vote that he was not entitled to citizenship will be considered in more detail in a separate analysis of kin as witnesses (Humphreys, in press).

Deme members The deme was the smallest unit in the series of segmentary patri-clans into which the citizen body was divided: deme, trittys, tribe. There were 139 demes, of very unequal size, thirty trittyes and ten tribes. A boy was admitted to his father's deme, if accepted as the legitimate child of citizen parents, in his eighteenth year, and thereby acquired citizenship. Each deme had a local base and its own religious rituals, although not all members lived in the deme centre.

Testimonies of deme members often concern matters similar to those attested by *phratores*. They might appear as *synēgoroi*: in Lysias 27 *Epicrates* 12 the speaker says that fellow-demesmen of his opponent, the ambassador Epicrates (*A.P.F.* 4859) will probably come to speak in his defence. In Demosthenes 39 *Boeotus i* 4-5 demesmen testify that the opponent had sought registration under the name Mantitheus, and in Demosthenes 44 *Leochares* 44 they bear witness to the manoeuvres by which the opponent tried to transfer himself and his sons from one deme to another in order to maintain a claim to the estate of a deceased kinsman, Archiades. In Isaeus 2 *Menecles* 16 and 7 *Apollodorus* 27-8 demesmen testify to the registration of adopted sons (cf. Is. 9 *Asty.* 8). In Lysias 23 *Pancleon* 3-4 demesmen of Dekeleia, to which the opponent claimed to belong, testify that they do not know him.

Their competence extended to knowledge about female members of deme families. In Isaeus 8 *Ciron* 18-20 members of the speaker's deme testify that his mother had acted as archon at the Thesmophoria, a ritual performed by demesmen's wives (cf. Detienne, 1979, p. 199), and in Isaeus 3 *Pyrrhus* 80 they testify that Pyrrhus had never paid for a feast at the Thesmophoria — evidence that the mother of the speaker of Isaeus 8 was lawfully married and Pyrrhus' alleged 'wife' was not. In Isaeus 6 *Philoctemon* 10-11 demesmen testified that Euctemon, father of *d.c.*, had only one wife and family; in Demosthenes 57 *Eubulides* 40 fellow-demesmen of the speaker's matrikin testify to his mother's legitimacy[81]; in [Demosthenes] 43 *Macartatus* 35 fellow-demesmen of Polemon, the father of *d.c.* (Hagnias) and of his cousin (FBS)

Philagrus, ancestor of the speaker's wife, testified that Philagrus' wife Phylomache I was considered to be the full sister of Polemon and that he had no brother (cf. Humphreys, in press).

In some cases we can be fairly sure that the persons concerned lived in the territory of the deme, under the eye of its resident members. In Isaeus 9 *Astyphilus* 17-18 the speaker claims that his opponent's fellow-demesmen know of the fight over land division in which the speaker's stepfather Euthycrates was allegedly killed by his brother Thudippus of Araphen, the opponent's father, but they are unwilling to testify. The fight presumably took place near Araphen (modern Rafina, on the east coast of Attica), even though Thudippus had something of a career as a politician in the city, being son-in-law of the demagogue Cleon (*A.P.F.* 7252, 8674). Though understandably reluctant to commit themselves on the question of Euthycrates' death, the demesmen were prepared to support the speaker (whose own deme is unknown) with testimony that they did not know of a will of his matrilateral half-brother, Astyphilus, in favour of the opponent, Cleon II (§§ 8-9) and that Astyphilus and Cleon II had never attended deme sacrifices together. This is a typical case where the content of the witnesses' testimony is of little significance, but their presence in court is intended to convey to the jury that the speaker has the opinion of the local community on his side. Possibly the city interests of Thudippus and his son had aroused some resentment against them in the deme; but Cleon II probably had his own faction of supporting witnesses.

In Isaeus 2 *Menecles* 29-33 the speaker gives an account of a private arbitration between his adoptive father Menecles and his opponent, Menecles' brother, which ended with an oath of reconciliation at the altar of Aphrodite (cf. Croissant and Salviat, 1966) at Kephale in south-east Attica. He claims that the arbitrators, an affine (*kēdestēs*) of his opponent and friends (*philoi*) of both parties, were biased against Menecles; if they are unwilling to testify he will call 'those who were present', *hoi paragenomenoi.* This expression probably refers to friends whom Menecles invited to the arbitration as witnesses, as would normally be the practice; but if, as seems likely, the altar at Kephale was chosen because this was the brothers' deme, these witnesses may well have been — or have included — fellow-demesmen. In the same speech fellow-demesmen testify that the speaker had performed all the burial rites for his adoptive father in a sumptuous manner (§§ 36-7).

Military call-up was also organised through demes, and fellow-demesmen probably often messed together on campaign. In Lysias 20 *Polystratus* 23 we are told that 'the demesmen, who know' could testify that the speaker's father Polystratus had never missed a campaign. But no witness appears. Polystratus was over seventy (§ 10) and many of his coevals will have died; but the main reason for this lack of support was probably his involvement with the oligarchic governments of 411-410 as a registrar of those eligible for citizenship. Those whom he had not registered would be resentful, while those whom he had listed would not be over-keen to have the fact remembered.

The speaker of Lysias 16 *Mantitheus* had better relations with his fellow-demesmen, who testified (§ 14) that in the 390s, when there was much poverty in Attica, he had called on the richer hoplites in his deme to help poorer men outfit themselves for the Corinthian war, and had himself given two men 30 drachmas each for this purpose.[82]

If we had fuller information on deme affairs such examples of local patronage and the appearance of demesmen in court as supporters of rival deme factions would be multiplied. Eubulides and Euxitheus of Halimous, deme rivals and opponents in the case for which Demosthenes 57 was written, had already clashed in court on a previous occasion when Euxitheus had testified against Eubulides (§ 8); Euxitheus calls deme witnesses, who he says are hostile to him, in § 14 to testify to points of marginal relevance. These groups were small worlds in which paths inevitably crossed, in an interlacing network of often competitive relationships.

Fellow-tribesmen The tribe was a much larger, less intimate unit than phratry or deme, and probably met less often. Where fellow-tribesmen are called as witnesses or act as supporters the significance of their presence belongs to the level of city politics and administration rather than community affairs. There are references in Andocides 1 *Mysteries* 150 and Demosthenes 23 *Aristocrates* 206 to tribes appointing a commission of members to act as *synēgoroi* supporting a defendant; clearly a man had to be well-known in the tribe for his political activities or his wealth, and involved in a charge of some public significance, to be able to request such support.[83]

Wealth was, in fact, an important consideration. Many of the 'liturgies' in which the rich were induced to spend money in the service of the city were organised on a tribal basis, and this was a likely subject for testimony. In Isaeus 7 *Apollodorus* 36 fellow-tribesmen testified that the speaker had acted as gymnasiarch for the tribe at the festival of Prometheus, undertaking the expenses of training the tribal relay team for the torch-race. In Demosthenes 39 *Boeotus i* 23-4 the speaker, Mantitheus (*A.P.F.* 9667) called witnesses from the tribe Hippothontis, which was that of his opponent's mother's family, to testify that the opponent, Boeotus, his half-brother, had taken part in boys' choruses for Hippothontis and not for Akamantis, the tribe of their father — an indication that their father did not recognise Boeotus as legitimate. Other testimonies arise from the functions of tribes in the organisation of the polis, and their mechanisms for running their own affairs. In Lysias 16 *Mantitheus* 13 the commander of a tribal cavalry squadron testified that the speaker[84] had transferred himself voluntarily from the cavalry to the riskier infantry; in [Demosthenes] 58 *Theocrines* 14-15 fellow-tribesmen of the opponent were called by the speaker to testify that the opponent had been convicted of embezzling money belonging to the eponymous heroes of the tribes.

KIN

It is not possible here to analyse in detail the appearances of kin as witnesses in Athenian courts (see Humphreys, in press). For obvious reasons, they were called on especially when testimony on questions of legitimacy and inheritance was required, both because they could appear as well-informed witnesses on such matters and because it was important to a litigant to give the impression that his claims were considered valid by his kin group. [Demosthenes] 43 *Macartatus* is a particularly clear case of the mobilisation of a large number of kin to testify repeatedly to the same facts, with the aim of showing that family opinion, in an inheritance dispute which had lasted about twenty years (Humphreys, 1983b), was now firmly on the speaker's side. The speakers of Demosthenes 57 *Eubulides* and Isaeus 12 *Euphiletus* also call on numerous kin, to help them defend their entitlement to citizenship; in these cases solidarity was probably in the whole group's interest, since defeat of the speaker would leave his relatives in an embarrassing or perhaps even dangerous position.

Athenians who needed witnesses to their actions and transactions might naturally turn to kin for help, but to be supported only by close kin in dubious circumstances put the litigant in a weak position; his opponent would claim that the witness was lying, due to family loyalty. Even testators often call in an unrelated family friend as well as those kin who have an interest in the estate.

Except in cases directly concerned with inheritance or legitimacy, such as the three mentioned above, the range of kinsmen whose relation to the parties to the case is precisely identified is narrow. Parents and their siblings, step-parents, own siblings and half-siblings, first cousins, children and step-children, wife's parents and siblings and sister's and daughter's husbands appear quite frequently with precise identification, but outside this circle the number of references falls off rapidly and we are often left with vague references to 'kinsmen' — *syngeneis, prosekontes* — or terms which can cover both kin and family friends (*philoi, oikeioi, anankaioi, epitēdeioi*). Within the narrower circle of positively identified relationships affines are strongly represented, an indication of the enduring ties which women maintained with their fathers and brothers after marriage and their ability to exert influence behind the scenes, though they could not appear in court to testify. Often, too, a woman's second husband will help her sons by her first marriage, or they will support him. The importance of links through women in the networks of solidarity which can be traced through witness testimonies thus provides one of our few indications of the role which women could play in Athenians' private affairs. Their influence may often have been at work too in relations between neighbours, and perhaps in fostering ties with family friends, but here it is less easy to detect.

FRIENDS

Friendship is stressed particularly in the case of supporting speakers. When they could, litigants called on *synēgoroi* who were influential and skilled in public speaking, but such support was represented as a pure response to the claims of friendship. (The opposite side, as we shall see, might present a different interpretation: cf. Kennedy, 1968). It is often emphasised that the friendship has lasted for more than a generation. The general Cephisodotus who supported Demosthenes' claim to a trierarchs' prize (D.51 *Trier. Crown*, cf. *A.P.F.* 3597 XXII B) had been a friend of his father (*patrikos philos*, Aeschines 3 *Ctesiphon* 52). Isaeus 4 *Nicostratus* is a supporting speech in an inheritance case delivered by an *epitēdeios* of the claimants and of their father. Lysias 5 *Callias* is a supporting speech by a friend of the defendant; the speaker's father had been friendly with the family too. Isaeus 6 *Philoctemon* was spoken by a friend of the claimant, who had sailed to Sicily and been imprisoned there with him.[85]

A speaker might also represent his appearance in court as motivated by an inherited enmity, or the desire to avenge a wrong done to a friend. Lysias 14-15 (*Alcibiades i-ii*) probably rhetorical exercises but nevertheless indicative of Athenian conventions, are supposedly supporting speeches in a suit against Alcibiades IV (*A.P.F.* 600 IX-X), the first made by a speaker whose father had been at enmity with the defendant's father Alcibiades III, the second by a friend of the plaintiff (15.12). Lysias 26 *Euandrus* belongs to a suit brought against Euandrus, a protegé of the politician Thrasybulus of Kollytos, by a friend of Leodamas (§ 15) who had been prevented from holding office as archon by Thrasybulus.

As has already been said, the line between supporting speakers and witnesses was not sharply drawn. Acting as witness could lead to involvement in a subsequent perjury charge. The speaker of Lysias 10 *Theomnestus* was in danger of being prosecuted for perjury for having testified in an earlier (unsuccessful) suit that Theomnestus had lost his civic rights. Theomnestus in this previous suit had called the speaker a parricide, and he was consequently bringing a countersuit for libel (*kakēgoria*). Litigants who wish to suggest that their opponents' witnesses are lying sometimes stress the closeness of the ties between witness and litigant ([Demosthenes] 48 *Olympiodorus* 24-5), most noticeably in the case of kin witnesses. The long-standing character of friendship between litigant and witness was likely to be stressed when a defendant called witnesses to testify to his character and his generosity in performing liturgies (e.g. Lysias 19 *Aristophanes* 58, Demosthenes 18 *Crown* 267, D.36 *For*

Phormio 55, Isocrates 17 *Trapeziticus* 40-41?).[86] In *P. Oxy.* 2538 the speaker's friendship with his witnesses goes back to his schooldays; they testify that he and his half-brother were educated together (frag. 2 col. iv 9ff.). The speaker of Lysias 17 *Demos. Adik.* calls witnesses to testify to a loan made by his grandfather to the father of the man whose property he is claiming (§ 2) and to attest that his father had secured judgment against the debtor's son in a suit four years previously (§ 3). Family friends may also be called to give evidence on patterns of solidarity or hostility within a kin group, as probably in Isaeus 1 *Cleonymus* 15-16 and 31-32. The speaker of Isaeus 8 *Ciron* calls friends of his maternal grandfather to testify that he regularly invited the speaker and his brother to attend sacrifices with him (§§ 15-17).

In some cases business associates were also family friends. Therippides of Paiania, one of Demosthenes' guardians, who gave testimony for him in D.27 *Aphobus i* 19-22 and D.28 *Aph. ii* 12, had three slaves employed in the workshop owned by Demosthenes' father from whom he received a regular income; he was a friend whom Demosthenes had known from his childhood (*philos ek paidos*, D.27.4). The speaker of Isocrates 17 *Trapeziticus* calls friends to testify about his financial affairs (§§ 40-41). Pythodorus of Acharnai (*A.P.F.* 12413), who tried to help his fellow-demesman Apollodorus son of Pasion in his difficulties as trierarch by offering to guarantee the lease of Apollodorus' equipment to his successor Polycles, and subsequently testified to having done so ([D.] 50 *Polycl.* 27-8), was probably the grandson of Pythodorus the stallholder (*ho skēnitēs*) who had acted as agent for Apollodorus' father thirty years earlier (*A.P.F.* 11672,IV).

The friends of one's opponent are of course described in very different terms. Ariston, the speaker of D.54 *Conon*, describes the witnesses who support his opponent as Conon's 'fellow-drinkers' (*sympotai*, § 33; cf. above, pp. 331-2). The speaker of D.39 *Boeotus i* maintains that his half-brother, the opponent, is surrounded by a gang (literally 'workshop', *ergastērion*, § 2, cf. [D.] 40 *Boeot. ii* 9) of sycophants; in [D.] 40.28 he reiterates the point, rejecting their testimony concerning Boeotus' naming ceremony: they were not kin or *philoi* of Boeotus' father, and one was the same age as Boeotus and could therefore have had no knowledge of the matter (cf. § 58). The same image of a 'workshop' for manufacturing false testimony is used[87] in D.37 *Pantainetus* 39 of the witnesses who came with the opponent to challenge the speaker to hand over his slaves for torture (*tous meth' heautou, to ergastērion tōn synestōtōn*). The speaker of [D.] 48 *Olympiodorus* accuses his opponent of collecting professional speakers, *rhētores*, to support him.

Another popular tactic was to represent witnesses as friends both of the speaker and of the opponent, therefore structurally impartial and motivated only by a commitment to truth and justice. The speaker of [D.] 48 calls *oikeioi* both of himself and of his brother-in-law (WB) Olympiodorus to testify about Olympiodorus' loose morals and the amount of money he spends on his mistress (*hetaira*, § 55). It may well be the same witnesses who testify in §§ 3-4 that the speaker wanted to submit his dispute with Olympiodorus to private arbitration, but that the latter would not agree to this, and who in § 33 testify that the two brothers-in-law had divided Conon's estate equally between them while it was in their possession. It was important for the speaker to show that common kinsmen were on his side. It was even better if it could be shown — or suggested — that common friends had broken with the opponent while maintining good relations with the speaker. The speaker of D.37 *Pantainetus* points out that his associate Euergus, who had been a particular friend (*philos to malista*, § 15) of the opponent Pantainetus, had subsequently been sued by him. The speaker of Isaeus 1 *Cleonymus* calls an acquaintance of his opponent, Pherenicus, to testify that *d.c.* was on bad terms with Pherenicus shortly before his death (§§ 31-2). The speaker of Demosthenes 57 *Eubulides* calls supporters of his opponent to testify for him on non-controversial points (§ 14).

A great many witness testimonies, for which no indication of the relation between witness and litigant is provided, concern the types of transaction for which any prudent Athenian would provide himself with reliable friends as witnesses (Isaeus 3 *Pyrrhus* 19-21): summonses ([D.] 34 *Ag. Phorm.* 12-15); formal challenges of offers to hand over slaves for torture (Isocr. 17 *Trap.* 14-16; Is. 6 *Philoct.* 15-16, 41-2; D.30 *Onetor i* 26-30; D.37 *Pant.* 39-42; [D.] 45 *Steph.i* 61; [D] 46 *Steph. ii* 21; [D.] 47 *Euerg.* 10, 17; [D.] 53 *Nicostr.* 25; D.54 *Konon* 28); challenges concerning other matters such as oaths, wills, exchange of property, etc. (D.27 *Aph.i* 41; [D.] 42 *Phaen.* 5-9; [D.] 45 *Steph. i* 8; [D.] 47 *Euerg.* 51, 66, cf. 62; [D.] 48 *Olymp.* 34, 48-9; D. 55 *Callicl.* 35); statements made by opponents when formally questioned before witnesses (D.30 *Onetor i* 19-20, 24; [D.] 47 *Euerg.* 34); payments and admissions of receipt and release from liability (Lys. 17 *Dem. Adik.* 2; D.36 *Phorm.* 10, 24; [D.] 38 *Nausim.* 3, cf. 12-13; [D.] 47 *Euerg.* 64-66, 77; cf. [D.] 45 *Steph. i* 37); division of an estate between heirs (D.36 *Phorm.* 10, 35, 40; [D.] 40 *Boeot. ii* 14-15); the contents of a household at the time of its owner's decease (Is. 6 *Philoct.* 41-2); inspection and evaluation of opponents' estates [D.] 42 *Phaen.* 5-9, *oikeioi* and *philoi*; [D.] 43 *Macart.* 70) and of injuries to victims of attack ([D.] 47 *Euerg.* 67); disputes over the status of a slave (Lys. 23 *Pancleon* 9-11); deposit of documents ([D.] 48 *Olymp.* 8-11, 32, 47; cf. D.36 *Phorm.* 4, 7). The speaker of Lysias 1 *Eratosthenes* was claiming to have killed a man justifiably because he had caught him *in flagrante* sleeping with his wife; to prove that the act was unpremeditated he called as witnesses one friend (*epitēdeios* and *philos*) who had dined with him and left before the intruder was discovered (§§ 22-29), others whom he had roused at night to accompany him when he broke in on the guilty couple (§§ 23-4) and others whom he had tried to summon but who had not been at home (§§ 41-2; note that this is hearsay evidence by modern criteria).

Witnesses are often called to testify to the outcome of earlier legal proceedings (Lys. 17 *Dem. Adik.* 3; Isocr. 17 *Trap.* 12, 14; Is. 5 *Dicaeog.* 2, 4, 18, 20, 22-4; D.30 *Onetor i* 17-18, 32; D.39 *Boeot. i* 2-5; [D.] 40 *Boeot. ii* 35; [D.] 43 *Macart.* 31; D.55 *Callicl.* 34) or to judgments given by the public arbitrators ([D.] 40 *Boeot. ii* 17-18, cf. 39; D.41 *Spud.* 28) or by private arbitrators (testimony by arbitrators: Isocr. 18 *Callim.* 10; Is. 12 *Euphil.* 11; [D.] 34 *Ag. Phorm.* 18, 20; [D.] 59 *Neaira* 45-47;[88] testimony by persons present at the arbitration, Is. 5 *Dicaeog.* 31-3; D.36 *Phorm.* 16 and 24; [D.] 52 *Callipp.* 15-17, 30-1). Witnesses might also be called for testimony about occurrences during arbitration hearings ([D.] 52 *Callipp.* 15-17), about offers to settle disputes by private arbitration which were rejected ([D.] 40 *Boeot. ii* 44, [D.] 48 *Olymp.* 3-4), attempts at compromise (Andoc. 1 *Myst.* 122-3, Callias asks three friends of Andocides to act as mediators; [D.] 58 *Theocr.* 33, offer to withdraw a suit for a payment of 1000 drachmas), compromise settlements ([D.] 58. 42-3),or other conflicts (D.39 *Boeot. i* 19, [D.] 40 *Boeot. ii* 34-5).

CONCLUSIONS

As I indicated at the beginning of this paper, study of witness testimonies can tell us something about a society's theory of knowledge.[89] It can also tell us about theories of the person and of action: the relation of a deviant action to the offender's past life-style and future relationships, and of the individual to his associates and social milieu.

We can see that Athenians still expected to be able to rely on face-to-face knowledge of persons in judging situations. Speakers quite often appeal to jurors' personal knowledge of the parties and their doings; even when jurors did not know litigants personally they knew by sight or reputation the public figures who appeared in court — politicians, officials, doctors, bankers, trierarchs — and they were expected to perceive other witnesses as representing the social networks in which litigants were personally known. The support and good opinion of such social networks was very important for the litigant; an Athenian could not even imagine relying on official registration procedures, written documents and the interpretation by legal experts of an unambiguous body of written rules to define his status and secure him his rights. Questions of identity were phrased in relation to persons, living and dead: who are your kin, where are your ancestors' tombs?[90] The reliability of witnesses is judged in personal terms even where questions of professional qualification might come into play; a doctor is a useful witness because he is known to the jurors as a trustworthy man, not because he has been certified as professionally competent. On the other hand — and this is a point to which we shall return — the jurors now have to rely to a considerable extent on second-hand representations of interaction rather than on direct experience. They are trying to retain some of the qualities of village dispute-settlement procedures in an urban setting, and this leads to contradictions.

What kind of results did the system deliver? We are in a poor position to judge, because the speeches we have represent only litigants whose disputes were not settled by arbitration and who were, or employed, ambitious speech-writers. Nevertheless, these speeches do have some features worth noting. A reader accustomed to Anglo-American law will obviously be surprised at the absence of any opportunity to cross-question witnesses, which often makes it possible for litigants to present as supporters witnesses whose testimony deliberately avoids the main point at issue.[91] As I have suggested above, the reasons for this limitation may have been largely practical; before the invention of shorthand, it was difficult to obtain reliable evidence about witnesses' testimony for use in perjury suits except by prescribing that the witness should confine himself to a previously prepared written text. Other attitudes may however have contributed. A modern textbook on trial techniques (Mauet, 1980) notes that jurors tend to identify with witnesses and resent aggressive cross-questioning by advocates; jurors' dislike of seeing litigants and witnesses tied in knots by sophists may have led to a reaction against cross-examination, if it was ever used. The organisation of the Athenian courts also depended increasingly, as their workload grew, on the allocation of a fixed time for each case; lengthy cross-examination of witnesses could have upset calculations. The use of speeches prepared in advance by speech-writers, and the fact that each court case had previously been heard by an arbitrator or reviewed in outline by a magistrate (*anakrisis*) meant that surprise was not an important element in trial technique. The theatrical skills of the speech-writer lay in narrative and the depiction of character, the art of representing the litigant and his claims as part of a just and harmonious pattern disrupted by the adversary, rather than in engineering dramatic confrontations; the excitement came from the jury's task of choosing between two alternative versions of the same scenario rather than from direct clashes between the protagonists. And finally, the jury's attitude to witnesses was less past-oriented than that of modern Anglo-American courts.[92] The jury's task was not merely to 'find facts', but to find a just solution to an ongoing conflict; the witnesses were there not merely to reproduce past experiences stored in memory, but to indicate how the groups in which the litigants lived were reacting to their behaviour and would react to alternative settlements. Witnesses were expected to be partisan; on these assumptions cross-examination becomes less relevant.

Criticism of the way the courts functioned certainly existed in Athens; it is expressed in considered form in Plato's *Laws*, written probably in the 360s-350s. Strict penalties are laid down for those who speak on behalf of others, give advice on influencing courts, or sue too freely (937d-938). Civil cases are to be heard first by a panel of arbitrators chosen from the neighbours and friends of the disputing parties, since they are best informed about the facts at issue. Litigants dissatisfied with the arbitrators' decision may appeal to a tribal court of jurors selected by lot, and those dissatisfied with this court's decision may appeal to a supreme court in which the judges are a small body of ex-magistrates. Penalties for unsuccessful appeal are increased at each stage. The supreme court also has jurisdiction in capital cases. Accusations of damaging the interests of the state are made before the assembly, handed over to a committee of three senior magistrates for investigation, and returned to the assembly for sentencing if the charge is found to be substantiated.[93] Plato's system thus minimises the importance of trial by large juries selected by lot, although he recognises the value of making jury duty part of the experience of every citizen (766d-768d). Plato attempts to make judicial decisions more final by penalties for appeal, by making more effective provision for the execution of sentences (958a-c) and by specifying that conviction of witnesses for perjury does not justify re-trial unless at least half of the testimonies are thus invalidated. He recognises the need for expertise in some cases: those involving medical injury are to be tried by doctors (916a-c). He objects to the use of oaths by litigants,[94] but not to the disclaimer oath taken by witnesses as an alternative to testifying (948b-949b; 936e); it is not clear whether he tries to provide stronger sanctions against witnesses who fail to appear (936e-937a; cf. above, n.27). He eliminates the use of torture in securing evidence from slaves (Morrow, 1939, pp. 80-1). Slaves and children are permitted to testify in homicide cases only; women over forty can testify and act as *synēgoroi* in any case, and can sue on their own behalf (937a). Conditions to be fulfilled if documents are to be accepted as valid evidence are laid down (953e).

Plato sees law as essentially repressive. In an ideal society courts would be unnecessary because citizens would be perfectly socialised and would never engage in the kind of behaviour forbidden by law (853b-c). He believed (unlike Aristotle) that conflicts of interest in society could be eliminated. He admits that laws sufficiently detailed to cover every possible contingency and aspect of behaviour would be ridiculous (788a-b, 789d-790a), but one feels that the prospect nevertheless attracts him; the looseness and ambiguity of the Athenian legal code, which democrats claimed was due to deliberate choice on Solon's part, to give greater power to the courts ([Aristotle], *Constitution of Athens* 9.2), was not in his eyes a virtue. He is more confident in the educational value of a law code, provided each set of laws is prefaced by an explanation of its rationale (718b-723d) than in the educational value of courts.[95] Though justice is a social skill which all can practise, law-making requires specialised knowledge. Problem cases are to be dealt with by legal specialists, not by jurors' discretion as in Athens.

Plato was articulating a hostility to the jury courts and those who made money out of litigation which can be more widely recognised among the Athenian upper class (Carter, 1982). This class increased its power in the Greek cities after the Macedonian victories of the late fourth century, and speech-writing as an art addressed to a public of readers as well as jurors seems to have died out, although forensic oratory continued to be taught, advocacy became more common, and the speeches of the classical orators continued to be widely read (cf. R.W. Smith, 1974, for a recent survey). Judges tended to replace jury-courts, at least in the Hellenistic kingdoms, as the proportion of laws concerned with taxation and other administrative matters increased; the use of written documentation grew (Pringsheim, 1955; Préaux, 1964). But there is still a considerable gap between pointing out that these changes follow directions sketched out by Plato in the *Laws*, and concluding that they result from any general dissatisfaction with the Athenian system in the fourth century. Such general trends in the development of Hellenistic law resulted from the new political regimes of the period rather than from conscious programmes for reform, and in many places they may represent continuity rather than change; the use of jury courts may well have been confined to Athens and the democratic regimes which were introduced under her influence in the fifth century.

Legal institutions varied from one Greek city to another, and we cannot reconstruct the history of this variation by arranging practices documented in different places and periods along an evolutionary continuum whose trajectory is determined by the values and ideology of our own legal system. I have already argued that the unquestioned Athenian assumption that witnesses are supporters of those for whom they testify — "une procession d'amis, un défilé de connaissances ou de relations qui viennent apporter leur soutien" (Soubie, 1974, pp. 182-3) — is not a survival from the use of oath-helpers documented in Gortyn, but a response to the increased use of city jury-courts from c.450 B.C. onwards. It is related to the Athenian decision in 461 to eliminate judges (Humphreys, 1983c); the verdicts of Athenian courts are legitimated as the expression of community opinion, not as the rulings of an individual to whom authority has been delegated, and in forming their opinions jurors not unnaturally looked for evidence of the opinion of the more limited local communities to which litigants belonged.

In any case, the difference between Athenian and contemporary Anglo-American conceptions of witnesses is not as great as some scholars have imagined. In both instances only a selection of the evidence potentially available is presented in court; perhaps one of the main differences is that this selectivity was more obvious to the jury in the Athenian system. Unilinear theories of evolution exaggerate differences between archaic or 'primitive' and 'modern' institutions, and conceal similarities. They too often take ideology for reality at the 'modern' end of the evolutionary continuum and construct the 'primitive' end eclectically out of decontextualised scraps of historical and/or ethnographic evidence chosen to provide a suitably 'irrational' contrast to the supposedly rational institutions of modern society (cf. Van Velsen, 1969). Certainly there has been an overall trend in human history towards larger urban settlements, more rapid means of communication, greater spatial and social mobility, occupational diversification, divergences in social experience and increasing impersonality in social interaction. But this evolution has not abolished intimacy; it has merely made the contrast between Gemeinschaft and Gesellschaft more pointed and more accessible to conscious reflection. Theories of evolution have all too often derived their plausibility from representing as opposite ends of the evolutionary continuum contradictory ideals simultaneously present in the theorist's own culture: stability and opportunity, continuity and change, group solidarity and freedom from intimidation. I have suggested elsewhere (Humphreys, 1983c) that we may be better able to integrate the diversity of the detailed historical record with the long-term evolutionary trends which can also be discerned in it if we recognise that both in the unconscious drift of praxis and in moments of conscious reform societies are trying to maintain a balance between contradictory ideals.[96] In the case of legal process one ideal is perfect knowledge and the other is absence of bias. The Athenians preferred witnesses who had had many dealings with the litigants, in the course of which they had developed feelings of loyalty or hostility, to impartial witnesses who had only encountered the litigants occasionally. They also preferred a witness who had been deliberately invited to a meeting to observe and remember what took place, to the casual passer-by who arrives *in medias res* and puts his own interpretation on what he sees. Put this way, there is nothing very 'primitive' or archaic about their preferences.

If we compare the use of witnesses in Athenian law-courts with the modern Anglo-American system, using this perspective of the contradiction between full local knowledge and impartiality, we can see that Anglo-American law has gone particularly far in the direction of trying to ensure impartiality and thereby restricting the kinds of knowledge of which the court officially takes cognisance. Jurors are asked to decide whether the defendant has committed a particular act in the past, without considering the implications of their decision for the future relations of the parties concerned, without knowing whether the defendant has previous convictions, often without any evidence on character.[97] Witnesses introduced in court may well be chosen because they appear independent, lacking close ties to the defendant;[98] hearsay evidence is not allowed, except in closely specified circumstances. To see how artificial these limitations are we have only to look at what happens before and after the presentation of evidence to the jury. Police do not observe these restrictions while making investigations (McBarnet, 1981), and it is significant that detective novels go even further in the pursuit of complete knowledge; the amateur detective is valued for being able to penetrate into the local community like an anthropologist doing participant observation, and the world created by the novelist must be seen to be capable of re-forming and continuing to function after the dénouement. Courts, too, change their rules when they turn from verdict to sentencing; the offender's character, circumstances and previous convictions are taken into account, the effects of different penalties on family and associates are considered, relatives and employers or fellow-employees are often called as witnesses, and a much more holistic view of the person is taken (Shapland, 1981).

Those who have expressed surprise at the way in which witnesses were used in Athenian lawcourts have thus been misled by comparing ancient practice with modern theory. We might, instead, ask what questions this analysis of ancient practice could suggest to the student of the practice of modern courts. Remarkably little has been done so far in assessing the social factors which influence jurors' estimations of the credibility of witnesses. Lawyers have their 'folk models' of the effects of the social characteristics of jurors and witnesses (E.H. Smith, 1944; Simon, 1967, ch. 6; 1980, pp. 15, 32-36; Erlanger, 1970; Saks and Hastie, 1978, ch. 3), but these are kept out of academic discussions, partly because of the narrow definition of the role of witnesses in legal theory and partly because such judgments belong to the kind of 'common sense' knowledge of society, embedded in practice, which operates without conscious formulation (Bourdieu, 1977). Most studies of jurors and their reactions to witnesses rely on experiments using psychology students, and therefore start with a narrower sociological range than one would find in a court case (Erlanger, 1970; Saks and Hastie, 1978; Lloyd-Bostock and Clifford, 1983). Experiments show that jurors are influenced by witnesses' 'confidence' in giving testimony, and this has been correlated with studies of witnesses' speech patterns (Lind and O'Barr, 1979, cf. Scherer, 1979), but obvious questions about the relation of confidence and its linguistic correlates to education, social class and age are not being directly tackled.[99]

The Athenian experience is also relevant to another question currently of interest to lawyers, the advantages of 'neighbourhood courts' (cf. Sander and Snyder, 1979). It is clear from the Athenian evidence that a distinction has to be made — not always presented with sufficient clarity in modern discussions, e.g. Conn and Hippler, 1974 — between village courts in which judges and audience know the litigants intimately and have to continue living with them, and urban courts with lay judges, assessors or jurors who can be considered typical representants of the disputants' milieu and speak in the name of a moral community (cf. especially Yaffe, 1972), but are not usually directly involved in social interaction with those who appear before them. Communist countries have courts at both levels; I have however been unable to find any detailed ethnographic analysis of the relation between court proceedings and social interaction at the most local level of village, factory and apartment-block courts. In Moscow City courts (Feifer, 1964), where the area served is considerably larger, community involvement mainly seems to take the form of witness testimony about litigants' characters (verdict and sentence are combined, and a holistic view is taken of the persons being judged), although community members in the audience may also express opinions.[100] As in classical Athens and in modern English sentencing procedure (Shapland, 1981), the character portraits presented seem stereotyped, and the court is unlikely to get any detailed view of local networks and power structures.

Courts, in all societies which have them, form one of a range of alternative mechanisms for dealing with disputes and deviance which includes friendly discussion between the parties concerned, gossip, mediation, violence, public confrontation of various kinds, reports in mass media, and a whole range of literary and dramatic genres from shadow puppets to soap operas. Courts are inherently rhetorical and theatrical (Ball, 1975; Bennett and Feldman, 1981; Humphreys, 1983a, pp. 7-9); their sittings are public performances in which the audience has a part to play as well as the actors, re-presentations of action and of social responses to action in which idealised pictures of social behaviour are presented and tried out (cf. Peacock, 1968 on *ludruk*). At the same time, court verdicts have real results (cf. Redfield, 1975, pp. 162-5), and so the element of idealisation has to be concealed. Court practice both reflects and helps to shape conceptions of the person and of action; we should not allow the view presented by legal theorists of a succession of sociologically naked witnesses observing an equally isolated set of occurrences to obscure our everyday realisation that actions and persons can only be understood in context.[101]

Notes

1. In California in the mid-19th c. blacks, Indians and immigrant Chinese were not allowed to testify: Doo, 1973.
2. Bohannan, 1957, pp. 44-5. Tiv distinguish two forms of right speaking: speaking *mimi* is speaking in conformity with social relationships, speaking *vough* is truth-telling. When Bohannan says, "It is generally conceded ... that for a witness to speak *vough* is *ipso facto* to speak *mimi*. From the standpoint of the witness the 'right' thing to do is to smooth over social relationships and hence to report what actually occurred so that judges will have a way of knowing what the rights of the matter are", he is reporting court ideology rather than the views of litigants.
3. Note the use made of Bernstein's concepts 'restricted code' and 'elaborated code' in the field of law by Perry, 1977.
4. Impartial judgments can be given in a local court without institutionalised safeguards against bias, if a substantial sector of the community is neutral or if judges' class interests are not involved, but the only safeguard against bias in local courts is the fact that all parties concerned have to continue to live together.
5. Cf. Gernet, 1951, on early legal formalism as an extreme example of this process of selection. See Udovitch, below, for another analysis of the relation between law and local knowledge.
6. Cf. Calhoun, 1919a. It is difficult to tell how much cross-questioning was ever used. In Aristophanes *Wasps* 962-6 and Andocides 1 *Myst.* 14 (399 B.C.) witnesses are led through their testimony by questions from the litigant for whom they are testifying. In Isaeus 3 *Pyrrh.* 79 (c. 370?) the speaker urges the jury to question his opponent; I see this as an invitation to heckle rather than a reference to cross-questioning. On the other hand the case in Aeschylus *Eumenides* 585-673 is conducted entirely by questions directed by the plaintiff to the defendant and his witness, and questioning was certainly a well-known method of attacking an argument in non-legal contexts. Aristotle's discussion of the use of questions in forensic oratory (*Rhet.* 1418a 40-1419a 18) makes no mention of witnesses.
7. There was no office of public prosecutor in Athens and no official machinery for making investigations except in matters of public finance (the *logistai*). The Council could appoint a committee of investigators (*zētētai*) to examine cases in which a public denunciation (*eisangelia*) was made (Rhodes, 1972, pp. 158, 186-7). The right to torture slaves to obtain evidence pertains to their owners, not to the court; cf. Menander *Samia* 305-325 for the use of torture threats to obtain confessions from slaves in a domestic context. The rule that slaves' evidence could only be admitted in court if obtained by torture (a) represented a continuation and formalisation of domestic practice, (b) provided the slave with a legitimate excuse for testifying against his or her owner (cf. Soubie, 1974, p. 127 and the parallel use of oaths to 'compel' reluctant witnesses to testify among the Tiv, Bohannan 1957), (c) mitigates the contradiction between the slave's cognitive capacity as a human being and his lack of legal capacity *quâ* slave. Extant speeches contain arguments both in favour of the use of torture and against it, depending on the speaker's circumstances, but though challenges and offers to hand over slaves for torture are common, only *P. Oxy* 2686 (Hyperides) refers to an actual instance of slave torture (Thür, 1977, pp. 19, 23 thinks this passage refers to torture of non-Athenian free witnesses, as in Antiphon 5 *Herod.*). Plato abandoned torture in the *Laws*. For other problems posed by the slave's lack of legal capacity cf. the paper by Manuela Carneiro da Cunha in this volume.
8. For parallels to the judgment in turn by elders in the 'Shield' scene see Gluckman, 1955.

9. On D.18 see Treves, 1940; on Aesch. 1 (in which there are conflicts between text and witness testimony in §§ 41/50 and 63/68), Drerup, 1898. Drerup also suspects the documents and testimonies in D.21 *Meid.*, except for the laws in §§ 8, 10 and 94. Doubts have also been expressed about the documents in Andoc. 1 *Myst.* and D.23 *Aristocr.*, but cf. Dover, 1968, p. 4, n. 4, pp. 36-7. I have dealt with the question of the archon-date in the witness testimony of [D.] 43 *Macart.* 31 in Humphreys, 1983b.
10. Since Drerup's discussion (1898), epigraphic evidence has confirmed information given only in witness testimonies on the following persons:-

[D.] 43 *Macart.*	36, 44,	the sons of Straton (*A.P.F.* 2921)
ibid.	42	Phanostratus father of Stratius (Humphreys, 1983b)
[D.] 45 *Steph. i*	55	deme of Deinias: *I.G.* ii^2 1641 (*A.P.F.*11672,X)
[D.] 59 *Neaira*	40	Aristocrates of Phaleron (*A.P.F.*1926)
ibid.	61	Eualces of Phaleron (read Eualcos) *P.A.* 5264 Euphranor of Aigilia (read Angeleia) *P.A.* 6091; *Agora XV* 32.32 Nicippus of Kephale (*A.P.F.* 10833)
ibid.	71	deme of Nausiphilus (P.A.10601, *Agora XV* 8.1)
ibid.	123	Diophanes son of Diophanes of Alopeke (*P.A.*4406, cf. *Agora XV* 155.43)

Drerup was already able to report epigraphical confirmation on Phormio son of Ctesiphon of Piraeus ([D.] 35 *Lacr.* 13-14, *A.P.F.*11672, IX), Endius of Lamptrai ([D.] 45.8, *A.P.F.* 4810), Philostratus son of Dionysius of Kolone ([D.] 59.23, *A.P.F.*14734), Glaucetes of Kephisia ([D.] 59.40, *A.P.F.*2954), Deinomenes son of Archelaus of Kydathenai ([D.] 59.123, *A.P.F.*3188) and Deinias son of Phormius of Kydantidai ([D.] 59.123, *I.G.*ii^2 6609). On D.21 *Meid.* 82 and 168 see Vanderpool, 1966.
11. Cases involving less than 10 drachmas (approximately 10 days' wages) were dealt with by tribal judges, the *dikastai kata dēmous* (see Humphreys, 1983c). Magistrates had summary powers to arrest lower-class criminals (*kakourgoi*) and those caught *in flagrante*: see Harrison, 1971, pp. 221-232; Hansen, 1976.
12. On the date of the *Tetralogies* see Zuntz, 1949; Dover, 1950.
13. In § 1 the speaker says that 'we, Phormio's *epitēdeioi*', will speak for him; at the end of the speech (§ 62) he tells the court officials to pour away the rest of the water in the clock. Either he decided that supporting speeches were superfluous (cf. [D.] 45 *Steph. i* 6) or the plural in § 1 is rhetorical. It is far from certain that the speaker was Demosthenes himself (Schaefer, 1858, pp. 292-6).
14. On *synēgoroi* see Lavency, 1964; Kennedy, 1968; Dover, 1968, ch. 8.
15. Usher, 1976, disagrees with Dover but proves only that in some instances speech-writers supplied complete speeches and used them afterwards in teaching and for advertisement — which was not in doubt.
16. Kennedy (1963, pp. 57-8) suggests that the earliest rhetorical handbooks were substitutes for the services of the speech-writer. If one takes Dover's view of the speech-writer's advisory functions, a training in rhetoric would be complementary; it would have given the litigant a basic structural frame for his argument and a repertoire of *topoi* which would help him to deliver it with confidence. Cf. Yates, 1966, on the technique of memorisation involved. On the practical orientation of rhetorical education Johnson, 1959, has useful remarks.
17. Turner, 1951, pp. 19-21. On the formation of the Demosthenic corpus see Canfora, 1974.
18. Plutarch's statement (*Moralia* 852e-f) that this speech was written by Demosthenes for Apollodorus is accepted by e.g. Wolff, 1968. But the story was apparently unknown to Aeschines (Gernet, 1957, pp. 153-4).
19. On the distinction between *diké* and *graphé* — which does not fully correspond either to the civil/criminal or to the private/public law distinction — see Harrison, 1971, pp. 75-8.
20. The speaker of D.57 *Eub.* was presumably primarily interested in persuading his 80 fellow-demesmen. Bystanders could attend trials (Dover, 1968, p. 182) but speakers might well wish to reach a wider, though still restricted, public. For interest in major cases among non-Athenians see Dorjahn and Cronin, 1938.

21. Attributions were often based on very slender grounds. Apollodorus' speeches found their way into the Demosthenic corpus at least partly because [D.] 45-6 *Steph. i-ii* arose from Demosthenes' successful speech for Phormio (D.36) and [D.] 50 *Polycles* was linked in theme to D.51 *Trier. Crown.* [D.] 58 *Theocr.* entered the corpus because of its references to Demosthenes (§§ 35-44, cf. 23), although the hostile tone of these clearly excludes Demosthenic authorship. In some cases, as Dover suggests (1968, ch. 8) attributions may have been based on informed gossip. Cf. Drerup, 1899. The number of surviving classical forensic speeches and substantial fragments (excluding some which were clearly not intended for delivery in court) is just over 100, divided between ten orators.
22. On modification of speeches between delivery and publication see Wilamowitz, 1923a; Dorjahn, 1935; Dover, 1968, pp. 168-172, 187-193.
23. Quotations of laws are often selective and do not necessarily follow the original text verbatim: see Bonner, 1927, p. 177. This aspect of the speech-writer's technique deserves further study.
24. For a more detailed treatment see Harrison, 1971.
25. In practice, in the 4th century magistrates were probably little inclined to use their powers to reject questionable suits (cf. Calhoun, 1919b). Possibly they had employed them more energetically in earlier periods.
26. On the differences between arbitrators' hearings and *anakrisis* (preliminary examination) by magistrates see Bonner, 1905, ch. 8; Laemmli, 1938, ch. 2; Dorjahn, 1941; Harrison, 1971, pp. 94-105.
27. Ruschenbusch (1968, pp. 61-2) argues that in early times magistrates judging *eisangeliai* or *graphai* could summons witnesses by *klēteusis* and impose summary fines on those who failed to appear. Aesch. 1. *Tim.* 46 seems to refer to such a fine, but the procedure was in all likelihood obsolete by the 4th century, though its use is still threatened, rhetorically, in Lyc. 1 *Leocr.* 20, [D.] 59 *Neaira* 28, Aesch. 2 *Emb.* 68 and D.32 *Zen.* 30. The last case was a *dikē*; we have to assume, on Ruschenbusch's theory, that the precise conditions for using *klēteusis* had by this time been forgotten — which is not unlikely. In practice litigants had to provide themselves with witnesses who could be trusted to appear (see [D.] 58 *Theocr.* on alleged attempts by opponents to persuade witnesses to default). It is not clear to me whether Plato *Laws* 936e-937a proposes stronger powers to compel witnesses to attend than were available in Athens (Morrow, 1960, p. 285 thinks not). References in texts to compelling reluctant witnesses to testify or take an oath of disclaimer refer to witnesses already present in court (see below, n. 30).
28. Cf. above, n. 14. Brief remarks by *synēgoroi* at end of speech, [D.] 58 *Theocr.* 70; cf. [D.] 19 *Emb.* 290.
29. Is. 2 *Men.*, 3 *Pyrrh.*, 6 *Philoct.*; [D.] 44-47 (*Leoch., Steph. i-ii, Euerg*); [D.] 29 *Aph. iii* if genuine (below, n. 70). The procedure for suing witnesses for perjury may have developed in the context of *diamartyria*, in which the content of the testimony was not in doubt (cf. Gernet, 1927; Harrison, 1971, pp. 124-31; below, n. 33). For an example of a very casuistic attack on a witness testimony, see [D.] 45-6 *Steph. i-ii.*
30. Aesch. 1 *Tim.* 67; [D.] 45 *Steph. i* 59-60; D.54 *Conon* 26; Is. 9 *Asty.* 18; cf. [D.] 29 *Aph. iii* 16, if genuine. For refusal to testify (apparently without oath) as a way of getting testimony 'in the record' without risk of perjury suits, see Anaximenes *Ars Rhetorica* (*Rhet. ad Alex.*) 15.7.
31. On 'bystander' witnesses see below, pp. 330-333.
32. The total city population within the Long Walls linking Athens and Piraeus may have been as high as 200,000 during the Peloponnesian war but is not likely to have exceeded 70,000 in the 4th century (cf. Gomme, 1933; Osborne, 1982). The proportion of slaves and resident aliens in the population was higher in the city than in the countryside.
33. Shack, 1979, provides a recent comparative study of oath-helping; Wendy Davies' paper in this volume shows how closely interrelated the activities of testifying, oath-helping and judging can be. For the view that oath-helping left its traces in Attic procedure see Meister, 1908; Gernet, 1927; Pringsheim, 1951; Sautel, 1964; Soubie, 1974, p. 125. Cf. also (with caution) Glotz, 1904, pp. 288-298. Gernet's paper, whick linked oath-helping and *diamartyria*, has had a considerable influence (cf. also Laemmli, 1938, ch. 4; Wolff, 1966,

pp. 121-131); but on a close examination the introduction of the idea of oath-helping turns out not to be essential to his reconstruction of the history of *diamartyria*, and seems to me to be out of place. Oath-helping is essentially a means of reaching decision in court, while *diamartyria* is designed for use outside courts. Gernet rightly stresses that uses of *diamartyrein* and *diamartyresthai* must be studied together; both refer to formal protestations in public — the former before a magistrate, the latter in the presence of witnesses — which supposedly become immediately effective by virtue of their publicity (or are opposed by an equally public counter-claim which leads to adjudication). *Diamartyresthai* is always, and *diamartyrein* sometimes, used of the person whose claim is being asserted (or his or her legal representative); understandably, there were circumstances in which use of a patron or person of more substance to makes a *diamartyria* was preferred (*e.g.* when a *graphē aprostasiou* was being brought against a metic, cf. Harpocr. *s.v. diamartyria*; the speaker of Is. 2 *Men.* used an older man, his father-in-law), but basically the term seems to be used of affirmation *before* witnesses rather than *by* a witness. The man who makes a *diamartyria* does not give evidence, he makes a formal statement to a magistrate, who is obliged to take note of it.

34. The social status of Philocleon and Bdelycleon in the *Wasps* is somewhat ambiguous: the father needs his juror's pay but the son is a smart young-man-about-town. A comic poet cannot be pressed too far for consistency, but the discrepancies are lessened if we assume that the father has had to leave his land and that the son has been earning a cash income in town, perhaps as a soldier. On the social status of 4th century jurors see Kroll, 1972, pp. 261-7: about 2/5 of the attested jurors are also known from other sources.
35. The speaker seems to represent himself as an arbitrator rather than a juror. Cf. also Isocr. 8 *Peace* 53 (character of metics judged by their *prostatai*) and Herodas *Mimiambi* ii 10-12.
36. Sandys and Paley (1896, p. 101) think that Apollodorus offered Deinias the testimony given in § 55 and Deinias took an oath of disclaimer, but Deinias was not a hostile witness (cf. above, nn. 27, 30); when Apollodorus says that Deinias was not prepared to swear to the truth because he did not wish to injure his nephew (§ 56) he means that Deinias was not prepared to give a positive testimony in his own favour.
37. Citizens paid neither poll-tax nor land-tax, so the state had no reason to keep a census or tax register; most taxes were collected by tax-farmers working as independent entrepreneurs. It is very doubtful whether formal land registers were kept (Finley, 1952, pp. 14, 207-8; Thompson, 1971). Demes kept lists of their members and of resident aliens domiciled in their area, and were certainly well informed about land ownership, but their records were not above suspicion (D.57 *Eub.*; Haussoullier, 1883, pp. 32-55).
38. Officials probably also gave evidence in Lys. 30 *Nicomachus* 20 (city finances), D.19 *Emb.* 211-214 (scrutiny of magistrates), [D.] 42 *Phaen.* 3, 9 and possibly Is. 3 *Pyrrh.* 43 (courts), although the identity of the witnesses in these passages is not stated.
39. Doctors and teachers received stipends from the state in some cities, but we have no evidence of this in classical Athens; the city was large and prosperous enough to attract doctors and teachers without such inducements. Cf. Cohn-Haft, 1956; on the doctor's need to make himself known, and his methods of doing so, see also Edelstein, 1967, pp. 87-90 [1931].
40. Euthydicus is mentioned again in Aesch. 1 *Tim.* 40; Timarchus is said to have pretended to be a student in his clinic (*iatreion*) in Piraeus, while actually living as a male prostitute.
41. A doctor who appeared as a witness would of course name himself when giving evidence, but speech-writers on the whole seem to avoid loading their texts with names unless these are likely to be familiar to the public. However, this question needs further investigation. Doctors are more explicitly recognized as 'experts' in Plato *Laws* 916a-c and in Roman Egypt (Nanetti, 1941; Cohn-Haft, 1956, pp. 70-1).
42. After the introduction of special procedures for suits concerning sea trade, in which distinctions of status were effectively disregarded, slaves could testify and indeed even appear as litigants in such suits (Gernet, 1950), but it is not clear whether the same was true of suits concerning mining, banking and tax-farming, for which revised procedures were also introduced in the middle of the 5th century (Gernet, 1938). On the challenge to deliver a slave for torture in D.37 *Pant.* 40-42, a mining suit in one party's view of the case, dated in or after 346/5, see Thür, 1977, pp. 214-232.

The statement in Isoc. 17 *Trap.* 2 that banking transactions took place without witnesses should not be taken too literally, *pace* Pringsheim, 1955 (cf. Bogaert, 1968, pp. 382-3); the speaker had reasons for keeping his dealings with Pasion's bank secret.

43. In several of the passages referred to the witness testimonies have not survived, and it is not therefore certain that every transaction listed in the text was confirmed by witnesses.
44. By *diadikasia* (Harrison, 1971, pp. 214-17) or, if he claimed to be a mortgagee, by a *dikē exoulēs* (ibid., pp. 217-221). The term *ōneisthai* used in [D.] 40.58 can refer to mortgage as well as sale and the fact that only a part share is claimed suggests mortgage.
45. The witnesses in Isocr. 17 *Trap.* 37 may have testified that Stratocles had been repaid.
46. Apollodorus intended to sue this delinquent witness for damages (*blabē*, not *lipomartyria*), but the procedural situation is far from clear: see Harrison, 1971, pp. 141-3, and n.27 above.
47. In such circumstances one would expect Timotheus to have been borrowing from personal friends (cf. Finley, 1952, pp. 83-5) who would remain loyal to him; but the seriousness of his financial difficulties in the late 370s (*A.P.F.* 13700, pp. 509-10) has to be taken into account.
48. The same witness may however have given evidence for Aphobus that others had a claim on the bed-making establishment which Demosthenes' father had acquired from him (D.27.25); his transactions with Aphobus seem to have been rather complex. In [D.] 52 *Callipp.* 20-21 the speaker calls a witness who had been involved in a legal dispute with *d.c.*, Lycon, to testify that Lycon had no dealings with the speaker's adversary Callippus. As an ex-opponent of Lycon this deponent looks like an impartial witness — but we have no means of knowing what his relations with the speaker or with Callippus may have been.
49. Similarly, the institution of partnership was not well developed, and we have no instances of testimony from business partners. The only example of testimony arising from an economic 'partnership' is Nicocles' testimony for his co-guardian Phormio in [D.] 45 *Steph. i* 37; clearly it was in Nicocles' interest to testify that the two guardians had behaved correctly.
50. Harrison, 1968, pp. 189-99; Gauthier, 1972; pp. 126-7, 132-56 (cf. D.M. Lewis, 1975); Whitehead, 1977, pp. 89-97. The main function of the patron was to guarantee that his client was entitled to metic status, which by the late 5th century could also be established in other ways (proof of tax payment). Metics continued to need citizen patrons for other reasons (*e.g.* as guarantors, cf. Plut. *Alc.* 5), but did not necessarily maintain a permanent relationship with one 'officially' recognised *prostatēs.*
51. In [D.] 53 *Nicostr.* 17-18 the speaker relates that he was attacked near the stone-quarries while returning to the city from Piraeus and rescued by passers-by who heard his cries for help; presumably they were among the witnesses who gave evidence in § 18. In Isocr. 18 *Callim.* 8 it is not clear who gave evidence about the seizure of Callimachus' money by the speaker's friend (*epitēdeios*) Patrocles.
52. The companion was 'held back' by one of Conon's group during the fight (§ 8) but apparently was not personally injured; it was probably he who looked about, when released, to collect witnesses. As Mensching, 1963, points out, it is suspicious that Ariston did not call him as a witness.
53. The Anaschetus whose testimony is impugned in Hyperides 2 *Lyc. ii* fr. v (*P. Oxy.* 1607) may be the brother of this Archebiades (*A.P.F.* 819). Another witness, Chaeretimus, appears in a tribal list of the middle of the 4th c. (*I.G.* ii^2 2385, 1. 104), but its purpose is unknown.
54. Pringsheim, 1961, p. 267 (1949), notes that it was more permissible for a magistrate to enter a private house and take possession of goods than for an ordinary citizen to do so. Possibly the speaker had asked for a magistrate to accompany him and had been given a slave instead. Whether public slaves could testify without being tortured is uncertain: Harrison, 1968, p. 177; 1971, p. 150; Thür, 1977, p. 162.
55. The origins of the oath of disclaimer in Athenian process are obscure, but there is no reason to regard it, as Harrison does (1971, pp. 143-4) as a survival of oath-helping. Witness testimonies were normally agreed with witnesses before they came to court; the option of

taking this oath protected the witness from a litigant's attempt to manipulate his testimony, and offered litigants some safeguard against changes of testimony by witnesses (cf. Lyc. 1 *Leocr.* 20, [D.] 58 *Theocr.* 7). References in court speeches (above, n. 30) are to the rhetorical use of challenges to opponents to give testimony damaging to their own case or swear ignorance; the oath was actually administered to a hostile witness in Is. 9 *Astyph.* 18, Aesch. 1 *Tim.* 67.

56. Apparently Astyphilus did not die in battle, since the funeral was private.
57. In Isocr. 17 *Trap.* 19-20 an agreement concerning arrangements for the end of a voyage is deposited with a fellow-traveller.
58. On torture of free non-Athenians see Thür, 1977, pp. 15-25.
59. He was challenged to testify in D.19 *Emb.* 198-200.
60. According to scandal, Anytus himself had been one of Alcibiades' lovers (Plut. *Alc.* 4; *A.P.F.* 1324). He and Andocides were in the same situation, both trying to escape the backlash of hostility which threatened (despite the amnesty law of 403, the efficacy of which has been much exaggerated) to strike anyone who had been connected with the oligarchic coups of the late 5th c. Andocides was also supported by Cephalus (*P.A.* 8277), who had taken his side in the Council when he was first accused (Andoc. 1 *Myst.* 115-6).
61. There is no particular reason to assume with Davies (*A.P.F.*, *l.c.*) that Demos had died in Cyprus. The witnesses who gave evidence in [D.] 50 *Polycl.* 13 about the honours which Apollodorus had received from the *demos* for his services as trierarch, and those who testified in Dinarchus 1 *Dem.* 27 about the misdeeds of Demosthenes, were presumably also significant public figures.
62. For other witnesses in this case see [D.] 59.25 (two members of wealthy families, *A.P.F.* 1969 and 9574), *ibid.* § 28 (an actor), §§ 32, 34, 48 (two more wealthy men, *A.P.F.* 4322, 8908).
63. He and his brother jointly manumitted two slaves c.330 at the age of about 70 (D.M. Lewis, 1959, B.335-342); it was unusual for brothers to keep property undivided unless one was childless (cf. [D.] 44 *Leoch.* and the case of Timarchus' blind uncle, Aesch. 1 *Tim.* 102-4).
64. The wording of the testimony is lost; the testimonies in our present text are late insertions.
65. Cf. above, p. 322 and n.30. For attitudes to homosexuality and male prostitution see Dover, 1978.
66. One of these witnesses, Callicrates, may have been the son of the well-known politician Callistratus of Aphidna (*A.P.F.* 8157, IV).
67. He testified for Pasion's opponent; we do not know if he also gave evidence for Pasion.
68. Cf. the *topos*, 'My enemies are bearing witness against themselves', used in pointing out damaging admissions by an adversary (D.28 *Aph. ii* 14), and the use of testimony from the opponent's witnesses on non-controversial points in D.57 *Eub.* 14.
69. See Schaefer, 1858, pp. 113-129; Treves, 1936, pp. 252-8; Sealey, 1967. The *hypothesis* to [D.] 25 is probably based on the speech of Lycurgus which this piece supposedly followed. Dinarchus 2 *Aristogiton* 8-10 (cf. 18) says that when Aristogiton was allotted the office of port superintendent, witnesses testified at his scrutiny that he had not looked after or buried his father and had stolen from his fellow-prisoners; Treves, *l.c.* thinks that Dinarchus' speech depends on [D.] 25, but the reverse relation seems more likely. Aristogiton's half-brother is said to be standing ready to speak in his defence despite their quarrel (§ 55); the dilemma of the brother expected to show family solidarity in an unworthy cause attracted composers of rhetorical exercises.
70. [D.] 29 is supposedly a defence of Phanus, a friend and fellow-tribesman of Aphobus who had testified for Demosthenes and whom Aphobus had indicted for perjury. Gernet (1954, pp. 68-70) considers it a collection of genuine Demosthenic fragments which were never used in court; but see Harrison, 1968, pp. 105-6, n.5.
71. On the possibility that Micon was a kinsman of the speaker see *A.P.F.* 1904.
72. Cf. [D.] 47 *Euerg.* 48, where trierarchs testify that they, like the speaker, have had to seize proerty from defaulting fellow-trierarchs — ostensibly a display of solidarity and approval of the speaker's behaviour, but also an opportunity to air old grudges.
73. The speaker says that Stephanus sued Phrastor for the return of the girl's dowry when he

divorced her, and Phrastor in retaliation brought a *graphē* charging him with passing a non-citizen woman as his legitimate daughter, in order to force Stephanos to drop his suit; Phrastor's testimony reverses the order of the two suits so that the *graphē* (which he admits he dropped) appears to have been motivated by righteous indignation. The speaker furthermore promises that Phrastor will give evidence that after he had expelled Phano, being ill and childless and on bad terms with his kin, he tried to introduce the child she had borne him to his *genos* and phratry; but in the upshot, not surprisingly, it is only the *gennētai* who testify to this (§§ 55-61).

74. In D.54 *Conon* 36-7 Ariston seems to imply that his witnesses testified that Conon's associates and witnesses had been involved in house-breaking, but we do not have the text of their testimony. Another hostile testimony, with no indication of motive, in D.18 *Crown* 137.
75. This would presumably have been hearsay evidence even by Athenian standards, which differed from those of Anglo-American law (Bonner, 1905, ch. 3).
76. Thrasybulus had been adopted, presumably after his father's death, by Hippolochides of Lousia, probably a patrilateral kinsman (*A.P.F.* 1395); he had inherited his father's estate and half that of his MB, and stood to inherit from his adoptive father too. The adoption did not affect his legal claim to inherit from Apollodorus, traced through his mother, but the accumulation of estates would have put him morally in a weak position. The division of his MB's estate may have left him on bad terms with the speaker's opponent, his MZ (represented by her husband).
77. Rules on presentation of female children may have varied from one phratry to another (cf. Is. 3 *Pyrrh.* 76). On marriage a woman was introduced to her husband's phratry with the sacrifice of *gamēlia*.
78. Priestly offices held by *genē* were often *de facto* hereditary, though not *de jure*. According to Ps.-Plutarch *Lives of the 10 Orators* 834B, Andocides himself was a member of the Kerykes; but Jacoby (*F.G.H.* 323a F 24) has shown that this is a mistake.
79. Cf. the similar case of Callias and the Kerykes, discussed above; no doubt the witnesses claimed to have voted against these illegal manoeuvres.
80. This refers to the celebration of the *meion* when the boys were young and their father was still alive. One of the weak points in their case, which they are trying to gloss over, is that after the death of his sons Ciron had made no attempt to introduce these grandsons to his own phratry and deme as his heirs (for other weaknesses see Wyse 1904, pp. 586-7).
81. Cf. Humphreys, in press. Some of Euxitheus' own fellow-demesmen (perhaps kin) testify in § 46 that he had been admitted to the deme — not a controversial point.
82. The money was to supply *epitēdeia*, either armour or provisions; the sum seems rather large for the latter purpose.
83. Cf. Hyp. 3 *Euxen.* 12. The decision to provide tribal support for an individual would presumably be made by a tribal assembly or authorised by tribal officials.
84. Probably no relation to the family of D.39-40 *Boeot. i-ii* (*A.P.F.* 9667).
85. § 1; some editors emend Chaerestratus to Phanostratus, making the speaker a friend of the claimant's father.
86. Some of these testimonies may come from officials or well-known public figures, as is perhaps the case in [D.] 34 *Ag. Phorm.* 38-9.
87. Perhaps even of the same man: one of the accomplices is called Mnesicles in both instances (*P.A.* 10307 (the second reference should read XL.9) and 10314).
88. Arbitrators were usually friends, or at least acquaintances, of both parties. In [D.] 59.45 there are three arbitrators, a friend of each of the two men competing for Neaira's favours, Stephanus and Phrynion, and a common friend of both. Very likely all belonged to the circle of Neaira's clients; Phrynion's arbitrator, Satyrus of Alopeke, married his daughter to Phrastor of Aigilia after the latter's abortive 'marriage' to Neaira's daughter.
89. Twining (1983, 1984) has pointed out that the Anglo-American theory of evidence currently rests on an empiricist epistemology which has long been rejected by philosophers. I should like to take this opportunity of thanking Professor Twining for helpful discussion and bibliographical advice; he is not responsible for the use I have made of it.

90. For the opposite extreme in conceptions of personal identity see Venezis, 1931.
91. Lord Devlin (foreword to Shepherd a.o., 1982) states categorically, "There is only one forensic weapon for testing the reliability of evidence and that is cross-examination. When that weapon is blunted, the advocate has no other to use." Morrow, 1960, believes that Plato introduces cross-questioning into his courts in the *Laws*, citing 766d and 855e-856a, but neither of these passages singles out the need to cross-question witnesses as a special problem; Plato wants courts to scrutinise the cases put to them more carefully (cf. *Apology* 37a-b), but he does not specify how such a scrutiny is to be carried out; he might well have considered cross-examination undesirably sophistic. On the possibility that Athenians used cross-examination before 378/7 B.C. see above, n. 6. *Eisangelia* trials at Athens could take two days (Rhodes, 1972, p. 164; [D.] 47 *Euerg.* 41-3), but we do not know how the extra time was used. Cf. Morrow, 1960, p. 282.
92. On the range of variation possible in courts' attitudes to time see Gernet, 1951, 1956. Note that the distinction between character and 'fact' witnesses is introduced in Aristotle *Rhet.* 1376a 24-5.
93. The procedure is not dissimilar to that of *eisangelia* in Athens, cf. n. 7 above; Morrow, 1960. Plato's supreme court is to consider its verdict on each case in three separate sittings.
94. Doubts are already expressed about this oath in Aeschylus, *Eumenides* 429-432.
95. In general, the gap between the abstract concept of justice and perceptions of legal institutions was wider in ancient Greece than in the rhetoric of our own legal tradition. Judges were not idealised (Humphreys, 1983c: Appendix); Antiphon the Sophist claimed that lawcourts were unjust because they produced hostility (Sprague, 1972, frag. B 92; 44 D.-K.).
96. Leach, 1954, uses a somewhat similar idea but attributes more clearly structured models to his actors than I would wish to hypothesise.
97. Character evidence can only be presented by the prosecution if it is also offered by the defence. In practice juries do not completely close their eyes to the relation between verdict and sentence (Kalven and Zeisel, 1966).
98. Practising lawyers note, however, that even 'independent' witnesses tend to identify with the side for which they are testifying (E.H. Smith, 1944).
99. Cf. Simon, 1975, p. 116. More work has been done on the effects of the witness's sex. It may be noted that although the law of hearsay is justified by reference to the importance to the jury of being able to observe witnesses' demeanour, 'demeanour' is currently defined in narrowly psychological terms (confidence/hesitation, etc.), while its sociological dimensions are ignored. Textbook advice on witnesses' 'character' is largely restricted to the question of previous criminal convictions (McCormick, 1972, ch. 17).
100. Cf. Greene, 1962, pp. 181-200 for similar points about Chinese courts. The effect of the presence of supporters in court is worth studying in modern England also; in one case I observed, in which a white boy was accused of knifing a West Indian, the defence lawyer pointed out the presence of his client's black girl-friend and her family in court, to prove that there was no racial prejudice involved.
101. On the need for a comparative study of concepts of the person see Lukes (in press), and the discussion of concepts of the person and of character in Greek tragedy and later dramatic theory in Jones, 1962. Another fruitful field of enquiry would be western medicine, in which the patient is normally treated without much consideration of his or her social milieu, and there is a tendency to focus on one organ or part of the body in isolation from the rest.

Abbreviations

Agora XV B.D. Meritt, J.S. Traill, eds., *The Athenian Agora XV. Inscriptions. The Athenian Councillors*, Princeton: The American School of Classical Studies, 1974.

A.P.F. J. K. Davies, *Athenian Propertied Families, 600-300 B.C.* Oxford: Clarendon Press, 1971.

Ath. Pol. Aristotle, *Athēnaiōn Politeia (Constitution of the Athenians).*
I.G. Inscriptions Graecae, Berlin: Reimer, 1873- .
P.A. J. Kirchner, ed., *Prosopographia Attica*, Berlin: Reimer, 1901-3.

Bibliography

Adkins, A.W.H. (1960) *Merit and Responsibility*, Oxford: Clarendon Press.

Ampolo, C. (1981) "Tra finanza e politica: carriera e affari del signor Moirokles" *Rivista di filologia* **109**:187-204.

Andrewes, A. (1961) "Philochoros on Phratries" *Journal of Hellenic Studies* **81**:1-15.

Ball, Milner S. (1975) "The Play's the Thing: an unscientific reflection on courts under the rubric of theater" *Stanford Law Review* **28**:81-115.

Bennett, W.L. and Feldman, M.S. (1981) *Reconstructing reality in the courtroom*, New Brunswick, N.J.: Rutgers University Press.

Biscardi, A. (1970) "La 'gnomē dikaiotatē' et l'interprétation des lois dans la Grèce ancienne" *Revue internationale des droits de l'antiquité* **17**:219-232.

Bogaert, R. (1968) *Banques et banquiers dans les cités grecques*, Leiden: Sijthoff.

Bohannan, Paul (1957) *Justice and judgment among the Tiv*, London: Oxford University Press.

Bonner, R.J. (1905) *Evidence in Athenian Courts*, Chicago: University Press.

Bonner, R.J. (1927) *Lawyers and litigants in ancient Athens*, Chicago: University Press.

Bourdieu, Pierre (1977) *Outline of a Theory of Practice*, Cambridge: University Press (original ed. Droz, 1972).

Brown, P.R.L. (1975) "Society and the supernatural: a medieval change" *Daedalus*, **104.2**:133-151 (also in Brown, *Society and the Holy in late Antiquity*, University of California, 1982).

Bruns, Ivo (1896) *Das Literarische Porträt der Griechen im fünften und vierten Jahrhundert vor Christi Geburt*, Berlin: Hertz.

Calhoun, George M. (1919a) "Oral and written pleading in Athenian courts" *Transactions of the American Philological Association* **50**:177-193.

Calhoun, George M. (1919b) "Athenian magistrates and special pleas" *Classical Philology* **14**:338-50.

Calhoun, George M. (1927) *The Growth of Criminal Law in ancient Greece*, Berkeley: University of California.

Canfora, L. ed. (1974) *Discorsi e lettere di Demostene*, I, Turin: Utet.

Carter, Lawrence (1982) *Apragmosyne: a study in late fifth-century Athenian society*, Ph.D. diss., London.

Chalmers, A.F. (1976) *What is this Thing called Science?* St. Lucia: University of Queensland Press (reprinted Open University, Milton Keynes, 1978).

Cohen, Jerome A. (1968) *The Criminal Process in the People's Republic of China 1949-1963: an introduction*, Cambridge: Harvard University Press.

Cohn-Haft, Louis (1956) *The Public Physicians of ancient Greece*, Northampton, Mass.: Smith College.

Conn, Stephen and Hippler, Arthur E. (1974) "Conciliation and arbitration in the native village and the urban ghetto" *Judicature* **58**:228-235.

Connor, W.R. (1971) *The New Politicians of fifth-century Athens*, Princeton: University Press.

Croissant, F. and Salviat, F. (1966) "Aphrodite guardienne des magistrats: gynéconomes de Thasos et polémarques de Thèbes" *Bulletin de correspondance hellénique* **90**:460-71.

Detienne, M. (1979) "Violentes 'eugénies'. En pleines Thesmophories: des femmes couvertes de sang", *La cuisine du sacrifice en pays grec*, ed. M. Detienne and J.-P. Vernant, Paris: Gallimard, pp. 183-214.

Doo, L.-W. (1973) "Dispute settlement in Chinese-American communities" *American Journal of Comparative Law* **21.4**:627-63.

Dorjahn, A.P. (1935) "Anticipation of arguments in Athenian courts" *Transactions of the American Philological Association* **66**:274-95.

Dorjahn, A.P. (1941) "On the Athenian anakrisis" *Classical Philology* **36**:182-5.

Dorjahn, A.P. (1953) "Evidence by torture in Athenian courts", *Studi in onore di V. Arangio-Ruiz*,

IV, Naples: Jovene, pp. 77-9.
Dorjahn, A.P. and Cronin, J.F. (1938) "Outside influence on Athenian courts" *Philological Quarterly* (Iowa State University) **17**:18-25.
Dover, K.J. (1950) "The Chronology of Antiphon's Speeches" *Classical Quarterly* **44**: 44-60.
Dover, K.J. (1968) *Lysias and the Corpus Lysiacum*, Berkeley: University of California.
Dover, K.J. (1974) *Greek Popular Morality in the time of Plato and Aristotle*, Oxford; Blackwell.
Dover, K.J. (1978) *Greek Homosexuality*, London: Duckworth.
Drerup, E. (1898) "Über die bei den attischen Rednern eingelegten Urkunden" *Jahrbuch für Philologie*, Supplementband **24**:221-366.
Drerup, E. (1899) "Antike Demosthenesausgaben" *Philologus*, supplement **7**:533-88.
Edelstein, Ludwig (1956) "The professional ethics of the Greek physician" *Bulletin of the History of Medicine* **30**:391-419 (Edelstein 1967, pp. 319-48).
Edelstein, Ludwig (1967) *Ancient Medicine*, Baltimore: Johns Hopkins University Press.
Erlanger, H.S. (1970) "Jury research in America: its past and future" *Law and Society Review* **4**:345-70.
Fallers, Lloyd A. (1969) *Law without Precedent*, Chicago: University Press.
Feifer, George (1964) *Justice in Moscow*, London: Bodley Head.
Finley, Moses I. (1952) *Studies in Land and Credit in ancient Athens, 500-200 B.C.; the horos-inscriptions*, Brunswick, N.J.: Rutgers University Press.
Finley, Moses I. (1980) *Ancient Slavery and Modern Ideology*, London: Chatto and Windus.
Gastaldi, Silvia (1981) *Discorso della città e discorso della scuola*, Florence: Nuova Italia.
Gauthier, Philippe (1972) *Symbola. Les étrangers et la justice dans les cités grecques*, Nancy: Université.
Gernet, Louis (1917) *Recherches sur le développement de la pensée juridique et morale en Grèce*, Paris: Leroux.
Gernet, Louis (1927) "La diamartyrie procédure archaïque du droit athénien" *Revue historique du droit français et étranger*, series 4, **6**:5-37 (Gernet, 1955:83-102).
Gernet, Louis (1938) "Sur les actions commerciales en droit athénien" *Revue des études grecques* **51**:1-44 (Gernet 1955:173-200).
Gernet, Louis (1939) "L'institution des arbitres publics à Athènes" *Revue des études grecques* **52**:389-414 (Gernet 1955: 103-119).
Gernet, Louis (1948) "Jeux et droit" *Revue historique de droit français et étranger* **26**:177-88 (Gernet 1955:9-18).
Gernet, Louis (1950) "Aspects du droit athénien de l'esclavage" *Archives d'histoire du droit oriental* **5**:159-87 (Gernet 1955:151-72).
Gernet, Louis (1951) "Droit et prédroit en Grèce ancienne" *L'Année sociologique* 1948-9:21-119 (Gernet 1968:175-260).
Gernet, Louis (1954) *Démosthène. Plaidoyers civils* I, Paris: Les Belles Lettres.
Gernet, Louis (1955) *Droit et société dans la Grèce ancienne*, Paris: Sirey.
Gernet, Louis (1956) "Le temps dans les formes archaïques du droit" *Journal de psychologie* **53**:379-406 (Gernet 1968:261-87).
Gernet, Louis (1957) *Démosthène. Plaidoyers civils II*, Paris: Les Belles Lettres.
Gernet, Louis (1959) "Note sur la notion de délit privé en droit grec", *Droits de l'antiquité et sociologie juridique, Mélanges H. Lévy-Bruhl*, Paris: Sirey, 393-405.
Gernet, Louis (1960) *Démosthène. Plaidoyers civils IV*, Paris: Les Belles Lettres.
Gernet, Louis (1968) *Anthropologie de la Grèce antique*, Paris: Maspero.
Gernet, Louis, and Bizos, Marcel (1926) *Lysias. Discours II*, Paris: Les Belles Lettres.
Giles, Howard, and St. Clair, Robert N., eds (1979) *Language and social personality*, Oxford: Blackwell.
Glotz, G. (1904) *La solidarité de la famille dans la Grèce ancienne*, Paris: Fontemoing.
Gluckman, Max (1955) *The Judicial Process among the Barotse of Northern Rhodesia*, Manchester: University Press.
Gomme, A.W. (1933) *The Population of Athens in the fifth and fourth centuries B.C.*, Oxford: Blackwell.
Greene, Felix (1962) *The Wall has Two Sides*, London: Cape.

Gulliver, P.H. (1963) *Social control in an African Society*, London: Routledge & Kegan Paul.
Gulliver, P.H. (1969) "Dispute settlement without courts: the Ndendeuli of Southern Tanzania", *Law in Culture and Society*, Laura Nader, ed. Chicago: Aldine, 24-68.
Hamnett, Ian, ed. (1977) *Social Anthropology and Law*, London: Academic Press.
Hansen, M.H., (1976) *Apagoge, Endeixis and Ephegesis against Kakourgoi, Atimoi and Pheugontes*, Odense: University Press.
Harrison, A.R.W. (1968) *The Law of Athens, I. The Family and Property*, Oxford: Clarendon Press.
Harrison, A.R.W. (1971) *The Law of Athens, II. Procedure*, Oxford: Clarendon Press.
Haussoulier, B. (1883) *La vie municipale en Attique*, Paris: Thorin.
Humphreys, S.C. (1978) *Anthropology and the Greeks*, London: Routledge & Kegan Paul.
Humphreys, S.C. (1983a) *The Family, Women and Death: comparative studies*, London: Routledge & Kegan Paul.
Humphreys, S.C. (1983b) "The date of Hagnias' death" *Classical Philogy* **78**:219-25.
Humphreys, S.C. (1983c) "The evolution of legal process in Attica", *Tria Corda, studi in onore di Arnaldo Momigliano*, E. Gabba, ed., Como: New Press: 229-256.
Humphreys, S.C. (in press) "*La Solidarité de la famille:* kin as witnesses in ancient Athenian courts".
Johnson, R. (1959) "Isocrates' methods of teaching" *American Journal of Philology* **80**:25-36.
Jones, John (1962) *Aristotle and Greek Tragedy*, London: Chatto and Windus.
Kalven, Harry, and Zeisel, Hans (1966), *The American Jury*, Boston: Little, Brown and Co.
Kennedy, George (1963) *The Art of Persuasion in Greece*, London: Routledge and Kegan Paul.
Kennedy, George (1968) "The Rhetoric of Advocacy in Greece and Rome" *American Journal of Philology* **89**:419-36.
Kohler, J., and Ziebarth, E. (1912) *Das Stadtrecht von Gortyn*, Göttingen: Vandenhoeck and Ruprecht (reprinted Hildesheim: Gerstenberg, 1972).
Kroll, John H. (1972) *Athenian Bronze Allotment Plates*, Cambridge: Harvard University Press.
Kuhn, Thomas S. (1962) *The Structure of Scientific Revolutions*, Chicago: University Press.
Kurczewski, J., and Frieske, K. (1978) "The social conciliatory commissions in Poland", *Access to Justice, II. Promising Institutions*, I, M. Cappeletti, ed., Milan: Giuffré, 153-427.
Labarbe, J. (1953) "L'âge correspondant au sacrifice du *koureion* et les données historiques du sixième discours d' Isée" *Academie Royale de Belgique, Bulletin de la classe des lettres et des sciences morales et politiques*, sér. 5, **39**:358-94.
Laemmli, Franz (1938) *Das attische Prozessverfahren in seiner Wirkung auf die Gerichtsrede* (*Rhetorische Studien*, 20), Paderborn: Schoningh.
Lanza, Diego (1979) *Lingua e discorso nell' Atene delle professioni*, Naples: Liguori.
Lavency, M. (1964) *Aspects de la logographie judiciaire attique*, Louvain: University.
Leach, E.R. (1954) *Political systems of Highland Burma*, London: Athlone Press.
Lewis, D.M. (1955) "Notes on Attic Inscriptions (II)" *Annual of the British School at Athens* **50**:1-36.
Lewis, D.M. (1959) "Attic Manumissions" *Hesperia* **28**:208-38.
Lewis, George Cornewall (1849) *An Essay on the Influence of Authority in Matters of Opinion*, London: Parker.
Lewis, George Cornewall (1852) *A Treatise on the Methods of Observation and Reasoning in Politics*, London: Parker.
Lind, E. Allan and O'Barr, William M. (1979) "The social significance of speech in the courtroom" in Giles and St. Clair, eds., 1979, 66-87.
Lloyd-Bostock, Sally, and Clifford, Brian R., eds. (1983) *Evaluating Witness Evidence*, New York: Wiley.
Lukes, Steven, a.o., eds. (in press) *Marcel Mauss and the Idea of the Person*, Cambridge: University Press.
McBarnet, Doreen J. (1981) *Conviction. Law, the State and the construction of justice*, London: Macmillan.
McCormick, Charles T. (1972) *McCormick's Handbook of the Law of Evidence*, 2nd ed., ed. Edward R. Cleary, St. Paul, Minnesota: West Publishing Co.
Malinowski, B. (1913) *The Family among the Australian Aborigines*, London: University Press.

Mathieu, Georges (1947) *Démosthène. Plaidoyers politiques. IV*, Paris: Les Belles Lettres.
Mauet, Thomas A. (1980) *Fundamentals of Trial Technique*, Boston: Little, Brown and co.
Meister, R.M.E. (1908) "Eideshelfer im griechischen Rechte" *Rheinisches Museum* **63**:559-86.
Mensching, Eckart (1963) "Zu Demosthenes' 54. Rede" *Rheinisches Museum* **106**:307-12.
Moore, Sally Falk (1977) "Individual interests and organisational structures: dispute settlements as 'events of articulation'" in Hamnett, ed., 1977, 159-88.
Moore, Sally Falk (1978) *Law as Process: an anthropological approach*, London: Routledge and Kegan Paul.
Moore, Sally Falk (1981) "Chagga 'customary' law and the property of the dead", *Mortality and Immortality*, eds. S.C. Humphreys and H. King, London: Academic Press, 225-48.
Morrow, Glenn R. (1939) *Plato's Law of Slavery (Illinois Studies in Language and Literature*, 25.3), Urbana: University of Illinois.
Morrow, Glenn R. (1960) *Plato's Cretan City*, Princeton: University Press.
Nanetti, Ofelia (1941) "Ricerche sui medici e sulla medicina nei papiri" *Aegyptus* **21**:301-14.
Nock, A.D. (1933) *Conversion*, London: Oxford University Press.
Osborne, Robin (1982) *Rural structure and the classical polis: town-country relations in Athenian Society*, Ph.D. diss., Cambridge.
Peacock, James L. (1968) *Rites of Modernization. Symbolic and social aspects of Indonesian proletarian drama*, Chicago: University Press.
Perry, J.A.G. (1977) "Law-codes and brokerage in a Lesotho Village" in Hamnett, ed., 1977, 189-228.
Pierart, M. (1971) "Les *euthynoi* athéniens" *L'Antiquité classique* **40**:526-73.
Préaux, Claire (1964) "La preuve à l'époque hellénistique, principalement dans l'Égypte grecque" *Recueuils de la Société Jean Bodin* **16**:161-222.
Pringsheim, F. (1949) "The Greek law of sale by auction", *Scritti Ferrini* 4, Milan: Vita e Pensiero, 284-343 (German text in Pringsheim, 1961.2, 262-329).
Pringsheim, F. (1951) "Le témoignage dans la Grèce et Rome archaïque" *Revue internationale des droits de l'antiquité* **6**:161-75 (= Pringsheim, 1961.2, 330-8).
Pringsheim, F. (1955) "The transition from witnessed to written transactions in Athens" *Aequitas und Bona Fides. Festgabe A. Simonius*, Basel: Helbing and Lichtenhahn, 287-97 (= Pringsheim, 1961.2, 401-9).
Pringsheim, F. (1961) *Gesammelte Abhandlungen* 1-2, Heidelberg: C. Winter.
Rea, John, a.o., eds (1962) *The Oxyrhynchus Papyri*, **27**, London: Egypt Exploration Society.
Redfield, James M. (1975) *Nature and Culture in the Iliad. The tragedy of Hector*, Chicago: University Press.
Revillout, E. (1892) "Une importante découverte" *Revue égyptologique* **7.1**:1-21.
Rhodes, P.J. (1972) *The Athenian Boule*, Oxford: Clarendon Press.
Ruschenbusch, E. (1961) "Ephesis" *Zeitschrift der Savigny-Stiftung* (Römische Abteilung) **78**:386-90.
Ruschenbusch, E. (1968) *Untersuchungen zur Geschichte des athenischen Strafrechts*, Koln/Graz: Böhlau.
Ruschenbusch, E. (1982) "Der Urspring des Gerichtlichen Rechtsstreits bei den Griechen", *Symposion 1977*, ed. J. Modrzejewski and D. Liebs, Koln/Wien: Böhlau, 1-8.
Saks, Michael J., and Hastie, Reid (1978) *Social Psychology in Court*, New York: Van Nostrand Reinhold.
Sander, Frank E.A., and Snyder, Frederick E. (1979) *Alternative Methods of Dispute Settlement - a selected bibliography*, Washington, D.C.: American Bar Association (Committee on Resolution of Minor Disputes).
Sandys, J.E., and Paley, F.A. (1896) *Select Private Orations of Demosthenes*, II, 3rd. ed. (1st ed. 1875), Cambridge: University Press.
Sautel, G. (1964) "Les preuves dans le droit grec archaïque" *Recueuils de la Société Jean Bodin* **16**:117-60.
Schaefer, A. (1858) *Demosthenes und seine Zeit, III. 2. Beilagen*, Leipzig: Teubner.
Schaefer, A. (1885) *Demosthenes und seine Zeit*, 2nd ed., Leipzig: Teubner.
Scherer, Klaus R. (1979) "Voice and speech correlates of perceived social influence in simulated

juries" in Giles and St. Clair, eds, 1979, 88-120.

Sealey, R. (1960) "Who was Aristogeiton?" *Bulletin of the Institute of Classical Studies*, London **7**:33-43.

Sealey, R. (1967) "Pseudo-Demosthenes XIII and XXV" *Revue des études grecques* **80**:250-5.

Shack, William A. (1979) "Collective oath. Compurgation in Anglo-Saxon England and African States" *Archives européennes de sociologie* **20**:1-18.

Shapland, Joanna (1981) *Between Conviction and Sentencing. The process of mitigation*, London: Routledge and Kegan Paul.

Shepherd, John W., Ellis, Hadya D., and Davies, Graham A., eds (1982) *Identification Evidence*, Aberdeen: University Press.

Simon, Rita J. (1967) *The Jury and the Defense of Insanity*, Boston: Little, Brown and co.

Simon, Rita J. (1975) *The Jury System in America. A critical overview*, Beverley Hills and London: Sage.

Simon, Rita J. (1980) *The Jury: its role in American society*, Lexington, Mass.: Lexington Books.

Smith, E.H. (1944) "Some things about witnesses" *Kentucky State Bar Journal* **8**:37-44.

Smith, Robert W. (1974) *The Art of Rhetoric in Alexandria*, The Hague: Nijhoff.

Soubie, André (1973-4) "Les preuves dans les plaidoyers des orateurs attiques" *Revue internationale des droits de l'antiquité* **20**:171-253, **21**:77-134.

Sprague, R.K., ed. (1972) *The Older Sophists*, Columbia: University of South Carolina Press.

Talamanca, M. (1975) "La Legge di Dem., 'or.' 21,94" *Bulletino dell' Istituto di Diritto Romano* **17**:93-159.

Thompson, W.E. (1968) "An oratorical fragment. *P. Oxy.* 2538" *Rivista di filologia* **96**:149-50.

Thompson, W.E. (1971) "The deme in Kleisthenes' reforms" *Symbolae Osloenses* **46**:72-79.

Thompson, W.E. (1981) "Athenian attitudes to wills" *Prudentia* **13**:13-24.

Thür, G. (1977) *Beweisführung vor den Schwurgerichtshöfen Athens. Die Proklesis zur Basanos*, Vienna: Österreichische Akademie (*Sitzungsberichte*, 317).

Treves, P. (1936) "Apocrifi Demostenici" *Athenaeum* **14**:233-66.

Treves, P. (1940) "Les documents apocryphes du 'Pro Corona'" *Les études classiques* **9**:138-74.

Turner, E.G. (1951) *Athenian Books in the Fifth and Fourth Centuries B.C.* (inaugural lecture), London: University College.

Twining, William (1983) "Identification and misidentification in legal processes: redefining the problem" in Lloyd-Bostock and Clifford, eds, 1983, 255-83.

Twining, William (1984) "Evidence and Legal Theory" *Modern Law Review* **47**: 261-83.

Usher, Stephen (1976) "Lysias and his clients" *Greek, Roman and Byzantine Studies* **17**:31-40.

Van Gulik, Robert (1956) *T'ang-yin-pi-shih, "Parallel cases from under the pear-tree". A thirteenth century manual of legal jurisprudence*, Leiden: Brill.

Van Velsen, J. (1969) "Procedural informality, reconciliation and false comparisons" in Max Gluckman, ed., *Ideas and Procedures in African Customary Law*, London: Oxford University Press, 137-50.

Vanderpool, E. (1966) "Some Attic Inscriptions" *Hesperia* **66**:274-83.

Venezis, Elias (1931) *To Noumero 31328*, Athens: Hestia.

Westermann, A. (1850) "Untersuchungen über die in die attischen Redner eingelegten Urkunden. II. Prüfung sämmtlicher in die attischen Redner eingelegten Zeugenaussagen" *Abhandlungen der philologisch-historischen Classe der Königlich Sächsischen Gesellschaft der Wissenschaften* **1**:61-136.

Whitehead, David (1977) *The Ideology of the Athenian Metic*, Cambridge: Philological Society (supplementary vol. 4).

Wilamowitz-Moellendorff, U. von (1923a) "Lesefrüchte CLXXI" *Hermes* **58**:57-61.

Wilamowitz-Moellendorff, U. von (1923b) "Lesefrüchte CLXXII" *Hermes* **58**:61-69.

Willetts, R.F.C. (1967) *The Law Code of Gortyn*, Berlin: De Gruyter.

Wolff, H.-J. (1966) *Die attische Paragraphe*, Weimar: Böhlau.

Wolff, H.-J. (1968) *Demosthenes als Advocat*, Berlin: de Gruyter.

Wolff, H.-J. (1969) "Methodische Grundfragen der rechtsgeschichtlichen Verwendung attischer Gerichtsreden", *Atti del II. Congresso Internazionale della Società Italiana di Storia del Diritto (Venice, 1967)*, Florence: Olschki.

Wyse, William (1904) *The Speeches of Isaeus*, Cambridge: University Press.
Yaffe, James (1972) *So Sue Me! Story of a Community Court*, New York: Saturday Review Press.
Yates, Frances A. (1966) *The Art of Memory*, London: Routledge and Kegan Paul.
Zuntz, G. (1947) "Once again the Antiphontean Tetralogies" *Museum Helveticum* **6**:100-3.

Law and Local Power

The benevolent proprietor and the property law: A British-Indian dilemma

ELIZABETH WHITCOMBE

National Hospital for Nervous Diseases, London

British Indian revenue policy determined British-Indian property law. It was essential to establish a class of landed proprietors, entitled by law to collect rents from their tenants, from which in turn government could legally assess its revenue demand. Revenue was principally settled with the zamindars, who had had rights to a share in agricultural produce which carried a duty to meet government's revenue demand recognised by the Mughal government. The zamindars were redefined unequivocally as landlords by the British-Indian property law. Their estates were assigned on the basis of existing records and were composed for the most part of disparate shares in villages. Such estates were essentially not economically viable; the social and domestic circumstances of the zamindars further compromised the management of their estates. Government intended that the landlords should become progressive farmers, but conditions, as much a product of legal enactment as of economic reality, frustrated that aim. The history of the nineteenth century administration of British India illustrates the dilemma of government, and the conflict between conservatism in the rural sphere and the pursuit of progressive policies. The radical reform of the zamindars' estates, namely the drastic curtailments which took place under the zamindari abolition statutes under the Congress government's programme for land reform, has paradoxically achieved for independent India that which the government of British India struggled throughout a century and a half to achieve: the creation of the progressive proprietor.

WITH THE CONSOLIDATION of the East India Company's power in the quarter-century following Plassey (1757), certain practical matters demanded immediate attention. Stable government required an assured source of revenue and, therefore, a legal system by which the staple source of taxable wealth — the land — might be regularly assessed and collected. A law of property was fundamental to the business of government, a law which defined proprietary right in land and, consistent with that right, the liability of the proprietor to meet the revenue demand levied by government: "there can be no public Revenue without private Property", as Sir Philip Francis, one of the most imaginative of the Company's savants, succinctly expressed it. [1] Govern-

History and Anthropology, 1985
Vol. 1, pp. 373-379
0275-7206/85/0373-0241 $18.50/0

ment's task, in drawing up its revenue settlements, was first to identify the proprietor; second, to award him right, title and interest in a landed estate; and third, to define and physically demarcate that estate, the whole procedure providing the legal basis for the just and equitable assessment of land revenue.

In the rural community, bewildering and archaic as it seemed to the Company's officials now beset with the problem of disentangling a mass of rights relating to land in order to redefine them, certain figures stood out as answering most closely to the description of 'proprietor': the zamindars. The *zamindar* — the word literally means "holder of land" — held rights, collectively known as *zamindari*, which had been recognised, if not bestowed, by the Company's Mughal predecessors. These rights applied to a village and the lands it encompassed, rather than to a parcel of land as such; most zamindars held rights pertaining to a number of villages, commonly scattered at considerable distances. Inheritance over many generations had further complicated the distribution of zamindari rights; the majority were shared by coparcenaries, several zamindars thus holding rights in the same village or villages. The possessors of zamindari rights were classified in the Mughal revenue books as distinct from and superior to the cultivating peasantry, or ra'iyats. Zamindari and *ra'iyati* were not necessarily co-extensive; villages existed in the Company's time which were the exclusive preserve of ra'iyats, in which case government settled the revenue directly with them. But in the great bulk of the Company's possessions — Bengal, the North-Western Provinces (later, with Oudh, the United Provinces) and a considerable part of the Madras Presidency — zamindars were dominant and here zamindari was unequivocally held to be a right superimposed upon ra'iyati. The official significance of zamindari was that it entitled its holder to claim, with government's express consent, a share in the produce of the land in satisfaction of the payment to government of government's own share as revenue. The arrangement with local government had taken various forms. In Bengal, the zamindar paid authority a fixed sum for the revenue assessed on a village and made his collections from the peasantry at rates fixed by custom, or by himself (the two being frequently indistinguishable). Elsewhere, local government officials fixed the revenue rates with which the zamindar complied; in addition he levied a separate rate for his own purposes. Integral also to zamindari was a prescriptive right to levy a variety of charges distinct from the revenue demand and exempt from official assessment — charges on houses, markets and bridges, for example, and on births and marriages, in the villages under the zamindar's jurisdiction. [2] It is clear that the package of rights constituting zamindari could change hands, in whole or in part; it was heritable and alienable but the personal laws of the Hindu and Moslem communities restricted alienation to certain conditions: sale, for example, under the law of the joint Hindu family, of coparcenary property could only be countenanced in response to distress, necessity or benefit of the family.

It would have been necessary for the Company, had the zamindar not existed, to invent him, given that the satisfaction of the revenue demand depended upon the presence of a proprietor possessing an estate. As it was, the Company redefined the zamindar they encountered in the revenue-books of the Mughal government and quantified his zamindari in terms of proprietary right in the land of the villages under his jurisdiction. Adherence to the records of the former government was nothing if not scrupulous and from the painstaking business of redefinition and demarcation, which meant ultimately the physical measurement of the greater part of British India, the proprietorial estate emerged to take its place in the new model revenue book. It was indeed a creation of British-Indian law. The zamindar now legally owned his land, but rarely in any coherent form; his estate might typically comprise three villages A, B, and C, together with one-quarter of village D, one-sixteenth of village E (two miles distant), one-thirtieth of village F (four miles across the river), one-ninety-sixth of village G, and so on; title to as little as one nine-hundredth of one-third of an acre, a literally quantified coparcenary share, went down in the record as legally valid. With immense industry, estimates were drawn up of the income this estate, disparate in all essential features, could be expected to yield; upon these estimates, government in turn assessed its revenue demand.

The duty of the proprietor, however, was not merely to discharge his revenue obligations. It was explicitly intended that the newly recognised landowners should be the spearhead of progressive agriculture, that they should primarily be concerned with the care and improvement of their estates, thus ensuring the welfare of the Indian people — and the prosperity of government. To this end, certain concessions were written in to the revenue laws: that the demand should be moderate and that it should be assessed in perpetuity, as in Bengal and parts of Madras, or, at the very least revised at intervals of no less than a decade, as in the North-Western Provinces, the least disturbance of the proprietary body's security being the stated aim. The zamindars were to be thus encouraged to devote their attention to their estates and the cultivators, their tenants, free of government harassment.

The provision made for the benevolent proprietor to safeguard and improve upon his and government's interests was however cruelly frustrated, by the very nature of the institutions the revenue laws had so carefully created. The estate cobbled together in the revenue record possessed no claim to coherence in reality; it was therefore virtually impossible to manage with any degree of efficiency, let alone enlightenment. Moreover, such income as this chaotic entity produced had, by the force of tradition preserved by the British Indian government, to sustain not merely the zamindar and his style of life commensurate with a commanding social position, the stability of which government was committed to ensure in the interests of its own security; a multitude of claimants also depended upon the state for livelihood — the joint family and innumerable hangers-on. The persistent drain on resources under the head of 'domestic establishment', being largely unofficial, was insufficiently accounted for by the government revenue department. Meanwhile, the early revenue settlements, prosecuted with the zeal which distinguishes pioneering enterprises, tended to err, as was later admitted, on the side of severity in their assessments. The zamindars were therefore commonly caught between the millstones of society and government: in keeping up appearances in the grand manner to maintain their status, their extravagant, even profligate, way of life conflicted with the fiscal requirements of government, and government did not bend. Ruin was staved off largely by windfalls — the occasional bumper harvest — and by a system of remittances. Younger sons, brothers and cousins were, throughout the first fifty years of the nineteenth century, employed readily in the Company's civil and military establishments: by the 1840s, as many as forty thousand young men are thought to have taken service thus from the eastern districts alone of the North-Western Provinces. Regular remittances from their salaries were crucial to the survival of the 'parent' zamindari estate.

In hundreds of cases, however, zamindars were overwhelmed by debt, despite such remedies. Government had made ample provision for this contingency; it was not to be deterred, at the outset, from putting its provision into practice. Its inflexibility was underwritten by moral as well as economic purpose. The spendthrift proprietor was an impediment to practical progress, to which government was committed. Sound commercial principles enacted in the law would see to his removal and replacement by the purchaser of his estate who, insofar as he possessed capital sufficient for the purchase, could be expected to conduct his affairs as an efficient, progressive entrepreneur, capable of advancing his estate in accordance with the acceptable order of things, with "the laws of Commerce," in Burke's phrase, "which are the laws of Nature, which are the laws of God". The revenue codes therefore carried the stipulation that estates were liable to be sold at auction to meet arrears of revenue; by 1830, the principle of compulsory sale in satisfaction of debt was extended to the civil jurisdiction. The way for clearance was legally opened.

According to official records, hundreds of estates belonging to perhaps thousands of improvident, impoverished zamindars in the North-Western Provinces alone changed hands in response to the working of the revenue and civil laws of debt and insolvency in the first fifty years of the nineteenth century. But the confident expectation that the embarassed proprietor would steadily become a rarity, an image progressively dispelled by vigorous, solvent auction-purchasers who would nurse their newly-acquired estates into financial health and set on foot a train of improvements, was defeated by circumstances. Chief amongst these was the apparently insoluble problem of the nature of the estates thus acquired. The 'new men', in buying up the old, bought no better right, title and interest than the latter had owned and found themselves saddled, more often than not, with the possession of a ramshackle, unworkable collection of proprietorial rights somewhat euphemistically labelled an estate. Furthermore, most auction purchasers, being men of ready capital, were to be found lodged where such ready capital was to be found, that is to say, in the bazars. Their interest in the land took the form commonly of absentee landlordism; the realities of estate 'management' tended to reinforce this tendency. On rare occasions when auction-purchasers ventured into the rural hinterland to take charge of their new acquisitions, they encountered former proprietors, with the full strength that the coparcenary and its domestic establishment could muster, legally dispossessed by the sale at auction, but not physically displaced. The traditional status of the zamindar in his community, guaranteed it will be remembered by government, tended to make eviction an idle threat. The problem of how the progressive landed proprietor might be established could not be solved.

The upheaval of the Mutiny complicated matters further for the Crown government which took over from the Company finally in 1857-58. The confiscation and, in some cases, the destruction of the property of rebellious zamindars engendered nothing but lasting bitterness: no enlightened phoenix rose from those ruins. But it was the wholesale disbandment of the 'native' civil and military establishments which created the most serious difficulties for the rural community, and for government. Overnight, the flow of remittances was stopped and, in addition, crowds of brothers, sons and cousins were driven back to dependence on the chronically unmanageable estates. Government, entering upon its tasks with imperial vigour, revised the revenue settlements, but less in accordance with the realities of the rural scene and the overpopulated zamindaris that in strict adherence to new, scientific standards of assessment based on the classification of soils and estimates of productivity.

The zamindars' predicament, which was also government's, deepened. It was now not only clear that the law of compulsory sales could not be relied on to steer the proprietary body into progressiveness. The Mutiny, in demonstrating the horror of rebellion, had made any prospect of social revolution, such as the widespread dispossession of the landed classes must necessarily entail, unstomachable. The logical outcome of the debt laws could not be countenanced. Such laws had to be countermanded, and were; and, as befitted a government to whom the rule of law was paramount, the countermanding was done itself by legislation. Compulsory sales remained on the statute-book and in the revenue codes but, from the 1860s, a series of grace and favour reliefs in the form of enactments for the relief of indebted and insolvent proprietors and the temporary management of their estates under government supervision took their place beside them. For the situation which government had legally created, a legal remedy at least was now provided; the status quo of the landed classes was honourably if not triumphantly upheld by the rule of law.

Government had however in no way dispensed with the notion of fostering progress in rural India. It took over the Company's inheritance and, principally in the field of public works — irrigation and the railways — prosecuted the large-scale development of agricultural resources along the lines its predecessor had established. The Crown government, from 1877 constituted the imperial government of India, saw itself, in innumerable public pronouncements, as the proprietor-in-chief of its vast British-Indian estate; its public works, chief amonst them the great irrigation canals which by the 1880s commanded over two million acres of northern India alone, were the very embodiment of benevolent proprietorship: "an enterprise not less lucrative than dignified", in the apt phrase of Lord Hastings, the Company's Governor-General in the first decade of the nineteenth century. But the financial burdens of government increased with its self-appointed tasks; by the late nineteenth century, the lucrative aspect of irrigation works was compromised by the debts incurred in their construction and maintenance. The proprietor-in-chief's estate itself took on the look of an embattled and financially embarrassed zamindar's. Only by delegation of proprietorial responsibility could the costs of agrarian progress be borne.

It was now established that agricultural policy, which received its new expression in the formation in 1870 of the Government of India's department of agriculture, while still under the aegis of the revenue administration, was henceforth to concentrate on technicalia, and on the economically viable. It was a policy of pick and choose. The irrigation districts were the focal point; the frustrating complexities of the property laws were ignored; the officials of the agricultural department set up a handful of farms for experimentation in the design of implements, the selection of crops, in tillage and well-digging, and sought out zamindars in possession of estates, or parts of them, which were small, coherent and productive and could therefore benefit from the fruits of successful experimentation. The policy could be seen at its clearest on the Court of Wards' estates, which the insolvency relief statutes brought under government management for the express purpose of improvement and the safeguarding thus of the minor's interests. Agricultural associations were formed, in which progressive proprietors could further the cause.

By the turn of the century, the demonstration zamindar had come into existence. His example, representing a tiny minority even of the proprietorial classes, was doomed to be of limited significance since the underlying problem of the zamindars' debt-in-perpetuity and of the unworkability of their estates as enshrined in the property law persisted; and was to persist throughout the remaining years of British rule. Questions of land tenure, so crucial to the improvement of Indian agriculture, were ruled out of court for the agriculture department: the most comprehensive review of the state and prospects of agriculture in India, the royal commission chaired by Lord Linlithgow in 1927-28, had land tenure removed from its terms of reference before any evidence was heard.

Within their limits, meanwhile, the minority of economically viable zamindars consolidated their position. The depression and concomitant slump in world cereal production provided Indian farmers with the opportunity, if they had the means, to capitalise on government's incentives and increase grain production. The introduction of sugar-cane into the northern irrigation districts was already by the 1930s an enormous boost to the fortunes of the small-scale progressive farmers — by then numbering perhaps a few thousand in a total population of over 300,000,000.

Such was the state of affairs at Independence, in 1947. The new Congress government, however, had been committed to a policy of radical land reform since the 1920s. It lost little time, on its accession to office, and seized the property bull by the horns: by a series of statutes in the 1950s, it abolished the zamindars. But more than a little of the imperial legacy remained. It was again a matter substantially of redefinition. The ex-zamindar was entitled to retain, for his own use, a home farm of his own choosing from his former estate, to comprise not more than forty acres. He thus took sole possession of the heartland of his former property, in a compact and usually highly productive block. The odds and ends which constituted the remainder of his former estate were now sold off to a multitude of cultivating tenants, amongst whom the insuperable difficulties of an unviable smallholding persisted with a vengeance. Meanwhile, with the understandable intention to dampen down zamindars' discontent at the stripping of their estates, provision for compensation was hurried through the legislature. The ex-zamindar was now relieved of the impracticable clutter of his outlying properties, which had been parcelled out amongst his ex-tenants, and was left in possession of a shrunken estate, perhaps a tenth, perhaps even a thousandth of his former zamindari, but compact, productive and as such constituted ideally for improvement; compensation now gave him the means by which to develop it, as government policy under first the five-year plans and, in the later 1960s, the high-yielding varieties programme, indicated. Once more, thorny questions of the impracticality of small-holding were put out of sight. Progressive farming had come of age in India, although still of necessity confined to a tiny minority of the rural population. But the imperial dilemma of the creation of the benevolent proprietor had been solved.

Notes

1. Philip Francis to W. Young, 5 July 1778: Francis MSS, 51 (41), 41 (India Office Library).
2. Habib, I., *The Agrarian System of Mughal India*, London: Asia Publishing House, 1963 pp. 136-159.

Law, arbitrariness and the power of the Lords of North Lebanon

MICHAEL GILSENAN

Magdalen College, Oxford

The paper focuses on the role of arbitrariness and violence and their relation to law-in-practice. The locus is the semi-feudal society of North Lebanon and more widely the Lebanon as a whole. Weber and others have suggested that the arbitrary is an important element in the characterisation of specific political types of domination such as patrimonialism. There are ambiguities in this kind of treatment which are explored for the case of the beys of the Akkar region of the north. A system of status honour, founded originally on military control and taxation, identified personal might and personal right. Modern social changes in the Ottoman and French Mandate periods and up to the present have combined to produce a social world in which violence has become more systematically important in local power. A fragmented and weak state formation has reinforced such processes and the use of law as a visible instrument of individual and group domination enshrining arbitrariness at the heart of society.

ORDER AND THE ARBITRARY

'ÉTONNANTE PUISSANCE de l'homme!' said the French writer Amedée Guillemin, 'il arrive à reconnaître l'ordre au milieu d'une confusion apparente.' The great nineteenth century social theorists show us confusion (not to say illusion, fetishism and historical irony) at the centre of the life experience of people under modern capitalism. They also show us that it is a confusion whose property is to mask the forces and structures that produce it. In this topsy-turvy world things must be 'stood on their head' to become comprehensible; the veil of what seems to be must be torn aside to reveal what is.

The sociologist demonstrates that the dis-order of the social system derives from an order. The in-coherent can be made to reveal a coherence, and in doing so be transformed into structure — privileged metaphor of the privileged discourse of science.

That we might equally modify Guillemin's dictum and come to recognise

History and Anthropology, 1985
Vol. 1, pp. 381-400
0275-7206/85/0102-0381 $18.50/0

the confusion at the centre, not of an apparent order only but also of an apparent disorder, seems almost sociologically impolite. Yet perhaps we should upend our own assumptions. If writers such as Pierre Bourdieu can properly insist on the double nature of social phenomena as always structured and structuring, we can also insist that they are always both destructured and destructuring.

The interpenetration of order and disorder, determinacy and indeterminacy in the different dimensions of social life takes on a particular relevance when a society is in seeming anarchy, as is the contemporary Lebanon. A certain grim sociological curiosity is all the more intense when the uneasy suspicion exists that such anarchy is not merely the false reflection of a deeper, organised level of reality, but is rather a direct expression of something chaotic within the basic conditions of existence of that society.

The classical literature in fact contains many explications of political, economic and social arrangments that are held, at least in part, to be defined by some core element of what I shall call by the blanket term of 'the arbitrary'. Weber's characterisations of patrimonial and patriarchal domination, for example, both incorporate such an idea. I shall quote him here at some length because what he says is central to the problem of the relationships, or lack of them, between power, property and the law that I wish to investigate.

1) Of patrimonial regimes: 'There is a wide scope for actual arbitrariness and the expression of purely personal whims on the part of the ruler and the members of his administrative staff.' (Weber 1968: vol.1, p.239)

2) Of patriarchal domination: 'Essentially it is based on a strictly personal loyalty ... Such personal authority has in common with *impersonally* oriented bureaucratic domination stability and an "everyday character" ... The master wields his power without restraint, at his own discretion and, above all, unencumbered by rules in so far as it is not limited by traditions or by competing powers.' (*ibid.* vol.2, pp.1006-1007, his emphasis)

3) Of the Turkish 'feudal' system: 'The Turkish feudal system remained much more prebendal with regard to claims of inheritance, since the power of the Sultan and the *beglerbeg* continued to be largely arbitrary despite all of the rules and regulations.' (ibid., p.1075)

Two major points arise. The first, on which Weber seems to me to be ambivalent, is the question of whether arbitrariness is to be regarded as essential to such political forms or merely accidental. Is the 'wide scope' of example (1) nonetheless relatively well defined and restricted, or is it more variable and constantly varying? Can it be both, or the first at one state of development and the second at another? Is there some oscillation between poles or a directional change? Such questions entail consideration of whether there is any broader analytical notion of determination by the political of other dimensions of society, as is hinted at in his model, and if so what the significance of arbitrariness is for those other dimensions. We would need to go on to inquiries such as: Can these kinds of 'systems' be said to be stable and self-ordering, or is instability and disordering one of their basic characteristics? Are there continuous and predictable processes that somehow reassert themselves over intermittency and unpredictability? And if there are not, what are the implications for both model and society?

This links us to the second point. Weber was engaged in the construction of ideal types. Notoriously, the line between ideal type and particular historical reality is not always clear, especially in terms of changes or transformations in that reality. When we are dealing with these forms of domination as concrete historical phenomena, we have to ask whether they possess their own dynamic and evolutionary tendencies. If they do, and if arbitrariness is essential to that dynamic overall rather than, let us say, characteristic only of a particular phase, are the evolutionary tendencies necessarily towards a state of chaos?

The Oriental Despot

Since we are going to deal with a former province of the Ottoman Empire it is worth recalling how much nineteenth century Western historiography identified despotism, notably in its 'Oriental' forms, as static, non-dialectical, or in some way ossified and incapable of changing from within. This stasis was seen to be closely related to, or even caused by, the arbitrary quality of power and this quality might be given very great explanatory weight. At the same time it was frequently seen as a, if not indeed the major cause of the ruin and decay of the Ottoman State in economic and social as much as any other terms. So an idea of stasis was actually linked with more processual and causal notions, though the separation and the linkage were not always clearly made.

More than this, arbitrary power has been invoked to answer negative questions of the type: why did capitalism not develop in the Ottoman Empire? Answer: in part because of the randomness and irrationality of arbitrary authority manifested in the confiscation of the wealth of the merchants, thus inhibiting the growth of a strong merchant class which might act as the motor of capitalist development. In this perspective arbitrariness blocks certain kinds of historical potentialities.

We can cite another nineteenth century view, but this time from the Sublime Porte itself, from the centre rather than from outside.

> Dans ce system l'administration civile et financière d'une localité est livrée à l'arbitraire d'un seul homme, c'est-à-dire quelque fois à la main de fer des passions les plus violentes et les plus stupides, car si ce fermier n'est pas bon, il n'aura d'autre soin que son propre avantage (Chevallier 1971: 104).

Thus the *Hatt-i Cherif* of Gülhane (concerning tax-farming) read on 3rd

November, 1839 before the young Sultan Abdulmegid. Here we have not only the attempt to regularise the collection of taxes to the benefit of the beleaguered state exchequer, but also a complaint that *local* arbitrariness is having an adverse effect on the Empire as a whole, not least in the randomness and unpredictability of its regional administrations.

As the French consul in Tripoli in Syria sourly remarked in 1856 of the 'chefs indigènes' who gathered taxes, executed state laws and regulations, and maintained order: 'Leurs actes sont sans contrôle; leur pouvoir, quoique défini par des règlements, est en réalité arbitraire, sans autre limite que la force de résistance qu'ils peuvent rencontrer chez les habitants' (Ismail 1976: vol.10, 71).

In the view of many writers and participants, therefore, arbitrariness defined political relations. It is seen in different ways. For the Porte this was a particular condition that had come into being in certain areas of the Imperial system and should be eliminated. For others it was a given of that system as an entirety, intrinsic to order in a society where for many reasons group violence was endemic, difficult to contain and indeed represented in cultural practice as being of the very nature of social relationships coded by honour and violence.

Dominique Chevallier suggests that brutality and cunning were fundamental to successful claims to authority in nineteenth century Lebanon, and that a 'real leader' was one who could impose himself by whatever means on those constantly threatening to overturn or thwart him: 'pouvoir être dur, arbitraire, c'était aussi être capable d'assurer plus d'ordre public.' (Chevallier, *ibid.*: 98). Having argued that only the chief who was able by force to protect people from the miseries of endless internecine quarrels would be respected he goes on: 'Là où le libéral européen dénoncait l'asservissement au "despotisme", l'oriental appréciait la protection relative de l'humble et du plus grand nombre contre des maux plus fâcheux' (*loc.cit.*). In this perspective it is suggested that arbitrariness and violence were the best protection against arbitrariness and violence; law, or certainly regulation, was a function of institutional disorder.

Nor is this only a western view of the expectations and *mentalité* of orientals. Gibb and Bowen quote the celebrated nineteenth century Egyptian historian al-Jabarti on the Egyptian peasantry:

> If the peasants were administered by a compassionate *multazim* (tax farmer, MG), they despised him and his agents, delayed payment of his taxes, called him by feminine names, and hoped for the ending of his *iltizam* and the appointment of some tyrant without fear of God or mercy for them, so as to gain by that means their private ends by the alighting of his violence upon some of their number. (Gibb and Bowen 1950: vol.1, pt.1, 205)

It is certainly true that such analyses of the master-servant relationship, which tend here to show an 'inherent' indifference and fatalism of the fellah as well as his total incorporation into a system dominated by coercion, raise many problems. This example is very much the perspective of a member of the notable stratum. Gabriel Baer is certainly correct to say that in the light of the record of revolts by the Egyptian peasantry in the eighteenth and nineteenth centuries such an account of their supposed passivity is 'highly improbable', though a wonderful justification for a harsh *multazim* (Baer 1969: 105).

Yet it can be argued that if, as explanations of a supposedly 'natural' peasant submissiveness and appreciation of brute force, such views are as interesting for what they reveal about their writers as for what they tell us about their subjects, they do nonetheless highlight very basic traits in conceptions of authority and order. In this social and cultural world the law-giving, or rather the law-guarding power, part of whose function is the ensuring of constraint and the following of religious prescription, state decree and locally sanctified tradition, is also precisely that which goes beyond restraint, violates sacred custom, breaks the bounds of honour, kinship, neighbourhood, oath and covenant, or may do so. It does not 'keep the faith'. Rulership, both in theory and in practice, is in tension, sometimes acute and sometimes latent, between the demands of Islamic law and custom and those of domination and power. The classical orthodox position may have been that the community of believers (the *umma*) should obey even the unjust ruler, but this reflected rather than resolved the contradictions in the relationship between the community and its masters. Law, which should be the very foundation of order, opposes in its nature if not its practice the whole principle of arbitrary power. Yet that power of the Prince combines both violation and preservation.

THE RULE OF THE BEYS

I want now to examine the outworkings of some of these very general themes in Lebanese society. Contemporary events give an all too great aptness to such an inquiry but my focus will be essentially on the period preceding the Civil War and on internal rather than external factors.

The beys (or lords) of the Akkar region of North Lebanon were outsiders to the area and were established there by the Ottoman state essentially as a military presence with an additional tax-gathering function. They were to control a key strategic zone between the Alawite mountain to the north and the Lebanese mountain to the south, both inhabited by unruly and troublesome tribal groupings. The lords themselves and the majority of the population were and are Sunni Muslim.

The plain of Akkar itself was dotted with small, scattered settlements, probably surrounded by collective lands, and it was here and in the foothills of the northern Lebanese mountain overlooking the coast and controlling routes to the heights that in the eighteenth century the lords eventually established their own fortresses.

Fiscality and force appear to have been quickly linked to direct control of agricultural production and the equally direct exploitation of labour power. As the effective sole representatives of the state in a marches area far from the great centres of Aleppo or Damascus the beys were of peripheral concern to the imperial centre or the pashas and governors of Acre or Sidon or Beirut as long as they performed their limited functions.

This freedom of local manoeuvre was crucial as Ottoman land codes of 1858 came into force, enabling them to control the processes of registration and take over for all practical purposes the legal title to large tracts of land that became their personal estate domains. Land reform assisted the consolidation of a quasi-feudal rule, which was certainly not the hoped-for result, and served to extend local dynastic and personal domination. A dispossessed rural population was brought systematically under their sway. Collective rights disappeared and the lords in many cases came to own whole villages, including in some zones the dwellings, draught animals and implements. Competition was probably as much for labour as for land, if not more, in conditions of low population density, thus relating the coercive nature of their domination yet more closely to production.

In this context law-in-practice was the word and act of the bey. It proceeded from his particular will and his capacity to impose that will upon the subjugated strata. The necessary force was both directly mobilised in the different lineages and descent groups of the 'family', claiming to derive ultimately from the same pair of Kurdish brothers, and by the use of other groups, also originally outsiders and mostly it seems of Circassian origin. These latter, the aghas, second in rank below the bey, were and to some extent still are the other privileged stratum in local conceptions of a three-tiered system of status honour (in the Weberian sense of the term).

The discourse of status honour and the individual is above all expressed in terms of violence, symbolic and/or physical. This in turn is intimately linked with the notion that it is part of the very 'being' of the privileged and constitutes the final legitimacy of their superiority and rule. That 'being' acknowledges only such restraints as honour is held to provide. The acts of the men of honour, what it pleases them to do, are characteristically acts in which they impose themselves upon others.

Political, economic and cultural space thus came to be integrated in representational terms of status honour and absorbed into the practice of domination. That domination was immediate, personal and visible. It operated on production as well as on individual and collective identity. The sanctification of force in status honour enshrined the arbitrary at the centre of the lords' mode of control. Law was contained and exercised in the *geste* and the *parole* of the bey or agha.

The whole point here is that the rules were whatever the lord chose to apply under whatever conditions. His authority was itself like an external force. He was an 'outsider' who derived his power from elsewhere, an 'other' source than that available to the disprivileged (according to the ideology). In this sense the lords went beyond the limits and boundaries framing the lives of others. Indeed, creating images of strength and authority consisted in violating the integrity of others, rupturing the normal, dislocating the universe of the dominated, or being thought to have that capacity and potency.

The impact of the French Mandate period (1919-1943) was effectively, and ironically though by no means untypically, to consolidate this mode of domination in a new political context. Some of the French agronomists wished to destroy the power of these 'hacienda owners' as they called them, to rationalise taxation and develop agricultural production and technology using what it was hoped would become a new small peasant stratum as the class vehicle of rural change.

This fantasy faded away in the harsh light of political realities. The beys were the sole guarantors of local taxation and even if they could be in some way 'removed' the whole social fabric might unravel with them. French rule was uneasy and insecure. The nineteen-twenties saw many minor and not so minor uprisings and nationalist incitements. French administrative, technical and military personnel were very difficult to get. The lords might be an obstacle to development and rationalised agricultural practice but they were socially and militarily crucial. Forces they mobilised could do basic local police work in the Alawite mountain and on the plain. Since the beys were the real local masters the French officer in the small district capital thought it sound policy to give permits or guns only to the aghas. The means of coercion, entering a new technological era, were thus firmly in the lords' hands as instruments of the new, 'modern' legality.

The cadastral survey and registration of private property in land which the French carried out in the area merely gave additional and more complete legal title to the full private ownership of land by the beys, another far from intended consequence. Even residual peasant land rights seem to have almost vanished in many regions.

The net effect of the contradictions in Mandate policy and theory was a rationalisation and expansion of the estate-based domination of the lords. They were being incorporated into what became the state of Greater Lebanon, in which the region of Tripoli and Akkar was joined to Mount Lebanon, the eastern valley of the Bekaa, and what is now the southern region centred on Sidon. They monopolised access to the parliamentary forms introduced by the Mandate authority and to the booty to be furnished by the state apparatuses in terms of growing patronage networks in all areas of the bureaucracy, judiciary and military. These apparatuses never ceased to be subordinate to the direct control of the ruling groups. Power was still personalised, even if its 'class' base was slowly changing, and it was fragmented on regional and confessional lines as well.

Neo-feudalism now crossed with more recent capitalist interest, both French and indigenous. The great lord figures of the nineteen-twenties and after could combine 'feudal' social relations with increasingly capitalist investment in agriculture. They could also invest in urban property and commercial companies, in competition with local and national rivals.

Law and power in the modern state

I cannot here trace out the intricacies and implications of these processes in any detail. Suffice it to say that the French period welded property, capital and domination together in ways whose social and political expression remained 'feudal' in the peripheral zones of the great landowners, and indeed often intensified the coercive and exploitative aspects. Personal power was more central even though, or precisely because, the overall system was changing. The operations of law were firmly within the purview of the beys and remained largely absorbed in the practice of their rule.

The Lebanese state failed, for many reasons, to develop an autonomous existence. This meant that ruling groups, particularly in the marginal agricultural regions away from the rapid commercial and later financial transformations of which Beirut was the focus, could maintain what was usually called 'traditional' rule, while participating to the full, if they were successful, in the lifestyle and politics of the new bourgeoisie of bankers, professional and business men.

'The state', that half-imaginary and elusive Lebanese creature, was a resource to be exploited in local controls. Moreover it continually helped to reproduce its own weaknesses as its apparatuses and resources were manipulated to fund and strengthen those forces which dispersed and fragmented power. Tendencies to centralisation and autonomy of the state were weak. Arbitrariness was given wider scope by this peculiar form of political modernity. Its ideological-cultural underpinnings were buttressed. And the *capitalisme sauvage* that was becoming a marked feature of Lebanese society chimed well with the display, competition and mobilisation of support that the older neo-feudal forms contained.

At the level of regional and national leadership such developments of a modern parcellated and dispersed sovereignty also meant that as a matter of functional necessity leaders or big men had to have their own staffs and apparatuses to defend, administer and expand their zones of influence and control. This was as true of the urban notable with his strong-arm men as it was of the rural estate owner or tribal sheikh. They operated in dissimilar universes and in dissimilar ways, but the basic principle was the same. Those of the professional middle class and higher bourgeoisie who played or sought a political role of their own were compelled to adopt such means.

This is the context for my suggestion that leadership and authority are represented directly in the ability of an individual to go beyond the limits of others, of the ordinary, of custom and tradition, into realms where he alone is his own measure of action (the late Bashir Gemayal was the perfect realisation of the type). Violation goes hand-in-hand with protection. What counts is the capacity for *transgression* as a measure to impose one's order on others.

The man of power in the Akkar has been a figure bestriding the domains of order and disorder, master of both and creator of both. For his arbitrariness disorders and throws out of kilter the worlds of others. The highest representatives of the collective, who are at the same time its most singular figures, concentrate these two domains in their person and agency. On the one hand the least predictable in their actions against opponents, they are on the other hand the most reliable for those tied to them by services and clientship. They are the fountains of protection and largesse.

In his role as champion and challenger of order, the bey of Akkar is at one with the practice of visible, personal power in the highly 'subjectified' Lebanese state. An incoming President may mark his accession to office, not by an amnesty (though that may be granted), but by surrendering so many wanted men 'at his hand' to the state of which he is becoming the embodiment. This is a public mark of his capacities as a leader and patron and of the fact that he can bring them in. He is a potent figure, intimately linked to their violence, which exists in the shadow of his own. 'Justice' and 'order' are framed by such a *geste* which is interpreted by others as the act of a ruler, a man who can deliver men up when he wishes.

Those surrendered come in not as 'criminals' but as 'wanted men' under the protection of the leader. Some of the acts for which they are wanted may well have been acts committed at the leader's behest, or they may be from families linked to him by long standing ties. Their place and the conditions of their sentence, not to mention its length, will be looked after with solicitude. Monthly allowances of cash are made, help to the family if required, the placing of a brother in a position, the keeping of a post open, all the standard modes of maintaining relations with one's clients and subordinates or those whom one is hoping to put in a position of obligation for services rendered. The notion of criminality in this aspect of the public realm, as also in cases of honour-associated violence, virtually disappears. The instrumentalities of power erase its significance.

To give men up to the state of which you are the highest representative is not to put yourself within the law and embody it, though there is an element of such cloaking. It is rather to show how much larger than the law you are. Your social and personal honour derive from sources beyond it, your strength is greater. The surrender of the outlaws marks your own personal potency as transgressor.

People are all in one degree or another therefore caught in the web of violence. They participate or have vital interests in the operations of power in all its modalities, the cultural-symbolic as much as the political-economic. It is those who do not have connections with the various levels of men of influence and leaders who are left to the more mechanical workings of the legal system, victims and losers who have not been able to get access to or to construct the lines of dependency and services that they might activate at the crucial moment.

At the most extreme such a one may be selected for a gruesome demonstration of power. The regimes of both Suleiman Franjieh (1970-76) and Amin Gemayal (1983-) began with the hanging of a 'murderer'. Both executions were carried out under semi-public conditions. Both were intended as witness of the state's stern justice. Both criminals came from families with no patronage connections. Most Lebanese seem to have judged these ghastly charades of legal order with the cynicism they deserved. The only exemplary value lay, not in any real transformation of politico-legal practice, but in the revelation of the character of a system in which such essentially futile spectacles depend on caprice and the almost random operations of protection or the lack of it. It need hardly be said that in the context of the endless atrocities of the Civil War the second execution appeared even more bizarrely inequitable than the first, though here it was seen particularly as inequity coming from an essential weakness in the president's position and perhaps a failure to decide just what would constitute a sign of authority in those circumstances. The reactions to both cases showed also how difficult it is to make a gesture of power that is taken to be specifically law-full and in obedience to some transcending legitimacy. The botched rhetorical appeal of the executions if anything highlighted the failure of the state and its personification, and in that way at least pointed to a reality of Lebanese politics.

Law is thus demonstrably a weapon in the hands of the law-less, the ruling but unruled. There is little space in which an impersonal, neutral and bureaucratic legal system, or even a semi-convincing simulacrum of one, might come into existence. Law-in-practice is not masked or transformed by majestic ritual, discourses, and apparatuses, or seen as being above individuals and collectivities. It is manifestly a means, one of many means, of arbitrariness.

LAW IN THE PRACTICE OF POWER, PROPERTY AND HONOUR

I have tried to show that law in its practical sense has been a very visible weapon in the armory of power in north Lebanon (and in the society as a whole). The lords embodied rule and judgement in local society. Ottoman and French regulations were directly implicated both in their military and coercive role and in fiscal and property relations with the other social strata. A distinction between *de jure* and *de facto* has been very difficult to sustain either in life or in analysis. The act of the ruler constituted its own justification and the arbitrary was legitimised at many levels.

Since specifically religious law seems to have been even more subordinated in its actual function and social representation, and was not really a source of alternative authority to which appeal might be made, there was no transcendental quality to the operations of law. Ottoman and French codes and reforms could serve the lords in the conditions of expansion of their form of domination, and in that sense were part of the totalising and closures of power. To the fellah law-in-practice was strictly a resource of and for the powerful, used in personal and intermittent ways, and as inseparable from the beys' status honour as from their rights in land. To put it another way, we could say that the legal order — not even truly constituted as an order — was a piece in the game rather than the framework of rules. In our case, though it might be taken as a limiting one, the powers of command were claimed, not so much by virtue of law as in terms of the 'nature' of the ruling groups; their powers were represented as being self-legitimating.

Aesthetics, routine and trickery

I can best illustrate the relationship between what Weber called the 'beauty and excellence' of the privileged, law and property, by reference to an emblematic moment in the life of one of the great lords (d.1958) and his greatest agha (d.1939).

A rival bey was engaged in a dispute over land with the lord (the period was sometime in the mid-1930s but I could never pin it down to a precise date, which is not locally relevant). The agha, a man already renowned for his awesome bravery and honour, set out to retrieve the property titles to the disputed land over which the opponent had somehow gained possession. He went straight to the reception room of the rival, who lived in another village, and in front of his bodyguards, attendants and clients seized the documents. Reaching the door, he turned to the stupefied and intimidated witnesses and said: 'if there is a real man amongst you I shall be seated beneath the great tree smoking my *nargileh* (water pipe).' He walked out, with his back to them and rode to the spot beneath the tree where he sat in the shade and smoked his pipe 'at his ease'.

No one came. The lord regained, or gained, the property and offered the agha a grove of olives 'out of respect'.

Even in this simplified form the story, in its direct and almost legendary way, highlights local cultural representations of the nature of power and authority. It is at once celebratory, exemplary, and a demonstration of the 'innate' qualities of the true chevalier. The apparent point about the scene is that the agha is a man of so great a reputation that force is presented not as an act or agency but more as a kind of silent emanation; it is a potentiality that is only briefly and partially realised, so far does his weighty singularity overbalance the mere physical means available to the many amongst whom he so confidently strides. The narrative recreates the central cultural icon of a figure whose capacity for violence-in-honour is of such a dimension that his mere presence nullifies the force of others.

There is much that could be said in commentary on this concentrated and highly dramatic story. Here I want only to use it to point to the way in which the heroic cultural form draws together and aestheticises the relations between lordship, honour, force, property and law.

We should note that at this period the lords did in fact need the legal titles to the land over which they competed. Even if it is the *way* in which those deeds are seized that is given primacy in the story and is at the centre of its aesthetic, it is nonetheless the documents around which the whole episode revolves. The lord requires them. To obtain them he does not have recourse to lawyers and the courts but to the agha and his sense of honour. The tension between two apparently different logics, of 'traditional' force and 'modern' law is resolved and contained by the style and act of the man of honour.

It might have been tempting to call this a transitional moment, in which law and bureaucracy are recognised as impinging vitally on the aristocracy but are still subordinated to the glorified traditional mode of claim-making by the rulers, at least in this particular discursive representation given many years later. Tempting, but not really convincing. Transitional to what? The law has never triumphed and shows no signs of doing so. Rather we have the often inchoate and uneven development of what passes for the Lebanese state which is in no position to impose the law. In the case of north Lebanon at least seizure of property 'by main force' in disputes continues as one weapon in the hands of those of the dominant figures who are able enough and skilful enough to use it. Even they may find that the conditions under which force may be exercised are themselves unstable, and have to be rediscovered in practice on each occasion. But they do have the benefits of long experience to help in their calculations, and miscalculations.

Our story hymns the hero. It makes the more prosaic relations that lie behind it quasi-invisible. Less glamorously but far more typically I was told of (and in 1972 witnessed) incidents in which fellahin were sent by one bey to plough land also claimed by another, only to be driven off by hastily summoned armed men. This much duller but more normal kind of event, whose interest the contrasting scene of heroic seizure obscures by its brightness and allure, tells us quite as much by its very routine and uncelebrated character.

Here the far more conventional instruments in property claims are the quasi-servile labourers. It is they who are caught in the crossfire (literally, for this is Lebanon), between those mobilised as armed groups by the competing parties on clientelistic, kinship or cash terms, or a mixture of all three. This is a banal confrontation that is totally familiar because so often repeated. It is not at all the stuff of the rich cultural imagery of status honour for which it has almost no representational significance. It is not 'told'. As a way of creating and settling land disputes, however, it continues parallel to the use of legal machinery where one party judges that the latter may also be worth using.

It is nonetheless true that these legal documents and processes may act as constraints in relations of dispute among the ruling strata. Main force in one shape or another is routine, but it is not necessarily the final or chief arbiter, and in any case involves a whole series of tactical manoeuverings. Land-holding in Akkar is not just a matter of superior firepower, important though that is in economic organisation. Violence may well figure in delimited local cases between beys over property. But there are many other considerations that govern disputes over land and labour, produce and profit.

Manipulation, ruse and trickery are as much a part of the arsenal as overt coercion. They are even more important for those who do not dispose of all the clout and resources necessary to have a violence group at their disposal.

Certainly those whose lives are almost entirely linked with the sophisticated world of finance capital and modern business make a serious error if they assume that making a deal is a question only of economic calculation backed by legal guarantees.

Let us take what I shall call the case of the naive speculator as an example. Unlike our heroic tale it demonstrates what may happen when an outsider, unversed in local social logic, relies on the law for the success on his venture.

One of the Akkari beys of my acquaintance, who now lived in Tripoli just a few kilometres from his village of origin, came from a rapidly declining branch of the 'house'. They had gradually lost their never very extensive holdings and less extensive status, and he now lived by brokering shady deals of one sort or another, and making himself a useful tool of others more shrewd. Main chance was perforce his motto. One son had finally made it into the police and the fact that this was regarded by his father as a little masterpiece of fixing showed the extent and the limits of his ambition. Loss of class position and decline in status in his case went together.

This somewhat down-at-heel character managed to make an agreement with a well-to-do business man from another region, representative exactly of that class which by the early nineteen seventies had begun to invest in the Akkar in citrus groves and other usually capital-intensive projects. The man on the way down, the *déclassé* bey, meets the man on the way up, the new money entrepreneur.

The businessman outsider wished to speculate on the next season's olive harvest by buying the rights to the produce of a large grove several months ahead of time for a low sum from any owner who might be found who desperately needed cash and could neither afford to wait nor run the risk of a poor harvest. Such persons were not difficult to find, if you had someone with enough local knowledge and the right level of entrée to make the connection. This sort of deal happened all the time. It often involved hard hit members of the ruling group who were now being financially and politically squeezed.

The investor expected a hefty profit on the basis of figures furnished by his local contact the bey, who scouted around for the appropriate seller who would jump at the chance of the money. Estimations of the size of the crop, always a rich area of expertise giving scope for a wide range of possibilities and therefore ideal territory for the canny and far-sighted, might vary of course. But our bey assured his client that he was getting a real bargain. For he was paying the owner on the basis of a low assessment which was bound to be exceeded by three or four times when the olive harvest came in, and the price per kilo now was much lower than it would be later.

For a percentage the bey arranged the initial estimate and promised to see to all the organising of the labour and the different tasks, including the harvesting itself and the delivery to the businessman's own olive press. He also provided the all-important guards who would camp out in the grove when the time for picking grew near to stop the thieving endemic in the area.

All of these valuable services, without which it would be impossible to set up the deal at all, were detailed in a properly drawn up and certified legal agreement, duly signed and ratified. What more could one want? The speculator had only to sit back and wait to rake in the money from what was predicted to be a bountiful harvest (in the estimate done for him).

Everything was in the hands of the bey. Too much, perhaps. How could the estimates, not to mention the harvest itself, be checked? If the estimates should be wildly inaccurate what then? Even more to the point, how would the buyer know just how many olives had been harvested and that all the sacks had been delivered to him rather than finding their way to some illicit resting place? The assessment might be said to have been unfortunately far too optimistic and this would be difficult to verify. As an outsider he could not check with other locals. The links had to pass through our bey. The business man had nothing to rely on save our man's assurances and those of the attendant bodyguard-cum-watchman, who was the youngest brother of a prominent figure in the village and thus beyond reproach — was he not? No one would dare to try to steal where he was, since 'He was who he was'. That guaranteed that no villager would risk thieving since it would challenge the honour of the powerful family. But who would watch the watchman?

The speculator evidently became uneasy about his bargain, and with reason since both bey and watchman were in fact rogues of calibre. What could he do? He could not oversee the harvest with outsiders nor organise it himself. Suspicion appeared to lead to greater anxiety which more repeated visits to the grove and its attendant relentless but evasive tea-serving courtesy could not assuage. The sheer scope of possible trickery must have become obvious to him (through a rival bey?), as it always had been to everyone who knew locally about the deal.

Disputes between the two partners broke out; threats of legal action were made; written agreements were invoked. To no effect. For in any case the signed papers allowed for all sorts of practical uncertainties in such a situation of harvesting with its wide possible fluctuations. Soothing promises of deliveries would be made, but nothing ever arrived and another row would break out.

Eventually, in fact, the businessman got nothing whatsoever. The bey, with bodyguard in smiling attendance, dared the victim to do something about it. The latter had been comprehensively outmanoeuvered and found that the forms of law and personal wealth were of no help in such a predicament. Without a local network he was stymied. By treating the deal as he treated most of his business operations he made a cardinal error. That logic only seemed to apply, as the logic of the legal documents only seemed to run. The bey cheated the bourgeois, using his local connections, low cunning and the threat of the bodyguard, with all that that implied. Legal agreement was a bait to the trap, and a facade rather than an underpinning to the relationships involved. It was used partly because it was known to be what the outsider's practices required, but for its formal and not substantive meaning and function.

This case demonstrates that the changes in patterns of class ascendancy within the Lebanon as a whole, represented here by the impoverished bey and the investor, may translate themselves in many ways on the ground. The space exists for theft and trickery. Guards are drawn from the same strata as the thieves. There are 'gaps' everywhere in the possible patterns of possible relations and it takes a very high degree of skill to create them and negotiate your own space for manipulation while avoiding the traps and blocks set by others. The speculator's position as outsider outweighed any advantages he may have had.

Yet all this manoeuvering should not obscure the reality of the financial and political displacement imaged in these three figures of bey, agha guard, and businessman. In this particular instance the latter loses out. Yet the bey's shady dealing and play on ruse and local contacts is precisely the trickery of the displaced and *déclassé* reduced to living on his wits and finding victims among those whose ventures are sufficiently recent in origin and removed in place for them not yet to have developed the practical awareness necessary for making bargains in this kind of setting. The guard's complicity is that of a generation of aghas whose status honour no longer can be lived out in the grand gesture and violence of the hero figure but exists in a mundane world of employment and scouting around for openings here and there, usually of a dubious kind that would not once have been entertained.

Such little local triumphs for the declining members of the lord and agha strata do nothing to arrest the processes which the increasing presence of business interests 'from outside' signal. Wiser, more astute and more powerful figures may purchase their irrigated land outright, turn it into citrus or winter vegetables and bring in outside guards on a straight wage basis if needed. For they operate at a higher level of influence and attempting to trick them would be too dangerous a business. Their lines to other power holders, the appropriate officers in the local military and police, and alliances with still important beys are their real guarantee. They need make no manifestation of personal presence at all. Their dominance in the region is more purely at the economic level, and does not show itself save in the lines of trees planted as windbreaks round the orange trees now growing on that fertile land on the plain where only a few years ago such a lord had one of his most valuable holdings. Not infrequently such acquisition comes about as the sons of a recently deceased lord, already indebted and with no immediate resources since they too have sold the olives for the next one or even up to five seasons in advance, are the willing vendors of the once precious patrimony. Short term need contributes to long term elimination from the local scene and the burdens of unsustainable status.

In such instances, legal ratification does effectively hedge round the transaction because the relations within which it operates are of a different order from those of even twenty years before. They are still politically to be accomplished and cannot be assumed, it is true, but the commercial and financial aspects are somewhat more separated out from the local webs of conflict with all their ramifications.

'Somewhat' is the key word, a 'somewhat' that ten years of war have rendered ludicrously overstated. But in Lebanon this sense of grey zones, competing possibilities and the constant vigilance needed to reproduce one's social relations, even those one might apparently most be able to take for granted, is deeply embedded in expectations, practice and culture.

POSTSCRIPT

The oil-fed money boom of the nineteen-sixties and early nineteen-seventies went together with the development of the overwhelming dominance of the services sector in the economy. Already enormous, the gap between the centre of Beirut and the impoverished peripheral zones such as the Akkar expanded yet further. The state remained largely fictional.

Such an evolution by no means worked to the disadvantage of individuals, groups and institutions who in the free-for-all world of capitalism as realised in the Lebanon and through Lebanese interests on a global scale might benefit from the absence of constraints, financial, bureaucratic or political.

The apparent ossification and isolation of the social structures of the peripheries seemed to permit an easy coexistence between 'the modern and the traditional' rather than to threaten it.

Such glib assumptions were exploded in the Civil War, still continuing as I write, the Syrian occupation of the Akkar and the Bekaa, the Israeli invasion and occupation of the south, and the bizarre American intervention of 1983-84. It is banal to say, and yet it should be said, that during the whole period since 1975-76 the organisation of and disorganisation by violence has taken on a new and more complex aspect and scope. That such processes have occurred is in part because of the factors that I have so diagrammatically portrayed here. Arbitrariness in its many forms and in the many dimensions of the social world has not only coloured the everyday lives of the Lebanese at the level of the event, but has been revealed at the heart of whatever Lebanese society can be said to be. The *confusion apparente* of the initial quotation from Guillemin, is also a *confusion réelle*, structuring and destructuring relations from within.

Legitimacy and authority have been increasingly personalised, confessionalised and localised. Violence is sanctified anew. The state and the law have both contributed to their own atomisation in various ways. That so many of the greater and lesser powers of the world are deeply implicated in this disaster cannot disguise the importance of certain root factors within 'the Lebanon' itself.

At the level of the state it should be noted that sovereignty and the political order were always not only parcellated, as in feudal Europe for example, but also fragmented. No lones of fealty or feudal hierarchies existed to preserve the foundations of society (regardless of disputes and struggles for power). The end of the Ottoman Empire and the French Mandate combined to give a broader range for action by the different elements of what can be called the ruling alliances. Such alliances, shifting over time, were basically untrammelled by secular or religious legalities. Both bourgeois and landowner could enjoy the fruits of political and economic *laissez aller* in their own spheres. Fractions of the bourgeoisie may have begun to wish to consolidate their position in the first half of the nineteen-sixties by programmes of 'modernisation', mostly with limited impact on the periphery. Yet it is significant that the main political instrument of that reformist period should have been the *deuxième bureau*, with its own very special notions of administration and legality. It too was in practice one person's instrument; or it was at least very much the instrument of one loose set of groupings against others. Among the first acts of President Suleiman Franjieh (1970-76) was the dissolution of this apparatus and the attempt to set up his and his son's own intelligence service.

Bibliography

Baer, G. (1969) *Studies in the Social History of Modern Egypt*, Chicago: The University of Chicago Press.

Chevallier, D. (1971) *La société du Mont Liban à l'époque de la révolution industrielle en Europe*, Paris: Librairie Orientaliste Paul Geuthner.

Gibb, H.A.R. and Bowen, H. (1950) *Islamic Society and the West*, London: Oxford University Press.

Ismail, A. (1976) *Le Liban: Documents diplomatiques et consulaires*, Beyrouth: Éditions des Oeuvres Politiques et Historiques.

Weber, M. (1968) *Economy and Society*, Berkeley/Los Angeles/London: University of California Press.

The Legal Discourse: Speech and Silences

F

"Reading the Riot Act": The discourse of law-enforcement in 18th century England

W. NIPPEL

Fakultät für Geschichtswissenschaft, Universität Bielefeld, W. Germany

During the past two decades historians have devoted much attention both to the crowd as a socio-cultural phenomenon and a political force, and to the discontinuities between the increasingly Draconian legal discourse of the 18th century and the discretionary practice which accompanied it. This article combines both concerns: study of the working of the Riot Act in 18th century England, by focussing on the use of penal law against crowds rather than single offenders, brings into particularly sharp relief the contradictions of a legal system which depended heavily on the support of the general public both for law-enforcement and for the efficacious operation of the practice of 'exemplary' public execution of selected offenders. Government was particularly anxious in the case of riots that the law should be seen to be effectively enforced, yet reluctant to abandon the 'rule of law' for indiscriminate use of troops against rioters. The ambiguities of the situation are well reflected both in the ostensible respect for law which characterised debates on interpretation of the Riot Act, at all levels from the Privy Council to the popular press, and in the wide discretion tacitly used in applying the law by judges and juries.

INTRODUCTION

"READING THE RIOT ACT" is an almost proverbial phrase in contemporary English denoting the giving of a final warning. However, hardly anyone knows its origin. It goes back to the Riot Act of 1715, which had practical importance down to the 20th century and was only abolished in 1967.[1]

Scholarly literature on riots in 18th century England (and of course in other periods and elsewhere) has grown to an immense size during the last two decades (Stevenson 1979a: 1-5). Most of this work is concentrated on the social composition of rioting crowds, their aims, motives and legitimising rituals, and I shall deliberately not deal with these aspects in the present article. The problems of law-enforcement, however, have only recently been discussed from the point of view of social history.[2]

History and Anthropology, 1985
Vol. 1, pp. 401-426
0275-7206/85/0102-0401 $18.50/0

The Riot Act is particularly suitable for a case study of the implementation of penal law during the 18th century (I shall confine myself largely to this period). Its application reflects some peculiar aspects of the general system of law-enforcement. Its features (Baker 1977) include the crucial role of lay magistrates, who had to rely on assistance by private citizens if they wanted to employ coercive measures; the principle of private prosecution; trial by jury; the use of the death penalty for exemplary punishment as a method of deterring potential offenders.

The collective nature of the offence (which in itself was highly liable to conflicts over interpretation) made the application of penal law to rioters even more complicated than law-enforcement was in any case. The possibility of prosecuting depended on previous repressive measures, viz. the apprehending of rioters in the act. Rioting could be considered a legitimate protest against social grievances or an expression of the political will of the common people. In addition, the involvement of considerable parts of a community made the employment of penal law a delicate affair. Riots led to direct confrontation between local rulers and ruled, and central government could become involved as well. These various factors were connected with each other and with the respective attitudes of both authorities and common people towards the law and its appropriate application in a given situation. The niceties of the law and the ambiguous reactions aroused by its implementation influenced the practical conduct of all sides. Misconceptions of the law on the part of authorities as well as of crowds could lead to serious and sometimes literally fatal consequences; crowds often relied on the restrictions which the law allegedly imposed upon magistrates; authorities showed scrupulous observance of these restrictions, which did not exclude swift exploitation of legal loopholes once they were discovered.

The following discussion does not pretend to give a full-scale account of all the problems in question. It should, however, provide an outline of the more important questions and formulate some preliminary results.

THE RIOT ACT

The 1715 Riot Act is an early example of the general tendency towards increasing the severity of the penal code typical of the criminal legislation of the 18th century (Radzinowicz 1948-68.1). At Common Law (Lambard 1581; Pulton 1609; Dalton 1618; W. Hawkins 1716; Burn 1755) a riot was defined as a joint action of a private nature committed by three or more persons which amounted to an actual breach of the King's Peace or at least to the manifest terror of the people. (Each element of this definition is subject to casuistic qualifications which I cannot deal with here). The suppression of riots was the duty of the Justices of the Peace. Indeed, it was held that this was the primary function which had given birth to their office in the 14th century.These magistrates were authorised to command the assistance of any private citizen or to summon the *posse comitatus* (the force consisting of all able-bodied loyal subjects of the Crown in a county). It was also held that under extraordinary circumstances every private citizen was entitled to suppress a riot even if he was not acting under the direction of a magistrate (Popham 1656: 121-2). Legal authorities had warned, however, that such a citizen took the risk of being prosecuted himself if the assumption that he was suppressing a riot could be challenged (W. Hawkins 1716: 159). Nevertheless, the principle was endorsed when it seemed to be appropriate, as for example in suppressing Jacobites (Blackstone 1781.1:47-8). Participation in a riot was considered a misdemeanour at Common Law punishable by imprisonment, whipping or fines.

By the statute of 1715[3] rioting under certain circumstances was made a felony without benefit of clergy (Baker 1979: 422ff.) punishable with death. The act laid down that twelve or more persons were guilty of felony if they had not dispersed within one hour after a proclamation was made by a Justice of the Peace (or an equivalent magistrate) addressing the rioters "with loud voice". The text of the proclamation was prescribed by the statute itself; it read:

> Our sovereign Lord the King chargeth and commandeth all persons, being assembled, immediately to disperse themselves, and peaceably to depart to their habitations, or to their lawful business, upon the pains contained in the act made in the first year of King George, for preventing tumults and riotous assemblies. —God save the King.[4]

Any obstruction against the making of the proclamation was adjudged as a felony, too. One hour after "the reading of the Riot Act" (as the making of the proclamation was generally known thereafter), anyone who assisted a magistrate in apprehending rioters was guaranteed indemnity in case a rioter happened to be hurt or killed. Furthermore, it was adjudged as a felony if rioters "demolish or pull down, or begin to demolish or pull down any church or chapel, or any building for religious worship ... [registered according to the Toleration Act] ... or any dwelling-house, barn, stable, or other out-house."[5] Finally, it was enacted that the inhabitants of a hundred (a traditional division of a county) were held financially responsible for damages caused by the riotous demolition of buildings mentioned in the statute.

The passing of the Riot Act was caused by a series of High Church and Jacobite disturbances culminating at the time of the accession of George I.[6] The Riot Act was intended to fulfil a variety of functions. It was supposed to underline the responsibility of the magistrates to suppress riots. In many cases local authorities were suspected of encouraging or at least tolerating the anti-Hanoverian riots.[7] (Charges of this kind remain a familiar feature of all riots of the "Church-and-King" type [Hobsbawm 1959: ch.7; Rudé 1964: ch.9] during the 18th century). Furthermore, it was intended to serve as an instrument of general deterrence. This was accentuated by a provision of the statute itself, viz. that it was to be read publicly at all Quarter Sessions.[8] The aim of the reading of the proclamation was, of course, to give a final warning to rioters. And finally, the provisions on the death penalty gave an opportunity to impose draconic exemplary punishment. It goes almost without saying that the provisions of this statute seem appropriate — if at all — predominantly for small communities. Here the public appearance of a magistrate and the reading of the proclamation, or even the mere announcement that he was going to read it, could be supposed to have an effect. There were, indeed, many cases of smaller disturbances which could be stopped solely by the appearance of a magistrate and his warning that serious consequences might ensue. The effect was much more doubtful under the conditions of the crowded areas of the metropolis and later of the new industrial towns where it was difficult to evoke deference by such means (cf. Stevenson 1979b:45). (It was a problem to find "acting" magistrates in these areas at all: Munger 1979: 79ff.; Munger 1981: 128ff.) Numerous cases are known in which the reading of the proclamation had no effect at all, and often the magistrates themselves were attacked. A Middlesex Justice of the Peace in 1771 for this reason questioned the practicability of the procedure, which he seemed to consider almost counter-productive. Reporting to a parliamentary committee which was investigating a riot which had taken place near Parliament, he explained (*PH.* 17:228):

> Being asked, whether their attempting to read the Riot Act, was not the occasion of the mob throwing stones? — he said, they threw stones before it was attempted to read — that he believes it was after the second volley of stones that the Act was attempted to be read, whereupon the mob threw more stones, and the magistrates went in — that he thinks the threatening to read the Riot Act, an unlikely method to quiet the people; and wishes it were otherwise.

Controversy repeatedly arose in contemporary discussions, and especially in court proceedings concerning large-scale riots, about when and where the Riot Act had been read, if it was read at all. Evidence was notoriously contradictory. Sometimes even the "feeble voice" (Quinault 1974:196) of a magistrate was blamed for the confusion. In other cases magistrates announced in advance that they had the intention to make use of this remedy (Stevenson 1979b:45). Magistrates in Manchester in 1781 tried to establish certainty by an unusual method (Wadsworth and Mann 1931:373):

> They intimated that when the proclamation under the Riot Act was read a blue flag would be displayed, and that if the mob did not disperse within an hour, or committed any violence within that time, the display of a red flag would be the signal that force would be immediately used.

These apparently trivial questions indicate a serious problem. What were the consequences if the proclamation was read several times (as was the general practice of magistrates who tried to avoid the use of force) and at different places? Was the hour to be computed from the first reading (as was ruled later by a court, Carrington and Payne 1825-41.5:516ff.) and what were the implications of changes in the composition of the crowd between the reading of the proclamation and the actual use of force by magistrates? These questions were of special importance because people often assumed that the magistrates were not allowed to use force — and especially troops — until one hour after the reading of the proclamation had passed, and that one could rely on them to observe this alleged rule. The general obsession with the procedure of the proclamation tended to obscure — for the authorities as well as for the common people — the fact that the reading of the proclamation (and the expiry of the celebrated hour) was not a necessary precondition either for constituting a riot as understood at Common Law (W. Hawkins 1716:159) nor for making the demolition of buildings a felony as defined by the Riot Act.

I shall come back to discuss these problems at greater length since they became especially virulent in connection with employing soldiers. Before that, I should explain why the magistrates in many cases saw no alternative to calling out troops.

CIVIL FORCES

The regular forces of order (if that is the appropriate name), consisting of constables and night watchmen, were normally not suited to deal with riots of considerable scale. That was not only due to their small numbers, their organisation on a parish basis or the personal qualifications of their members — which gave rise to the well-known caricature of the illiterate, half-blind and lame and always drunken "policeman" of the 18th century. (It was common practice that more respectable persons — who were obliged in turn to take over these functions — engaged substitutes.)[9] They were normally not supposed to undertake the special duty of riot control. "The ordinary Police (had not) ceased to continue its function", comments an eye-witness on a scene during the peak of the Gordon Riots, when a watchman made his round and called the hour "as if in a time of profound tranquillity" (Wraxall 1904:199).

The proper provision at Common Law was that the magistrate had to rely on the help of private persons or alternatively to summon the *posse comitatus*. Furthermore, the Riot Act had unreservedly applied a centuries-old principle of Common Law, i.e. the collective responsibilities of hundreds,[10] to damages caused by rioters. Thereby a special incentive was given for the activity of citizens whose sympathies in many cases were likely to lie with rioters.[11]

Referring to the fact that this principle was deeply rooted in Common Law (going back allegedly to Anglo-Saxon times) Lord Chief Justice Mansfield declared in 1776, on the occasion of a decision on compensation for riot damages, that the provision of the Riot Act under discussion was a "way of inducement to the inhabitants to be active in the suppressing of such riots, which it is their duty to do; and which being thus made their interest too, they are more likely to execute" (Cowper 1784:488).

The practicability, efficiency and the pacifying effect of this method was, however, problematic. If a riot articulated the grievances of a community, it was unlikely that the magistrates would find support. Or it led to a confrontation between two sides in a social conflict. In other cases rioters even turned into forces of order.[12] And it was often difficult to draw a distinction between supporters of law and order and "loyal mobs" persecuting Catholics, Methodists, Dissenters or Jacobins.[13]

THE USE OF TROOPS

Because of the inadequacy and problematic nature of the civil forces available to them, in cases of major disturbances magistrates had to resort to calling out troops, units either of the militia or of the regular army. The militia was sometimes considered unreliable, especially when units were expected to act in the neighbourhood of their home base. There are, however, several cases in which militia units were employed to suppress riots, and the overall record does not necessarily suggest that the doubts about their reliability were justified.[14] The crucial role in suppressing large-scale riots was played by the army (Hayter 1978; Palmer 1978). There is of course an irony in this since opposition against a standing army and emphasis on the danger to liberty which it would represent at home was part of the standard repertory of 18th century English political ideology. Nevertheless, the army was frequently used as an agency of riot control. The decision to call out troops was, however, supposed to lie with the local magistrates. The magistrates often hesitated to take this step. During waves of riots the government sometimes put pressure on them to employ troops in good time (*CHOP* 1770-72:488). On the other hand, due to the small number of troops available, the government was always anxious to ensure that troops were not called for merely because a magistrate had lost his nerve (Hewitt 1779:9-10).

Apart from practical obstacles and the difficulties of communication between central and local authorities, there were serious problems arising from uncertainties about the legal situation.

From the very beginning, the view of the government had been that it was legal to use troops against rioters provided that it was the civil magistrates who called for the support of the armed forces. The basis of this opinion was that in such a case the soldiers were just following the call for assistance by a magistrate like any other citizen who was obliged to do so. As the Attorney General ruled in 1721: "by the Law any person may justify the assistance of the Civil Magistrate or Officer in keeping the Peace or executing Legal Process when required by such Officer or Magistrate, without distinction whether such a person is a Civil or Military man" (Clode 1869.2:621). The understanding was that in such a case they were not entitled "to repell Force with Force, unless it shall be found absolutely necessary" (Clode 1869.2:624).

What that meant in any given situation was far from clear. Government was always reluctant to commit itself to more unequivocal statements than the ruling, repeated again and again, that officers were advised to follow the instructions of the civil magistrates and to act generally with extreme discretion. The crucial question whether troops were allowed to fire on crowds was not answered.[15] The conviction of Captain Porteous in Edinburgh in 1736 was sometimes understood both by authorities and by commoners to have established that troops were not entitled to shoot (Hayter 1978:31ff.; Ellis 1980:338ff.). (Porteous was sentenced to death, and lynched by a mob afterwards, because he had ordered the City Guard to open fire on a crowd: Dickinson and Logue 1972).

Furthermore, both magistrates and soldiers had to consider that they rendered themselves liable to criminal prosecution by using force; on the other hand, magistrates could be charged with neglect of their duties if they could be accused of not having used sufficient means to suppress riots.

THE ST. GEORGE'S FIELDS "MASSACRE"

These ambiguities added to the general insecurity about the meaning of crucial provisions of the Riot Act. They led to serious consequences in the case of the so-called "St. George's Fields Massacre" of May 10, 1768 ([Anon.] 1769; Rudé 1962: ch.3; P.D.G. Thomas 1978). As on previous days, a large crowd had assembled outside the King's Bench Prison in Lambeth where the great popular hero John Wilkes[16] was serving his sentence, being thereby debarred from taking over the Middlesex seat in Parliament which he had won after his return from France. On the 10th of May Parliament met. As it was feared that Wilkes would be released by the crowd, a detachment of soldiers was sent there to defend the prison. Two violent clashes took place. Soldiers pursued and killed a young man called William Allen who had allegedly attacked them by wildly throwing stones (as the crowd in general were doing). As it happened, they probably killed the wrong man, and the killing appeared to have been deliberate. Another serious clash occurred in front of the prison. Soldiers fired on the crowd causing the death of some persons including, it was clear, passers-by returning home from work.[17]

The aftermath of these events was that one officer and two soldiers were charged with the wilful murder of William Allen and that Justice Gillam, who was responsible for the employment of the troops, had to face the same charge[18] with respect to a person who was killed by the fire of the soldiers.[19] Although these trials ended with acquittals, the mere fact that they had taken place was of great importance. Furthermore, the "massacre" had considerable repercussions in public opinion and led to heavy attacks on the government.

The proceedings at the trial of Gillam (*AR* 1768:227-33; *GM* 1768:323-5) show that there had been, as was to be expected, some confusion about the question when the Riot Act had been read and how its reading was related to the actual opening of fire by the soldiers.[20] It is indicated, however, that the Justice as well as the crowd — as on other occasions elsewhere (*AR* 1765:117; 1776:161ff.) — believed that only the reading of the proclamation would justify action against the mob (*AR* 1768:228):

(Constable Richard Nicholl) says, the people behaved very riotous, and threw stones at the soldiers, so that they could not keep their posts for them; Mr. Gillam, who was there, begged of the people to disperse, and go about their business; he told them that the riot-act had been read; some people there said, D-n you, we do not believe the riot-act has been read; Mr. Gillam said, If I thought that would appease you, I would read it again; upon which, he took a pocket-book out of his pocket, called out silence, and read it again, and he the deponent heard him read it. The people came round about, were pretty silent at that time, and afterwards he begged of them again to disperse.

Nevertheless, the judges in this case were apparently reluctant to bring the Riot Act into play when they delivered their opinions on the points of law involved (Clode 1869.2:630-5; *GM* 1768:324ff.). They preferred to base their unanimous view that Gillam's conduct was justified on the older principles of Common Law (*GM* 1768:324):

Hon. Mr. Justice Gould ... declared, that he thought Mr. Gillam perfectly justifiable ... His lordship quoted several established authorities, which proved beyond a doubt, that a magistrate, when there is any occasion to support the laws, has a right to demand assistance from all his majesty's subjects who are capable of bearing arms; that he is empowered to arm them with such weapons as are most likely to quell any riot, and that consequently, if he has a right to give them arms, he has a right to direct the use of these arms, as he judges requisite for the preservation of the peace. His lordship moreover observed that a magistrate, upon proper application to him, was obliged to take every possible method to suppress riots ... and therefore, as the magistrate was obliged to stand forth in time of necessity for the support of the laws, the laws had expressly declared, that he should be indemnified for any personal injuries, which in the execution of his duty should happen to the disturbers of the public tranquillity.

The same judge also points out that in such a case there is no legal distinction between soldiers and other loyal subjects (Clode 1869.2:631).

The interpretation of the law as given in the case of Gillam stirred public opposition. In a pamphlet published in the same year it was argued that the law provided indemnity to enable rioters to be seized and brought to trial, but not for "military execution" on the spot ([Anon.] 1768:28).

The main direction of criticism turned against the role of the government.[21] In December Wilkes was able to publish in a newspaper a letter of the Secretary of State to the Lambeth magistrates written on April 17. In it he had admonished the local authorities (Clode 1869.2:628):

> I need not add that if the public peace is not preserved ... the blame will be imputed to the want of prudent and spirited conduct in the Civil Magistrate. As I have no reason to doubt your caution and discretion in not calling for Troops till they are wanted, so, on the other hand, I hope you will not delay a moment calling for their aid, and making use of them effectually where there is occasion — that occasion always presents itself when the Civil Power is trifled with and insulted. Nor can a Military Force ever be employed to a more constitutional purpose than in support of the authority and dignity of Magistracy.

Wilkes, of course, construed this as a proof that the "massacre" had been premeditated (Cavendish 1841-2.1:106ff.; Free 1769:15ff.; Wilkes 1769.2:229ff.). Already during the trial of Gillam one witness had asserted that he had overheard Gillam say that "he had orders from the ministry to fire upon the people, and there must be some killed, and it was better to kill five and twenty today than have a hundred killed tomorrow" (*OBP* 1768:280-1).

The public was also aware of a letter in which the Secretary-at-War had already on May 11 congratulated the troops on behalf of the King for their conduct, assuring them that "in case any disagreeable circumstance should happen in the execution of their duty, they shall have every defence and protection that the law can authorize and this Office can give" (Clode 1869.2:629; *GM* 1768:244). In fact, Crown lawyers took over the defence of the soldiers later; it was further suspected that the government helped one of the accused soldiers to escape (*AR* 1769:61ff.).

All this supplied ammunition for a fierce attack on the government by Edmund Burke in Parliament in March 1769 amounting to the accusation of an overthrow of the constitution: by introducing a "martial police" into the administration of justice the government had "expressed a desire and design of incorporating the military with the civil constitution of this country" (Cavendish 1841-2.1:308).

Apart from stressing the necessity to quell riots, the spokesmen for the government again adopted the position that "by the law and constitution of this country, there is no such thing as a military force, *quasi* a military force; that every man in this kingdom is bound to give his assistance to the execution of the laws" (Cavendish 1841-2.1:320).

The proposal of Burke that an Act should be passed to regulate the conditions in which troops might be employed was defeated. Parliament was content with the assertion "that as to the relation betwixt the civil and the military it stood on as good grounds now as it well could: the civil magistrate could call out the military to his assistance when he wanted it, but if he used them improperly it was at his own peril" (*PH* 16:603).

THE GORDON RIOTS

The aftermath of the "St. George's Fields Massacre" had laid open the legal and political risks to which the employing of troops exposed authorities. The awareness of this problem had its effect twelve years later in the handling of the Gordon Riots. The riots in the metropolis between the 2nd and 9th of June 1780 were the most serious disturbances of the century. The Protestant Association, led by an eccentric Member of Parliament called Lord George Gordon, staged a mass lobbying of Parliament petitioning for the repeal of the Catholic Relief Act of 1778, which led to attacks on Members of Parliament. The following days saw a wave of riotous incidents. Catholic chapels, houses, shops, and public houses were demolished or set on fire, as were houses of magistrates and prominent politicians; prisons were stormed, prisoners released, Newgate prison was set on fire, the Bank of England was rumoured to be the next target . . . the facts are too well known to be repeated here.[22]

It was obvious that the dramatic increase in rioting was at least partly rendered possible by the lack of action by the magistrates of the metropolitan area (especially those of the City of London). Their attitude was partly due to sympathy with the anti-Catholic sentiment, partly due to timidity. But it was also assumed that the *cause célèbre* of Gillam had had its impact on their conduct: "Such a precedent could not but tend, in similar emergencies, most dangerously to enfeeble the power of the executive government" (Belsham 1795.2:22).

Magistrates called for troops in some cases but were not prepared to appear in person at the scene of the rioting. Accordingly the soldiers did not intervene (Aikin 1816.1:262; Vincent 1780:54) and the mob was relying on their passivity ([Anon.] 1780a:51):

> The military, after the civil power had called them in, were not used by them. The mob knew the military did not dare to fire without the command of the civil power. The military, seeing they were not to be used effectually endeavoured to keep upon good terms with those, who might with impunity, as they did, in many places, pull their noses and spit in their faces. Hence reports at the time, as if the soldiery had, in some measure, joined with the mob.

The troops considered themselves legally bound to act only on the command of a civil magistrate, who had to read the Riot Act (*OBP* 1780:386, 587). And that was also the opinion of the government. In a letter dated June 6 the Secretary-at-War complained to the Secretary-of-State about the conduct of magistrates who were not ready to attend troops for which they had called. "It is the duty of the Troops . . . to act only under the authority and by the direction of the Civil Magistrate". By the refusal of the civil authorities to act, the troops were left in a "defenceless and disgraceful situation" (Clode 1869.2:636-7).

A turning point was reached when the government reversed this position the next day. In a controversial discussion in the Privy Council, presided over by the King, the statement of the Attorney General turned the balance (Wraxall 1904:208-9):

Doubts existed whether persons riotously collected together and committing outrages might legally be fired on by the military power, without staying to read the Riot Act. Mr. Wedderburn ... who was then Attorney General, having been called in to the council table, and ordered by the King to deliver his official opinion on the point, stated in the most precise terms, that any such assemblage might be dispersed by military force without waiting for forms or reading the Riot Act. 'Is that your declaration of the law as Attorney General?', said the King. Wedderburn answering decidedly in the affirmative, 'Then let so it be done', rejoined his Majesty.

Accordingly an order was given to the troops, "to act without waiting for directions from the Civil Magistrates, and to use force for dispersing the illegal and tumultous assemblies of the people" (*AR* 1780:266; Horn and Ransome 1957:279).

The government later published the (conservative) figure of 458 casualties (*AR* 1780:262; de Castro 1926:236) — a number as unprecedented as was the scale of the riots.[23]

Neither the public nor the government as a whole were agreed on the legal basis of this decision. The public interpreted it as a declaration of Martial Law ([Anon.] 1780b:51; Vincent 1780:41; Clode 1869.2:167ff.). The notion[24] was understood as implying executions by military authorities without due course of law. This peculiar idea had indeed been raised in the Privy Council but had then apparently been dropped.[25]

The speech which the King delivered to both Houses of Parliament on June 19 seemed to suggest that he had made use of his royal prerogative in a situation of absolute necessity (*PH* 21:689; cf. Fortescue 1927-8.5:81). Although nobody criticised the decision as such, in the debate which followed the opposition was anxious that it could constitute a dangerous precedent. It is interesting to see that Lord North, the Prime Minister, even considered "to move for a Bill of Indemnity, for having called in the aid of the soldiery, because it might otherwise appear a measure that militated against the spirit of the constitution" (*PH* 21:700).

It was Lord Chief Justice Mansfield who in his speech in the Lords led the way to a conception that was to become the authoritative interpretation of the legal situation (*PH* 21:694-6):

It has been taken for granted ... that his Majesty, in the orders he gave respecting the riots, acted merely upon his prerogative, as being entrusted with the protection and preservation of the state, in cases arising from necessity, and not provided for in the ordinary contemplation and execution of law ... I take the case to be exactly the reverse ... It appears most clearly to me, that not only every man may legally interfere to suppress a riot, much more prevent acts of felony, treason and rebellion, in his private capacity, but he is bound to do it as an act of duty ... The persons who assisted in the suppression of those riots and tumults, in contemplation of law, are to be considered as mere private individuals, acting according to law, and upon any abuse of the legal power with which they were invested, are amenable to the laws of their country ... consequently, the false idea that we are living under a military government, or that the military have any more power, or other power, since the commencement of the riots, is the point which I rose to refute, and on that ground to remove those idle and ill-founded apprehensions, that any part of the laws or the constitution are either suspended or have been dispensed with. I believe this great mistake has chiefly arisen from the general understanding of the [Riot Act]".

The recourse to the citizens' rights and duties at Common Law had precedents, as discussed above. It had, however, never been applied to the action of soldiers in such an unreserved way, virtually implying the repeal of the provision that soldiers could only act under the direction of magistrates. It is worth mentioning that Mansfield himself is reported to have been doubtful about the legality of the decision taken by the King in Council on June 7 (Wraxall 1904:209 ff.). His public statement was considered by contemporary commentators to be a "new doctrine" (Vincent 1780: App. note L) and the dangerous consequence was immediately pointed out, viz. that it removed any legal restriction on the employment of troops by government (Vincent 1780: App. note L; *GM* 1780:368).

This legal position was confirmed in a charge which Lord Loughborough (the former Wedderburn, who had been promptly rewarded for his unequivocal advice) delivered to a Grand Jury sitting at a trial of Gordon Rioters (*AR* 1780:284):

I take this public opportunity of mentioning a fatal mistake into which many persons have fallen. It has been imagined, because the law allows an hour for the dispersion of a mob to whom the riot act has been read ... that during that period of time, the civil power and the magistracy are disarmed, and the king's subjects, whose duty it is at all times to suppress riots, are to remain quiet and passive. No such meaning was within the view of the legislative ... The civil magistrates are left in possession of those powers which the law had given them before ...

Mansfield's and Loughborough's view became the authoritative construction of the law.[26] It was soon adopted by the government (*PH* 21:736 ff.) and confirmed by courts on different occasions afterwards.[27] Indeed, it remained the legal basis for the employment of troops at least down to the late 19th century ([Anon.] 1833; Finlason 1868).

AFTER THE GORDON RIOTS

Certain ambiguities still prevailed and had their impact in practice on the conduct of all parties concerned in riots. That popular misconceptions of the law died slowly is indicated by the circumstances of the Bristol Toll Bridge Riot of 1793 (P.D. Jones 1980). After initial hesitation by the magistrates the militia eventually opened fire, shooting rather indiscriminately into the streets and thereby causing a considerable number of casualties.[28]

Contemporary accounts relate (J. Rose 1793a:8; J. Rose 1793b:6; [Anon.] 1793:11):

> (The magistrate) did not gain attention, neither did the riot act which was read tho'not heard by many (comparatively) and supposed by most to allude only to the rioters, in which class peaceable citizens could not think of including themselves: of course, though some of the most prudent went away, great numbers continued to look on ... The spectators (and even the rioters) had no idea that the military would fire, before the riot act had been read to them, as it was to others in the morning: They had no knowledge that its being read to others, *nine hours before*, was a legal warning to them; ... A report had been generally circulated amongst the rioters, that the soldiery could not *legally* fire upon them, and if they did, it must be with nothing but powder.

The situation continued to provide problems for the authorities as well. On the one hand, magistrates were obliged to oppose rioters — as was confirmed by the charge against the Lord Mayor of London because of his conduct during the Gordon Riots (Carrington and Payne 1825-41.5:282-96; *GM* 1781:144) — on the other hand they were (as was also always stated as well) liable to criminal prosecution if they could be accused of a misuse of power. The legal fiction that soldiers were nothing else than subjects wearing red coats meant that they too enjoyed no immunity from criminal prosecution.

Although the government sometimes made use of the newly discovered possibility of ordering troops to intervene without waiting for a call from the magistrates (Wells 1977a:729ff.), it was still held as a rule that soldiers should only operate under the direction of the civil authorities. In practice this repeatedly caused frictions concerning the actual division of responsibility between the civil and military officers (Radzinowicz 1948-68.4:ch.4; Darvall 1969:80, 261, 266ff.). The reaction to the Bristol Riots of 1831 demonstrates the point. The reluctance of the local authorities and consequently of the military officers led to large-scale riots comparable only to the Gordon Riots.[29]

THE RETURN TO CITIZEN SELF-HELP

Although I cannot deal with it at length here, it is worth stressing that the principle of collective responsibility and self-help from the citizenry could be invoked to promote endeavours which were expressly aimed at making the employment of troops unnecessary. This can be seen particularly in London. The City of London had always been anxious to defend its privileges against any encroachment by the government. The London authorities had on occasion demonstrated ostentatiously that they were able to secure law and order without having recourse to the assistance of troops.[30] During the Gordon Riots paramilitary organisations[31] of citizens were formed[32] to defend houses and to police the streets (de Castro 1926:198). It is revealing to see that the government tried to compel the City authorities to disarm these associations because they were encroaching on the military monopoly of the Crown. Still in apparent contradiction to the rules which it applied to the military, the government later came round to demanding that such associations should only act under the direction of a magistrate, whereas the City authorities were making precisely the same demand for the use of troops (*AR* 1780:266ff.; Sharpe 1895.3:183ff.). In Parliament the government had to face accusations that it was trying to deny Englishmen their constitutional rights (*PH* 21:691ff., 726ff.; Aikin 1816.1:263ff.). A number of publications in 1780 and the subsequent years suggest that the only way to avoid a "military dictatorship" was to reorganise citizen self-defence in a permanent manner on the basis of the much-praised principles of Common Law.[33] The endorsement of these principles by the "left wing" of the political spectrum is also illustrated by Joseph Priestley's resumption of the same proposals after the "Church-and-King" Riots in Birmingham in July 1791 (Priestley 1791:82, 87; R.B. Rose 1960).

Not surprisingly the most important implementation of these principles in practical terms took place on the "loyal" side. This was the formation of officially backed voluntary associations in reaction to the French Revolution. They were considered suitable for preventing both a French invasion and Jacobin insurrections at home (Western 1956). In fact their main business, from the 1790s onwards, turned out to be suppressing riots. In the long run their class character made the employment of voluntary forces more and more controversial.

Another version of the reactivation and adaptation of the Common Law principles was the engagement of special constables. Any private person could be sworn in by the magistrates even without his agreement. In many cases the summoning of special constables was more or less equivalent to the organisation of the "principal inhabitants" of a community. As in the case of the voluntary associations, the recruiting of members of the lower classes could sometimes fulfil the function of stabilising their loyalty.[34]

RIOT CASES IN COURT

Further aspects of the ambiguities underlying the implementation of the law on riots can be brought out by considering the application of the law in court. To generalise here is of course almost impossible. Some tentative remarks can, however, be made. In general the Riot Act had enlarged the choice of possible forms of prosecution, since charges based on the Riot Act provided an alternative to those at Common Law. Trials could take place either at Quarter Sessions or at Assizes. In some cases the Black Act[35] could also be employed.[36] In addition, of course, there was often the possibility of prosecuting for theft and assault committed in connection with riots. In principle, this enhanced the prosecution's chance of selecting the charge which seemed most promising. But this does not mean that the prosecution took advantage of the range of choices available in any specific case. In fact, rioters continued to be prosecuted for misdemeanour at Common Law (*CHOP* 1760-65:595; *GM* 1768:441). Charges according to the provisions of the Riot Act were obviously considered suitable only under extreme circumstances. The public outcry against the conviction of two and the actual execution of one unlucky participant in the Strand Riots of 1749 in London illustrates this point.[37] Defendants who were found guilty because they were seized more than one hour after the reading of the proclamation were likely to be punished leniently (*GM* 1739:602; 1749:34; *AR* 1832:60). The capital sentences imposed after the Gordon Riots were based on the felony of the demolishing of buildings as defined by the Riot Act.[38]

The tendencies of the construction of the law by judges are not uniform. In one case, someone who was present at a scene of rioting and had merely cheered on those who were actually demolishing a building was sentenced to death as a principal in the second degree.[39] In a later case, on the contrary, a judge ruled that the clause "beginning to demolish" could only apply if it was the perceptible "ultimate object of the rioters ... to demolish the house" (Carrington and Payne 1825-41.4:237ff.;5:510ff.). In general, the extreme observance of technicalities worked in favour of defendants. The mere omitting of words in the reading of the proclamation or in an indictment based on the Riot Act was sufficient to render them void (Carrington and Payne 1825-41.4:442;5:516ff.).

The actual prosecution of rioters reveals the discretionary nature of the handling of the penal law and the importance of the notion of deterrence. The conviction voiced again and again was that the speedy and exemplary punishment of ringleaders was the only adequate remedy. As George III wrote to his Prime Minister during the Gordon Riots: "indeed unless exemplary punishment is procured it will remain a lasting disgrace, and will be precedent for future commotion" (Fortescue 1927-8.5:73). That was also the crucial justification for the employment of troops. In 1768 the Secretary-at-War expressed his hope (Clode 1869.2:628)

> that whenever there shall be occasion to employ Troops to suppress Riots, the Civil Magistrates will take care that proper objects be seized and brought to punishment according to Law, without which no disorders of that kind will be quieted for any time, and the Forces will be continually wanted for a most odious service, which nothing but necessity can justify.

It can be assumed — although not, of course, demonstrated — that the idea of the conviction of ringleaders influenced the decisions of Grand Juries (*AR* 1758:105) and Juries as well. It also played an important role at the last stage, when the question arose whether a convict sentenced to death should be recommended to obtain a royal pardon or not. The Recorder of London informed one of the Gordon Rioters immediately after his conviction that "being the principal ringleader ... he could not expect mercy" (*AR* 1780:271). (Even Edmund Burke advocated in 1780 the careful selection of a small number of Gordon Rioters to be brought to execution in a most solemn way: Burke 1884-9.5:513-21). Furthermore, it was ordered that those Gordon Rioters who were in fact executed were hanged "near the spot where the felonies they were guilty of had been committed" (*AR* 1780:276; Dolman 1847:219) — a procedure which had some precedents.[40]

The freedom of judges to recommend pardons could also be brought into play as an inducement to stop riots, as happened in Warwick in 1756 (Hewitt 1779:1-2):

> Lord Chief Justice Parker, then on the Midland Circuit, sat on the crown bar at Warwick, the very same week of their commitment, before whom four of the rioters were tried on the Saturday, convicted and sentence immediately passed upon them; two of them were, on the Wednesday following, executed ... , two were reprieved, and others remained in custody, untried. The Lord Chief Baron, upon this, found it highly necessary to shew a spirit of determination and firmness; he adjourned the court until the Monday following, and declared his resolution that he would hold the assizes every Monday, until the rioters were dispersed: at the same time promised, provided those who were still rioting, levying contributions, and putting farmers etc. in continual fear, would return home to their respective habitations, giving assurances to remain peaceable, that those who were respited, as well as such that were detained, should have his Majesty's pardon, and be discharged: if they continued their riotous proceedings, every man that was apprehended and committed, should be executed the day after he was found guilty.

The final decision whether a pardon should be granted lay with the government. The use of its discretion "to make an example" of ringleaders could arouse opposition from public opinion, especially in cases when many petitions had been made to spare the life of the convict (Ward 1843:446). In consequence of the notion that exemplary punishment was necessary, however, rioters who were selected for punishment were probably more likely to be actually executed than felons were in general (Stevenson 1979b:46). To achieve speedy trials Special Commissions of judges would be sent, to avoid waiting for the next regular Assizes. The initiative could lie with government (*AR* 1766:143,149), especially when it was anxious to stop a wave of riots, or with local authorities, when they had special motives in asking for exemplary speedy punishment.[41] Sometimes the mere rumour that a special commission was to arrive had the effect of calming down rioters (D.E. Williams 1976:276).

The use made of the theatrical impact of the appearance of Assize judges should also be noted (Madan 1785:23ff.). In the case of the Hertford Assizes of Summer 1768 (*AR* 1768:153-4), the high-sheriff received the judges with uncommon ceremony; he doubled the number of javelin-men in livery who attended them from the frontiers of the county, and waited for them himself a mile further on the road than usual. On Tuesday he sent a turtle for their table, with burgundy instead of the common present of claret, and gave for a reason, that in these licentious times, when so many people had attempted to trample on the laws, he could not treat his majesty's chief ministers of justice with too much respect.

A contemporary summary of the handling of the wave of food riots in 1766 puts all these important elements together (*AR* 1767:40):

The magistrates being at length obliged to call in the military force to the aid of the civil; the rioters were easily dispersed, and the jails filled with persons. Judges were soon after sent to the counties where the riots had happened, with special commissions to bring the prisoners to immediate trial, in consequence of which several of the leaders, and other prisoners, the most outrageous of them, were condemned to die; most of these were however afterwards reprieved, several were transported, some got a free pardon, and some examples were made.

The severity of the law and the eagerness, especially of the central government, to see exemplary punishments was mitigated by the fact that the actual handling of the law lay in the hand of the local élites.

In cases of "Church-and-King-Riots" the sympathy local authorities often felt for the rioters might well amount even to the sabotage of justice by suppression of evidence, intimidation of witnesses and manipulation of the composition of juries; the juries themselves might deliberately ignore evidence.[42]

The case of food riots is more complicated. These involved considerable and — in most cases — "respectable" parts of the community. The smaller the community, the greater were the tensions criminal prosecutions would produce (Wells 1978:68-72; A.G. Rose 1963-4:67ff.). Furthermore, potential prosecutors and witnesses, and the magistrates themselves (who were also subject to pressures from the central government) were exposed to diverse influences and pressures — amounting to social outlawry and threats or deeds of revenge. On the other hand, prosecutions were encouraged by the offer of rewards.

Food riots could be construed as legitimate protest against encroachments on the "moral economy" (Thompson 1971; M. Thomas 1975:37-47). Justices of the Peace were inclined to enforce traditional paternalistic measures under such circumstances; they had, however, to face the charge that in doing so they were *de facto* encouraging riots.

It can be reasonably suggested that in cases of food riots magistrates, Grand Juries and Petty Juries were reluctant to institute preliminary proceedings, to find "true" bills of indictment and to convict, and that on the whole lenient sentences were imposed.[43]

Although I have not dealt with riots of this type here, it should be indicated that political riots, e.g. at elections, did not normally lead to harsh punishment (*GM* 1748: 378;1749: 88; Rudé 1962: App.11; Ellis 1980: 346ff.) whereas in the case of the early industrial conflicts, which took place under more violent[44] circumstances, the full severity of the penal code was more likely to be used.[45]

CONCLUSION

In conclusion, I can only briefly indicate some of the wider implications of the preceding discussion.

1) It shows that both the "rule of law" and a selective, discretionary application of the penal code are essential and complementary features of the system of law-enforcement in 18th century England. This holds true for the use of the penal law in general (Hay 1975; Brewer and Styles 1980:11-20). In the case of the riot law, however, the restrictive effect of the rule of law on the ability of authorities to enforce their will is even more significant since they had as a rule to rely on acceptance of and support for their measures from the citizenry. As in general, the authority of the law as such was not challenged by the common people. It is striking to see how far the opinions of both authorities and common people coincided with respect to the legal significance of the "reading of the Riot Act" during most of the period under discussion. The gap between the views of both sides as to what constituted an appropriate and just application of the law was likely to widen significantly, however, when the stage of instituting prosecution was reached. The clash of divergent opinions, interests and pressures in the complicated interactions between central and local government, local authorities and different parts of the community concerned, juries and judges, led to a variety of possible results in any given case. The difficulty of bringing rioters to trial was balanced to a certain degree by the determination to "make examples" of those who were actually indicted.

2) The law on riots was not inconsistent with the conditions of the rule of rural élites represented by the Justices of the Peace. For them the resort to coercion was only the *ultima ratio* when other attempts to appease crowds had failed. Nevertheless, they had to face growing difficulties later in the century in so far as the pressure from central government was increased and some property-owners were no longer prepared to accept the enforcement of paternalistic economic rules. The actual overtaxing of the system, however, took place in the metropolis and in the new industrial areas.

3) Growing problems of law-enforcement did not cause a direct transition to bureaucratic solutions. On the contrary, the resort to collective self-help on the part of citizens was not confined to the handling of riots but was also used with respect to the prosecution of "ordinary crime" (Hastings 1980; Shubert 1981; Curtis and Speck 1976). This suggests that the thorough changes which

were undertaken during the 19th century cannot be explained solely by deficiencies in the old system; they were also caused by new demands for public order in society.[46]

4) The English system of law-enforcement, based on a far-reaching autonomy of local authorities, private prosecution, and trial by jury, was, it is true, an exceptional case in early modern Europe. On the other hand, the lack of specialised agencies of law-enforcement and the necessity to make use of the army instead in critical situations was a common feature of continental states in this period as well. We are badly in need of comparative studies which overcome the tendency to base judgment on the standards of the 19th and 20th centuries, which in fact constitute the exception in terms of universal history. Furthermore, to understand the role of legitimate self-help and societal self-regulation in highly developed legal systems, the case of ancient and medieval states also has to be taken in consideration. In the long run, this should lead to a theory of law-enforcement in pre-modern societies.[47]

Notes

1. Probably the last application of the Riot Act occurred in Liverpool in 1919. See Brownlie 1968: ch.4; Keeton 1975: 52ff.; Ascoli 1979: 31 n.1 The serious riots of 1981 in British cities have led to some considerations of the usefulness of once again making rioting a statutory offence. See *Scarman Report* 1982: 188ff.
2. The fundamental work remains Radzinowicz 1948-68. It is biased, however, towards an often uncritical identification with the movement for the reform of criminal law and for the establishment of a professional police. A new approach has been provided by Hay *et. al.* 1975, especially Hay 1975, the contributions to Brewer and Styles 1980 and Philips 1980.
3. I Geo. I.st.2, c.5. The text is easily accessible in Horn & Ransome 1957: 271-75 and E.N. Williams 1960: 414-17.
4. These provisions clearly departed from Common Law practice. Two points of qualification should however be made. First, there had already been laws during the reigns of Tudor monarchs which defined conditions — comparable to those described in the Riot Act — under which rioting was treasonable. These laws had expired on the death of the monarch (Holdsworth 1956-72:8:327). Secondly, it should be pointed out that under certain specific conditions it had been the practice to interpret riots as treasonable (Luders 1810; Holdsworth 1956-72.8:307ff.). Although this construction was controversial within the judiciary itself (Hale 1736:139ff., 143ff.), it was still used in the aftermath of the Sacheverell Riots of 1709-10, when three rioters were found guilty of treason (Howell 1809-26.15:522-702).
5. In 1769, after a wave of food riots, mills were added by another statute (Radzinowicz 1948-68.1:620).
6. Critics soon raised the objection that the act should not have been passed without making sure that it was to expire after a certain period (Ryder 1939:93ff.; Bolingbroke in *The Craftsman*, vol.6, no.214, 8 Aug. 1730).
7. See the Royal Proclamation of 4 Nov.1714 and motion of the Commons, July 1715, *PH.*7:109ff.; and pamphlets like Rosewell 1715; Ferguson 1715: 50ff.; [Anon.] 1715.
8. The effect was doubtful. In 1781 the Attorney General asserted that the Riot Act "was more universally known than perhaps any act in the Statute book". He was probably correct as far as its existence was concerned, but the reply made on the same occasion that there was no "other subject on which so universal an ignorance prevailed" may have been equally true (Carrington & Payne 1825-41.5:285, 291). During the London Riots of 1794 it

was significant that the Home Office thought it necessary to send a copy of the Riot Act to the magistrates affected (Stevenson 1971: 48).

9. It should be mentioned, however, that considerable improvements of the system were achieved in the later eighteenth century (see Tobias 1979: ch.2).
10. See the chapters on "hue and cry" in Lambard 1581; Pulton 1609; Dalton 1618; W. Hawkins 1716; Burn 1755.
11. It is significant that during the eighteenth century this principle was also applied to damages likely to occur in connection with types of "social crime" which could find the support or toleration of a community; for example, arson, killing or maiming cattle, destroying of turnpikes, cutting hop-bins, destroying corn to prevent it from being exported. See the list in T. Williams 1812: 460. (These provisions were repealed in 1827 and only responsibility for riot damages was upheld, G.W. Hawkins 1875.)
12. In Norwich in 1766 rioters joined the *posse comitatus* before they were denounced to the magistrates, see Shelton 1973a: 53.
13. Thompson 1963: 74; Shelton 1973b: 102; Wearmouth 1945: ch. 1; Walsh 1972: 213-27. The Duke of Newcastle employed a "loyal mob" to oppose the Jacobites at the accession of George I. In retrospect he explained "I love a mob. I headed a mob once myself. We owe the Hanover succession to a mob" (*London Magazine or Gentlemen's Monthly Intelligencer*, 1768: 329). See also Ryder, 1939: 225: "I am extremely glad to find that the mob can be raised for the Government"; Fitts 1973; N. Rogers 1975 and 1978.
14. For the circumstances of a serious mutiny at the time of food riots see P. Horn 1979.
15. During the Sacheverell Riots of 1709-10 the captain commanding the Guards approached the Secretary of State, the Earl of Sunderland, and asked, "Whether he was to Preach or Fight the Mobb? If the first, he desired some better speaker might be sent along with him, for he was an indifferent Orator, if the latter, Fighting was his Trade, and he would do his best. To this the Earl reply'd, He must use his Judgment and Discretion, and forbear violent Means, except in Case of Necessity", Boyer 1703-13.8:266.
16. See Brewer 1976: ch.9 for a fresh assessment of Wilkes' popularity.
17. Some five to eleven deaths were reported. See Rudé 1962: 51.
18. See *GM* 1757: 430 for a previous case of prosecution brought against a magistrate.
19. The bringing of the prosecutions and the political exploitation of the affair was the work of the Wilkite organisations. See Brewer 1980: 132, 144ff.
20. "A stupid, over zealous Justice however thought proper to read the Riot Act, which not one hundredth part of the crowd knew had been done ... " Hickey 1913.1: 93.
21. The question had already been raised in Parliament in November 1768, *PH* 5: 18.
22. Sharpe 1895. 3: 178ff.; de Castro 1926; Rudé 1956; Stevenson 1979a: 76ff.; Davis 1973: 279ff.; Jaggard 1980.
23. Probably the most serious clash between rioters and soldiers had previously occurred in Hexham in 1761, when about 90 casualties had been counted. See *GM* 1761: 137ff.; Dickinson 1978.
24. The confusion was about the meaning of this in English law: see E.N. Williams 1960: 420ff.
25. Walpole 1859.2:408ff.; Romilly 1840.1:125, 131ff.; Vincent 1780: 42; de Castro 1926: 172ff. See, however, the report that troops, who had instructions to stop the wearing of blue cockades, the sign of the Protestant Association, had shot two persons dead who resisted them, [Anon.] 1780b: 44ff.
26. Vincent 1780: app.n.L; Romilly 1840.1: 372; [Ramsay] 1781: 4; [Perceval] 1792: 10, 15.
27. Carrington & Payne 1825-41.5: 294ff.; Bosanquet & Puller 1800-08.2: 264; Taunton 1810-23.4: 401-50; Starkie 1817-23.3: 90.
28. J. Rose 1793a gives the number of 10-12 deaths and 40-50 wounded persons.
29. S. Thomas 1974; Amey 1979. The juridical aftermath is also reminiscent of that of the Gordon Riots. The mayor was charged with neglect of duty and at his trial the precedent of the trial of the Lord Mayor of London was repeatedly cited (Howell 1809-26.3: 2ff.). A special commission imposed harsh punishments on the rioters ([Anon.] 1832a; [Anon.] 1832b).
30. As in the case of the execution of Bosavern Penlez in 1749 ([Anon.] 1749: 54ff.; [Anon.]

1780?: 50ff.; Linebaugh 1975: 99ff.) and others in 1769 and 1771 (see below n. 40).

31. The London Military Association already existed; for its role during the riots see *OBP* 1780: 465ff.; de Castro 1926: 125, 144ff., 166ff.
32. The example was given by the Inns of Court; it was followed by householders of various wards. See Romilly 1840.1: 51, 131ff.; *GM* 1780: 315ff.; [Anon.] 1780b: 40ff.; Fitzgerald 1888.2: 286ff.
33. [Ramsay] 1781; W. Jones 1780; [Anon.] 1780c; Sharp 1782; Blizard 1785.
34. For the role of the various volunteer units and of special constables as forces of riot control until c.1850, see Radzinowicz 1948-68.4: ch.4; Darvall 1969: 250-73; Teichman 1940; Mather 1958; Mather 1959: ch.3; Mather 1980: ch.4; Stevenson 1979b.
35. Different assessments of its origin appear in P. Rogers 1974 and Thompson 1975.
36. As in the case of turnpike rioters. See *GM* 1736: 353, 422; Albert 1979; Malcolmson 1980: 98ff.
37. In answering the criticism of [Anon.] 1749, Fielding 1749 was not successful in his attempt to demonstrate that both the riots and the person of the delinquent were proper objects for exemplary punishment.
38. *OBP* 1780: 358-640; [Anon.] 1780d: 1-168. Of more than 450 persons arrested during the riots, 160 were indicted, 85 found not guilty, 12 sentenced to imprisonment of between one month and five years, 62 sentenced to death and 25 eventually hanged; the others had their sentence commuted to life transportation (Rudé 1956: 99).
39. Burrow 1790.4: 2073-86, confirmed in Campbell 1811-16.3: 358-72.
40. There had been a case in 1716, see Boyer 1711-40.12: 235. The demand of the government in 1769 to have two convicted Spitalfields weavers executed near the place of their crime was opposed by the City authorities, who doubted its legality. Only after the judges had decided that the clause "usual place of execution" (*de facto* Tyburn) was not a constitutive part of the sentence did the City magistrates yield, insisting at the same time that they could handle the spectacle without troops: Leach 1815.1: 67ff.; *CHOP* 1766-69: 525-7; *AR* 1769: 181ff., 154ff., 159ff.; Stephens 1813.1: 109ff. Later the clause on the place of execution was omitted in sentences (*AR* 1769: 186). A further execution "on the spot" in East London was ordered in 1771 (*AR* 1771: 122, 142ff., 195).
41. As in Lancashire in 1779 when cases of machine breaking were considered to be endangering the continued presence of industry in the area, *GM* 1779: 609.
42. See, for example, the proceedings following the 1715 Riots in Bristol (Seyer 1823.2: 561ff.) and Newcastle (Briggs 1974: 74ff.), the reaction to an anti-Methodist riot in Exeter (Cennick 1745) and the case of the Priestley rioters of 1791 (Priestley 1791: 72ff.; Field 1791: 40; Romilly 1840.1: 443ff.; Hutton 1817: 275ff.).
43. *GM* 1758: 191; *AR* 1768: 140; Wells 1977b: 29-34; Wells 1977a: 736ff.; D.E. Williams 1976: 277ff.; Booth 1977: 105ff.
44. Violence as such did not necessarily provoke severe punishment. See the case of the sailors in Liverpool who in 1775 were allowed to avoid punishment by joining the navy, even though they had used firearms (Brooke 1853: 343ff.; R.B. Rose 1958).
45. Rudé 1962: App.3. By contrast, magistrates could adopt a different attitude when machine-breaking was directed against the property of nonconformists and the rioters were supporters of "Church and King": see Wykes 1978/79: 39-50.
46. I can only indicate here that the propagandists of a police force in the eighteenth century (like H. and J. Fielding and Hanway and Colquhoun) were especially concerned with the imposition of new moral standards on the urban masses to suppress idleness, drunkenness, prostitution, betting etc. The original hostility to the new police in the nineteenth century was due to the fear that they would encroach on the habits of daily life.
47. This article is based on part of the research I carried out during a year's stay at the German Historical Institute in London in 1980-81. My thanks are due to the Deutsche Forschungsgemeinschaft and to the Director of the Institute, Professor Wolfgang J. Mommsen, for enabling me to undertake this work, which I hope to pursue in the direction indicated.

Abbreviations

AR	*Annual Register.*
CHOP	*Calendar of Home Office Papers of the reign of George III* . . . , 4 vols. [1760-1765 ed. J. Redington; 1766-1769 ed. J. Redington; 1770-1772 ed. R.A. Roberts; 1773-1775 ed. R.A. Roberts], London: Longman & Co., 1878-1899.
GM	*Gentleman's Magazine.*
OBP	*Old Bailey Proceedings.*
PH	*Cobbett's Parliamentary History of England* (later simply called *The Parliamentary History of England from the Earliest Period to the Year 1803*).

Bibliography

Aikin, J. (1816) *Annals of the Reign of King George III*, 2 vols., London: Longman and Co.

Albert, W. (1979) "Popular Opposition to Turnpike Trusts in Early Eighteenth-Century England" *Journal of Transport History* (new series) **5**: 1-17.

Amey, G. (1979) *City Under Fire. The Bristol riots and aftermath*, Guildford: Lutterworth Press.

[Anon.] (1715) *An Account of a dreadful Mob at Manchester and other places in England*, Edinburgh: J. Mosman.

[Anon.] (1749) *The Case of the Unfortunate Bosavern Penlez*, London: Printed for T. Clement.

[Anon.] (1768) *Remarks on the Riot Act, with an application to certain recent and alarming facts*, London: G. Kearsly.

[Anon.] (1769) *A Collection of Pieces relative to the Inhumane Massacre in St. George's Fields on the 10th of May 1768*, London.

[Anon.] (1780a) *Fanaticism and Treason; or, a dispassionate History of the Rise, Progress and Suppression of the Rebellious Insurrections in June 1780*, London: G. Kearsly.

[Anon.] (1780b) *A Narrative of the Proceedings of Lord Geo. Gordon and the Persons Assembled under the Denomination of the Protestant Association*, London: J. Wallis.

[Anon.] (1780c) *A Plan of Association, on constitutional principles, for the Parishes . . . and Counties of Great Britain; by which the outrages of Mobs, and the necessity of a Military Government will be prevented*, London.

[Anon.] (1780d) *The Proceedings of the King's Special Commission of Oyer and Terminer for the County of Surrey*, London: Joseph Gurney.

[Anon.] (1780?) *The Liberty of the Subject and Dignity of the Crown, maintained and secured without the Application of a Military, unconstitutional Force*, London: Printed for G. Kearsly, J. Almon, B. White & N. Young.

[Anon.] (1793) *An Impartial History of the Late Riots at Bristol*, London: G.G.J. & J. Robinson.

[Anon.] (1832a) *A Charge delivered to the Grand Jury of Bristol*, Bristol.

[Anon.] (1832b) *Trials and Executions of the Unhappy Rioters of Bristol*, Bristol: J. Catnach.

[Anon.] (1833) "On the Suppression of Riots by Military Interference" *The Law Magazine* **9**: 66-82.

Ascoli, D. (1979) *The Queen's Peace: the origin and development of the Metropolitan Police, 1829-1979*, London: H. Hamilton.

Baker, J.H. (1977) "Criminal Courts and Procedure at Common Law 1550-1800", *Crime in England 1550-1800*, ed. J.S. Cockburn, London: Methuen, pp. 15-48.

Baker, J.H. (1979) *An Introduction to English Legal History*, 2nd ed., London: Butterworth.

Belsham, W. (1795) *Memoirs of the Reign of George III*, 4 vols., London: G.G. & J. Robinson.

Blackstone, W. (1781) *Reports of Cases Determined in the Several Courts of Westminster-Hall, from 1746 to 1779*, 2 vols., London: W. Strahan & T. Cadell.

Blizard, W. (1785) *Desultory Reflections on Police*, London: C. Dilly.

Booth, A. (1977) "Food Riots in North West England, 1790-1801" *Past & Present* **77**: 84-107.

Bosanquet, J.B. & Puller, C. (1800-08) *Reports of Cases . . . Courts of Common Pleas . . .* [1796-1807], 5 vols., London: J. Butterworth.

Boyer, A. (1703-13) *History of the Reign of Queen Anne Digested into Annals*, 11 vols., London: A. Roper, F. Coggan.

Boyer, A. (1711-40) *Political State of Great Britain*, 60 vols., London: The Author and T. Cooper.

Brewer, J. (1976) *Party Ideology and Popular Politics at the Accession of George III*, Cambridge: Cambridge University Press.

Brewer, J. (1980) "The Wilkites and the Law", in Brewer and Styles, 1980, pp. 128-71.

Brewer, J. & Styles, J. (1980) *An Ungovernable People. The English and their law in the seventeenth and eighteenth centuries*, London: Hutchinson.·

Briggs, J.H.Y. (1974) "The Burning of the Meeting House, July 1715: Dissent and Faction in Late Stuart Newcastle" *North Staffordshire Journal of Field Studies* **14**: 61-79.

Brooke, R. (1853) *Liverpool as it was . . . 1775 to 1800*, Liverpool: J. Maudsley & Son.

Brownlie, I. (1968) *The Law relating to Public Order*, London: Butterworth.

Burke, E. (1884-89) *The Works of the Right Honourable Edmund Burke*, 8 vols., London: Bell.

Burn, R. (1755) *The Justice of the Peace and Parish Officer*, 2 vols., London: A. Millar.

Burrow, Sir J. (1790) *Reports of Cases . . . King's Bench* [1756-1772], 5 vols., London: E. & R. Brooke.

Campbell, J. (1811-16) *Reports of Cases . . . Nisi Prius* [1807-1816], 4 vols., London: J. Butterworth.

Carrington, F.A. & Payne, J. (1825-41) *Reports of Cases argued and ruled Nisi Prius . . . King's Bench and Common Pleas* [1823-1841], 9 vols., London: S. Sweet, R. Pheney.

Cavendish, Sir H. (1841-42) *Sir Henry Cavendish's Debates of the House of Commons*, ed. J. Wright, 2 vols., London: Longman & Co.

Cennick, J. (1745) *An Account of a Late Riot in Exeter*, London: J. Lewis.

Clode, C.M. (1869) *The Military Forces of the Crown*, 2 vols., London: John Murray.

Cowper, H. (1784) *Reports of Cases . . . King's Bench* [1774-1778], Dublin: E. Lynch.

Curtis, T. & Speck, W.A. (1976) "The Societies for the Reformation of Manners" *Literature & History* 3: 45-64.

Dalton, M. (1618) *The Countrey Justice, conteyning the practice of the Justices of the Peace out of their Sessions*, London: The Societies of Stationers.

Darvall, F.O. (1969) *Popular Disturbances and Public Order in Regency England*, 2nd ed., London: Oxford University Press.

Davis, B.H. (1973) *A Proof of Eminence: The Life of Sir John Hawkins*, Bloomington, Ind. & London: Indiana University Press.

de Castro, J.P. (1926) *The Gordon Riots*, London: Oxford University Press.

Dickinson, H.T. & Logue, K. (1972) "The Porteous Riot, 1736" *History Today* **22**: 272-81. *History Society* **22**: 2-6.

Dickinson, H.T. & Logue, K. (1972) "The Porteous Riot, 1736" *History Today* 22: 272-81.

Dolman, C. (1847) "The Last Days of the Penal Laws and the Riots of 1779 and 1780", *Dolman's Magazine*, vol. 6.

Ellis, J. (1980) "Urban Conflict and Popular Violence: the Guildhall Riots of 1740 in Newcastle upon Tyne" *International Review of Social History* **25**: 332-49.

Ferguson, R. (1715) *The History of all the Mobs, Tumults, and Insurrections in Great Britain*, London: Printed for J. Moore.

Field, F. (1791) *Trials of the Birmingham Rioters*, Birmingham: Printed by J. Thompson.

Fielding, H. (1749) *The True Case of Bosavern Penlez*, London: A. Millar.

Finlason, W.F. (1868) *A Review of the Authorities as to the Repression of Riots and Rebellions*, London: Stevens & Sons; Chapman & Hall.

Fitts, J.L. (1973) "Newcastle's Mob" *Albion* **5**: 41-9.

Fitzgerald, P. (1888) *The Life and Times of John Wilkes*, 2 vols., London: Ward & Downey.

Fortescue, Sir J. (1927-28) *The Correspondence of King George III from 1760 to 1783*, 6 vols., London: Macmillan & Co.

Free, J. (1769) *England's Warning Piece . . . A Sermon occasioned by the untimely death of . . . William Allen*, London: The Author.

Hale, Sir Matthew (1736) *Historia Placitorum Coronae*, London: F. Gyles.

Hastings, R.P. (1980) "The Private Law Enforcement Associations" *The Local Historian* **14**: 226-232.

Hawkins, G.W. (1875) "The Law of Compensation for Damage by Riot" *The Law Magazine and*

Review (new series) **4**: 552-62.
Hawkins, W. (1716) *A Treatise of the Pleas of the Crown*, London: J. Walthoe, J. Walthoe jr.
Hay, D. *et al.* (1975) *Albion's Fatal Tree: Crime and Society in Eighteenth-Century England*, London: Allen Lane.
Hay, D. (1975) "Property, Authority and the Criminal Law", in Hay *et al.*, 1975, pp. 17-63.
Hayter, T. (1978) *The Army and the Crowd in Mid-Georgian England*, London: Macmillan & L.S.E.
Hewitt, J. (1779) *A Journal of the Proceedings of J. Hewitt, Mayor ... in the Year 1756, in the Suppressing of Riots and Tumults in the County of Warwick and the City and County of Coventry*, London: T.W. Pasham; Birmingham: C. Earl & R. Martin.
Hickey, W. (1913) *The Memoirs of William Hickey 1749-1775*, ed. A. Spencer, 4 vols., London: Hurst & Blackett.
Hobsbawm, E.J. (1959) *Primitive Rebels*, Manchester: Manchester University Press.
Holdsworth, W. (1956-72) *A History of English Law*, 17 vols., London: Methuen & Co.
Horn, D.B. & Ransome, M. (1957) *English Historical Documents 1714-1783*, London: Eyre & Spottiswoode.
Horn, P. (1979) "The Mutiny of the Oxfordshire Militia in 1795" *Cake & Cockhorse* **7**: 232-41.
Howell, T.B. (1809-26) *Cobbett's Complete Collection of State Trials*, 33 vols., London: R. Bagshaw; Longman & Co.
Hutton, W. (1817) *The Life of William Hutton ... written by himself*, 2nd ed., London: Baldwin, Craddock & Joy; Birmingham: Beilby & Knotts.
Jaggard, E. (1980) "A Cornish-Man's Impression of 'King Mob'. June 1780" *Devon & Cornwall Notes and Queries* **34**: 223-29.
Jones, P.D. (1980) "The Bristol Bridge Riot and its Antecedents: eighteenth century perceptions of the crowd" *Journal of British Studies* **19**, no. 2: 74-92.
Jones, Sir W. (1780) *An Inquiry into the Legal Mode of Suppressing Riots with a Constitutional Plan of Future Defence*, London.
Keeton, G.W. (1975) *Keeping the Peace*, Chichester: Rose.
Lambard, W. (1581) *Eirenarcha; or, of the Office of the Justices of Peace*, London: B. Newbery & H. Bynneman at the assig. of R. Tottell & C. Barker.
Leach, T. (1815) *Cases in Crown Law ... 1730-1815*, 2 vols., 4th ed., London: Butterworth.
Linebaugh, P. (1975) "The Tyburn Riots against the Surgeons", in Hay *et al.*, 1975, pp. 65-117.
Luders, A. (1810) "On Constructive Treason", *Tracts on Various Subjects in the Law and History*, Bath: R. Cruttwell, pp. 1-147
Madan, M. (1785) *Thoughts on Executive Justice*, 2nd ed., London: J. Dodsley.
Malcolmson, R.W. (1980) "A Set of Ungovernable People: the Kingswood colliers in the eighteenth century", in Brewer & Styles, 1980, pp. 85-127.
Mather, F.C. (1958) "Army Pensioners and the Maintenance of Civil Order in Early Nineteenth-Century England" *Journal of the Society for Army Historical Research* **36**: 110-24.
Mather, F.C. (1959) *Public Order in the Age of the Chartists*, Manchester: Manchester University Press.
Mather, F.C. (1980) *Chartism and Society, An Anthology of documents*, London: Bell and Hyman.
Munger, F. (1979) "Measuring Repression of Popular Protest by English Justices of the Peace in the Industrial Revolution" *Historical Methods* **12**: 76-83.
Munger, F. (1981) "Suppression of Popular Gatherings in England, 1800-1830" *American Journal of Legal History* **25**: 111-140.
Palmer, S.H. (1978) "Calling out the Troops: the military, the law and public order in England 1650-1850" *Journal of the Society for Army Historical Research* **56**: 198-214.
[Perceval, S.] (1792) *The Duties and Powers of Public Officers and Private Persons with Respect to Violations of the Public Peace*, [London ?]
Philips, D. (1980) "'A New Engine of Power and Authority': the institutionalization of Law-Enforcement in England, 1780-1830", *Crime and the Law: a social history of crime in western Europe since 1500*, ed. V.A.C. Gatrell, *et al.*, London: Europa, pp. 155-89.
Popham, Sir J. (1656) *Reports and Cases, Collected by the Learned Sir John Popham*, London: Thomas Roycroft for John Place.
Priestley, J. (1791) *An Appeal to the Public on the Subject of the late Riots in Birmingham*,

Birmingham: J. Thompson.
Pulton, F. (1609) *De Pace Regis et Regni*, London: Printed for the Companie of Stationers.
Quinault, R. (1974) "The Warwickshire County Magistracy and Public Order, c.1830-1870", *Popular Protests and Public Order: six studies in British History 1790-1920*, ed. R. Quinault & J. Stevenson, London: George Allen & Unwin, pp. 181-214.
Radzinowicz, Sir L. (1948-68) *A History of English Criminal Law and its Administration from 1750*, 4 vols., London: Stevens & Sons.
[Ramsay, A.] (1781) *Observations upon the Riot Act*, London: T. Cadell.
Rogers, N. (1975) "Popular Disaffection in London during the Forty-Five" *London Journal* **1**: 5-27.
Rogers, N. (1978) "Popular Protest in Early Hanoverian London" *Past & Present* **79**: 70-100.
Rogers, P. (1974) "The Waltham Blacks and the Black Act" *Historical Journal* **17**: 465-86.
Romilly, Sir S. (1840) *Memoirs of the Life of Sir Samuel Romilly written by himself*, 2 vols., London: J. Murray.
Rose, A.G. (1963-4) "Early Cotton Riots in Lancashire, 1769-1779" *Transactions of the Lancashire & Cheshire Antiquarian Society* **73-4**: 60-100.
Rose, J. (1793a) *An Impartial History of the late Disturbances in Bristol*, Bristol: Printed & sold by the editor.
Rose, J. (1793b) *A Reply to a Bridge Trustee*, Bristol: Printed & sold by the Editor.
Rose, R.B. (1958) "A Liverpool Sailors' Strike in the Eighteenth Century" *Transactions of the Lancashire & Cheshire Antiquarian Society* **68**: 85-92.
Rose, R.B. (1960) "The Priestley Riots of 1791" *Past & Present* **18**:68-88.
Rosewell, S. (1715) *The Unreasonableness of the Present Riotous and Tumultuous Proceedings*, London: M. Lawrence.
Rudé, G. (1956) "The Gordon Riots: a study of the rioters and their victims" *Transactions of the Royal Historical Society* series 5, **6**: 93-114.
Rudé, G. (1962) *Wilkes and Liberty*, Oxford: Oxford University Press.
Rudé, G. (1964) *The Crowd in History*, New York: John Wiley & Sons.
Ryder, D. (1939) *The Diary of Dudley Ryder*, ed. W. Matthews, London: Methuen.
Scarman Report (1982) *The Scarman Report*, Harmondsworth: Penguin Books.
Seyer, S. (1821-23) *Memoirs Historical and Topographical of Bristol and its Neighbourhood*, 2 vols., Bristol: Printed for the Author by J.M. Gutch.
Sharp, G. (1782) *Tracts concerning the ancient and only true legal means of natural defence by a Free Militia*, 3rd ed., London.
Sharpe, R.R. (1894-5) *London and the Kingdom*, 3 vols., London and New York: Longmans, Green & Co.
Shelton, W. (1973a) "The Role of Local Authorities in the Provincial Hunger Riots of 1766" *Albion* **5**: 50-66.
Shelton, W. (1973b) *English Hunger and Industrial Disorders. A study of social conflict during the first decade of George III's reign*, London: Macmillan.
Shubert, A. (1981) "Private Initiative in Law Enforcement: Associations for the Prosecution of Felons, 1744-1856", *Policing and Punishment in Nineteenth-Century Britain*, ed. V. Bailey, London: Croom Helm, pp. 25-41.
Starkie, T. (1817-23) *Reports of Cases ... Nisi Prius* [1814-1823], 3 vols., London: A. Strahan.
Stephens, A. (1813) *Memoirs of John Horne Tooke*, 2 vols., London: Printed for J. Johnson and co.
Stevenson, J. (1971) "The London 'Crimp' Riots of 1794" *International Review of Social History* **16**: 40-58.
Stevenson, J. (1979a) *Popular Disturbances in England 1700-1870*, London: Longman.
Stevenson, J. (1979b) "Social Control and the Prevention of Riots in England, 1789-1829", *Social Control in Nineteenth-Century Britain*, ed. A.P. Donajgrodzki, London: Croom Helm; Totowa, N.J. : Rowman and Littlefield, pp. 27-50.
Taunton, W.P. (1810-23) *Reports of Cases ... Courts of Common Pleas, 1807-1819*, 8 vols., London: J. Butterworth.
Teichman, O. (1940) "The Yeomanry as an Aid to Civil Power, 1795-1867" *Journal of the Society for Army Historical Research* **19**: 75-91, 127-43.

Thomas, M. (1975) "The Rioting Crowd in Derbyshire in the 18th Century" *Derbyshire Archaeological Journal* **95**: 37-47.
Thomas, P.D.G. (1978) "The St. George's Fields 'Massacre' of 10 May 1768: an eye witness report" *London Journal* **4**: 221-4.
Thomas, S. (1974) *The Bristol Riots*, Bristol: Historical Association.
Thompson, E.P. (1963) *The Making of the English Working Class*, London: Gollancz.
Thompson, E.P. (1971) "The Moral Economy of the English Crowd in the Eighteenth Century" *Past & Present* **50**: 76-136.
Thompson, E.P. (1975) *Whigs and Hunters. The origins of the Black Act*, London: Allen Lane.
Tobias, J.J. (1979) *Crime and Police in England 1700-1900*, Dublin: Gill and Macmillan.
Vincent, W. [pseud. for Thomas Holcroft] (1780) *A Plain and Succinct Narrative of the Late Riots and Disturbances*, London: Fielding and Walker.
Wadsworth, A. & Mann, J. De L. (1931) *The Cotton Trade and Industrial Lancashire 1600-1780*, Manchester: Manchester University Press.
Walpole, H. (1859) *Journals of the Reign of King George III from 1771 to 1783*, ed. J.R. Doran, 2 vols., London: R. Bentley.
Walsh, J. (1972) "Methodism and the Mob in the Eighteenth Century", *Popular Beliefs and Practice*, ed. G.J. Cumming & D. Baker, Cambridge: Cambridge University Press, pp. 213-27.
Ward, J. (1843) *The Borough of Stoke-upon-Trent*, London: W. Lewis and son.
Wearmouth, R.F. (1945) *Methodism and the Common People of the Eighteenth Century*, London: Epworth Press.
Wells, R. (1977a) "The revolt of the south-west, 1800-1801: a study in English popular protest" *Social History* **2**: 713-44.
Wells, R. (1977b) "Death and Distress in Yorkshire 1793-1802", *Borthwick Papers*, no. 52.
Wells, R. (1978) "Counting Riots in Eighteenth-Century England" *Bulletin of the Society for the Study of Labour History* **37**:68-72.
Western, J.R. (1956) "The Volunteer Movement as an Anti-Revolutionary Force, 1793-1801" *English Historical Review* **71**: 603-14.
Wilkes, J. (1769) "The Humble Petition of the Livery of the City of London", *English Liberty, or the British Lion roused*, 2 vols., London: T. Baldwin.
Williams, D.E. (1976) "Midland Hunger Riots in 1766" *Midland History* **3**: 256-97.
Williams, E.N. (1960) *The Eighteenth-Century Constitution*, Cambridge: Cambridge University Press.
Williams, T. (1812) *Every man his own Lawyer*, London.
Wraxall, Sir N.W. (1904) *Historical Memoirs of my own Time*, ed. R. Askham, London: Kegan Paul and co.
Wykes, D.L. (1978-9) "The Leicester riots of 1773 and 1787, a study of the victims of popular protest" *Transactions of the Leicestershire Archaeological & Historical Society* **54**: 39-50.

Silences of the law: Customary law and positive law on the manumission of slaves in 19th century Brazil

MANUELA CARNEIRO DA CUNHA

Department of Anthropology, University of São Paulo, Brazil

Historians have unanimously credited Brazil with a particularly generous law: any slave who offered his master his own value in cash acquired his freedom, the owner being obliged to accept the ransom. This law, however, never existed in writing, though the practice was widespread and can certainly be said to have been recognised as customary law. The absence of the rule in written law is not a mere omission to codify customary practice, but is the result of deliberate opposition to recording the rule in written form.

This raises the question of the relation between customary law and written law in a literate society. The author maintains that the deliberate silence of the written code on this point fits a society grappling with a chronic manpower shortage and anxious to control not only the slave labour force but also freed slaves. To represent the sale of freedom as dependent on the master's good will and as being, at least in theory, revocable if the slave showed ingratitude, helped to keep freedmen in a state of personal dependence.

The silences of the law have their meaning. Codified law is a discourse on society, a self-description constructed by the State. It is not the only possible discourse. Its silences supply, in intaglio, alternative descriptions of the same society. In 19th century Brazil this duality, this double-facedness, reflects the contradictions of a country which presents itself as liberal, but has a social structure still based for the most part on relations of personal dependence.

"Law is worn very loosely."
Kidder & Fletcher, 1857: *Brazil and the Brazilians*, p. 522.

The history of an error is always instructive.

It is well known that in their theses on the peculiar leniency of the slave system in Brazil, Tannenbaum and Elkins give the place of honour to the mediation of the State and the Church in the relations between masters and slaves. The alleged role of the State, in its turn, is said to be centred on the right to manumission granted any slave who could present a sum corres-

History and Anthropology, 1985
Vol. 1, pp. 427-443
0275-7206/85/0102-0427 $18.50/0

ponding to his own worth. Now it must at once be pointed out that this is one of the most successful errors in History. At first sight, it is a riddle: the custom of manumitting slaves who could pay their own price was indeed widespread. Yet it did not involve the State. Not that the State was opposed to it, but it was not allowed to sanction the custom in law, owing to the opposition of the very people who followed this customary practice. It is a riddle we shall attempt to decipher.

It is possible to retrace the vertiginous career of this historical misunderstanding. I believe it arose with the Englishman Henry Koster, who was a sugarcane planter in Pernambuco at the start of the 19th century, and, if not the best, was certainly one of the best sources on the Northeast of Brazil at that time. Koster writes:

> The slave can oblige his master to manumit him, on tendering to him the sum for which he was first purchased, or the price for which he might be sold, if that price is higher than what the slave was worth at the time he was first bought.
>
> (H. Koster, 1816: 404)

Immediately after this, however, Koster finds himself faced with the evident deviations from this rule he has affirmed, and which he now explicitly describes as being a law:

> This regulation, like every one that is framed in favour of slaves, is liable to be evaded, and the master sometimes does refuse to manumit a valuable slave; and no appeal is made by the sufferer owing to the state of law in the country, which renders it almost impossible for a slave to gain a hearing.
>
> (H. Koster, *ibid.*: 404)

One page further on, nonetheless, in a footnote where he is remarking on a refusal of manumission, Koster seems to be clearing up a doubt which has apparently occurred to him, as to whether or not this law really exists. He finally comes down in favour of its existence and imputes the glaring deviations recorded in practice to the fact that the law is being evaded:

> This instance of refusal, and some others of which I have heard, would make me very doubtful of the foundation upon which the custom of manumitting is placed, if I did not know how easily the laws relating to many other important points are evaded through the influence of wealth and power. I did not see a copy of the law or regulation on the subject, but I never met with any one who doubted that the slave had a right to appeal, if he thought proper; whether he would be heard or not was another question.
>
> (H. Koster, *ibid.*: 405, footnote)

From then on, this error had a rapid career, above all because Koster was a source for many of his successors, most of whom were reluctant to admit how much they had borrowed from him. Tollenare, a Frenchman living in Pernambuco at the same time as Koster, takes the law's existence for granted in his *Notas Dominicais* (L.F. Tollenare, 1956: 144), published in 1818. Robert Southey, the English poet and author of a major history of Brazil, speaks of the law in 1819 and quotes Koster as his source (R. Southey, 1819, Part 3, cap. XLIV: 783). From then on, it becomes common to mention the law of manumission by payment of the slave's own worth: it appears in almost all the travellers' accounts. In 1835, for example, Carl Seidler refers to it in his *Zehn Jahre in Brasilien* (1980: 255). In 1857, the Reverends Kidder and Fletcher mention it in their book *Brazil and the Brazilians* (1857: 133). Sir Harry Johnston returns to the affirmation in 1910 in his comparative book on slavery, and it is to him and to Kidder and Fletcher that Tannenbaum later refers in support of the existence of a legal right to manumission in Brazil (1947: 54, 56, 65). The error had by then become well established, and as far as I know, none of the arguments raised against the theses of Tannenbaum, or those of Elkins, who took them up later on, involved casting any doubt on the existence of such a legal right.

And yet this right had no basis in law until 1871, that is, until the "Free Womb" Law; and significantly this Law, which laid down that all children thereafter born to slaves would be free, heralded the beginning of the official dismantling of slavery.

It is true that before that time there had been exceptional circumstances in which the State would intervene with promises of manumission. In the 1821 War of Independence in Bahia, General Labatut promised to free any slaves of the region who joined up to fight the Portuguese. He thereby managed to antagonise all the slaveowners in the region, as well as the Governing Council, head-quartered in Cachoeira and in whose name he was fighting. Not that they stood to lose much, for the prevailing economic chaos and the promise of compensation were enough to reassure them as to any real losses (Braz do Amaral, 1957: 292, n. 3; 284-5). But, although the letters of manumission, even in this case of virtual expropriation, were granted by the slaveowners in question, they were highly resentful of this interference in their strictly private right to concede manumission.

In 1835, after the most important slave uprising of the 19th century, the rebellion of the *Malês* in Bahia, the government enacted a law intended to prevent further rebellions: this provided for special powers and included a promise to manumit any slaves willing to act as informers regarding the insurgents (Lei de 13 de maio de 1835, no. 9, art. 9). In Rio Grande do Sul, in 1838, manumission was offered to any slaves who would desert from the Republican forces of Bento Gonçalves. His proud reply to this was a reminder that in his Republic all men already *were* free (Determinação de 19-11-1838 do Governo Imperial, *apud* J.A. Goulart, 1971: 202).

At the time of the War of Paraguay (1865-70), promises were again made to free any slave who would join up, and the slaveowners again protested.

In the preceding century, the exceptional cases where the State intervened in manumission involved attempts to prevent smuggling of diamonds and, later on, of timber. Any slaves denouncing smugglers, even if to do so they informed against their masters, were to be manumitted. So were any who themselves found diamonds of more than 20 carats (A. Perdigão Malheiro, 1976 (1867), Vol. I: 98, §60, §70).

I believe that this completes the list of occasions when the government arrogated to itself the right to interfere in the granting of manumission; there were compelling reasons of State in all of them, and they were all seen as exceptional measures. In any case, the slaveowners were always paid compensation, and it was they who granted the letters of manumission. In short, barring exceptional circumstances, the slaveowner had the sole right to grant or deny his slaves manumission. In reality, it was customary law — "whose existence nobody doubted", as Koster puts it — that prevailed. We have some statistical indications of this. In Paraty between 1789 and 1822, 31% of manumissions were paid for. In Salvador between 1684 and 1888, the proportion was 48% (J.P. Kiernan, 1976; K. Mattoso, 1979: 211; S. Schwartz, 1974). In 9 municipalities of Paraíba State between 1850 and 1888, it was 25.6% (D.S. Galliza, 1979: 143). For Brazil as a whole, between 1873 and 1885, 30.6% of manumissions were paid for (R. Slenes, 1976: 517-18).

It is true that in some cases, where the owner was especially fond of the slave, he would accept less than the market value (D.S. Galliza, 1979: 152; n. 29 and 30 on pp. 161-2), but this practice does not seem to have been general. There were also cases where the opposite happened — the owner asked more than the market price, probably speculating with the private and untransferable interest of the slave in his own person. M.I. Cortes de Oliveira (1979: 207) publishes a will of 1810 from which it can be deduced that the slaveowner — actually himself a freedman — manumitted a female slave who had given him nothing but trouble in return for a much higher sum than she had been sold for two years before.

Some of these manumissions were paid for in cash, others in movable assets, which could even include slaves, or in real estate (D.S. Galliza, 1979: 150). What can be seen to be implicit in such practices is the fact that slaves have a peculium; although the law was also silent on this until 1871, it was widely prevalent under customary law. Whereas slaves were not allowed *de jure* to own anything, *de facto* there were even special ways, for example, to brand cattle which belonged to them (H. Koster, 1816; A. Perdigão Malheiro, 1976 (1867), Vol. I, p. 62, §34).

In view of the figures quoted above concerning paid manumissions, the silence of the law is what most draws attention. Why was there no regulation, until 1871, of such a widespread practice? And this in turn leads to further questions. What was the relationship between customary and positive law in 19th century Brazil? What was the significance of what remained unwritten? And more generally, what is the place and role of silence, of omission, of the unwritten, in a literate society?

The silence of the law certainly was not a mere question of oversight. Throughout the first half of the 19th century, almost all anti-slavery bills included in their proposals for legislation the compulsory deliverance of any slave able to pay his or her own worth.

José Bonifácio, in Article 5 of his famous Bill of 1823, which was to be put before the General Constituent and Legislative Assembly of Brazil; Moniz Barreto, in the Memoir presented to the King, Dom João VI, in 1817 (and published in 1837); José Eloy Pereira da Silva, in 1826; Dr. Caetano Alberto Soares in his Memoir of 1845, re-issued in 1862; the 1852 Bill proposed by the Society Against the African Slave Trade and for the Promotion of the Colonisation and Civilisation of the Indians, Part 3, Article 46 — all these proposed that the law make specific reference to a slave's right to manumission upon presentation of his or her value in money[1].

Yet with the same consistency, every one of these proposals was defeated. The Bill drafted by José Bonifácio, for example, was intended as a guideline for the Constitution, but this was replaced by the Charter decreed in 1824. Even in the Bill drawn up by the Constituent Assembly, which was finally dissolved, the role of the State was at the same time mentioned and watered down in a typically liberal formula, the irony of which has been so finely pointed out by Caio Prado Jr. (1963: 54): "Art. 265. The Constitution recognises the contracts between masters and slaves, and the government shall keep watch over their enforcement".

In the legal field, the argument used to refute these proposals was the right of property, guaranteed "in all its plenitude" in the 1824 Charter (Art. 179, §22). This plenitude implied that the master had sole discretion as to whether or not to manumit his slave, as he deemed fit.

During the liberal period which ran from 1827 to 1837, a time when profound legal changes were taking place [2], jurisprudence began, however, to recommend such manumissions: a declaration of intent which ultimately emphasises the absence of a basis in law. In 1830, for example, when dealing with a petition from two slaves whose mistress refused to free them, although they were prepared to pay their own price in cash, the Ministry of Justice refused to order them to be manumitted in order to avoid "coaction upon the right of the masters as permitted in law". It preferred to recommend the use of "docile and persuasive means" to induce the mistress to grant the freedom she had promised in exchange for a sum stipulated by herself (Justiça — 8 de março de 1830, no. 66, *Colleção das Leis do Império do Brasil*, 1830, p. 50).

Two further Notices of 1830 follow the same trend, in advising conciliatory means to persuade masters to accept payment of the value of any slaves who desire freedom. The second of these Notices recommends that the master be convinced of his slave's "right to seek his own manumission" (and here we should note that nothing is said of a right to manumission, but of the right to desire it) and of his "duty (as a master) to contribute to the happiness of the said slave ... " (Avisos, 17 de março de 1830/29 de julho de 1830, in Nabuco de Araújo, Vol. 7, pp. 158 and 187). But in the name of "humanity, philanthropy, Christian charity and the rights of man", jurisprudence ventured even further: a Notice of December 15 1831 ordered that, if peaceful means of achieving freedom in return for payment for the slave Eugênia should fail, the terms of the law protecting her were to be applied (Nabuco de Araújo, Vol. 7, p. 604). Precisely what law this Notice refers to is not specified. Followed as it was in 1837 by a Resolution which ordered the manumission of those slaves of the Emperor who offered to pay their own price, and in 1847 by an Ordinance which made the same provision for slaves of the Nation (Resolução no. 30 de 11 de agosto of 1837, art. 10; Ord. no. 160 de 30 de outubro de 1847), the 1831 Notice in fact paved the way for a whole series of speculations concerning the right to manumission, which were only to be halted by a peremptory verdict issued by the Section of Justice of the Council of State in 1855. This verdict, coming from a body which directly assisted the Emperor in an advisory capacity and was markedly reactionary at this time, called a halt to "humanitarian interpretations of established laws" and reaffirmed that no existing law could oblige a master to manumit his slave (C. Mendes de Almeida, 1870, pp. 1073-4; Aviso no. 388 de 21 de dezembro de 1855).

So Tannenbaum was mistaken: the State did not act as mediator in the relations between masters and slaves. Nor did the Church as an institution. Not only did the religious orders have their own slaves, practically until the eve of Abolition, but some even specialised in the reproduction of slaves — and they were probably the only undertakings of the kind in Brazil. The Carmelites, for example, had establishments for breeding slaves in the Province of Rio de Janeiro, as did the Benedictines in Ilha do Governador, also in Rio (Th. Ewbank, 1976 (1856): 276). A major role was played, however, by the religious brotherhoods. These were lay associations under the aegis of the established Church, organised on an entirely local basis without any centralisation; their aim was to defend the corporate interests of their members. Brotherhoods of slaves and freedmen, both black and mulatto, advanced money to their members to help pay for manumission (see e.g. J. Scarano, 1976; A.J. Russell-Wood, 1974). A number of specific brotherhoods had various privileges granted them by the King of Portugal. But they were brotherhoods of a particular Church in a particular town, and these privileges applied exclusively to their own members. In 1688, the Black Brotherhood of Our Lady of the Rosary, of São Salvador Church in Lisbon, had obtained the privilege of being entitled to buy the freedom of its members if their masters were willing to sell them outside the Kingdom; in 1779, the Brotherhood of São Benedito, of the Convent of Saint Francis in Lisbon, obtained the privilege of buying the freedom of its members in captivity [3] (Alvará de 22 de fevereiro de 1688, in J.J. Andrade e Silva, 1859: 154; Provisão de 29 de novembro de 1779, in C. Mendes de Almeida, 1870: 1022). But these can hardly be understood as instances of mediation by the Church: furthermore, in 1685, the King gave an elite brotherhood based in Angola permission to send 500 slaves to Brazil for sale for four consecutive years to raise funds for the construction of a church (Alvará de 31 de outubro de 1685, in J.J. Andrade e Silva, 1859: 48).

Although written law said nothing in favour of the right to paid manumission, customary law went its own way. "I understand," wrote a stern Councillor of State in the 1855 verdict referred to above, "that in the Province of Bahia it has become customary, when inventories are being made, to permit the ransom of any slave as soon as his value is offered. If this be true, I am quite ignorant of the basis upon which such a practice is carried out, for in my opinion it has no justification in the Laws by which we are governed" (Aviso no. 388, 21 de dezembro de 1855, in C. Mendes de Almeida, 1870, Vol. 2: 1073).

There is no doubt that there was more compliance with customary than with written law. It was common knowledge that the authority of written laws varied in inverse proportion to one's distance from the urban centres. In the interior, law was enforced by those with power, "the sugarmill owners, who refuse to bend before the law and are in fact accustomed to taking it into their own hands" (L.F. Tollenare, 1956 (1818): 194). It may also be asked how widespread knowledge of the legislation was. It is common sense that hardly any slaves can have been familiar with written laws, and indeed it is hard to see how they would have been able to obtain any knowledge of them. Moreover, there are indications that the legislation protecting slaves was deliberately hidden from them by the legislators themselves. An example: two Royal Decrees of 1688 obliged any master to sell a slave he was known to have punished with cruelty. But they also stipulated that knowledge of this must not reach other slaves (Carta Régia de 20.3.1688/23.3.1688).

What legal means were open to a slave to obtain his rights under these laws? To lodge a complaint, he had to go through his master[4]. If this were not possible, he could — according to only some interpretations[5] — resort to the offices of the Public Prosecutor or to those of "any one of the people". If even so he should manage to lodge a complaint against his master, which as we have seen did happen, what support could he expect from the judges[6]? In the passage quoted at the start of this article, Koster suggests that slaves did not resort to the courts because they had no hope of winning a lawsuit and feared their conditions would worsen (H. Koster, 1816: 404).

Unlike written law, customary law, according to Koster, was backed up by an alert public opinion. Priests, "men of the same class as the masters", and even the "lower orders", in whose eyes the masters did not wish to lose prestige, brought pressure to bear in support of it. This did not represent a totally effective instance of power, however. Licutan, one of the leaders of the

1835 *Malê* rebellion in Bahia, was a literate Muslim. His disciples amassed the sum corresponding to his worth, but his master refused to free him. Nina Rodrigues, who recounts this story based on the records of the trial, adds that "even today [i.e. in 1900] the surviving Africans attribute the reason for the insurrection generally known as the 'War of the *Malês*' to the slaveowners' refusal to free those Negroes who offered the sum then stipulated as the value of a slave's ransom" (R. Nina Rodrigues, 1976 (1910): 61-2, 56).

There are many other examples, besides those already mentioned, of the relative efficacy of customary law. What brought pressure to bear on slave-owners to enforce it was not so much public opinion, perhaps, as the ever-present fear that a slave whose hopes of manumission were frustrated would run away or commit suicide. The relative propensity of the various African races for suicide, which was believed to be an ethnic characteristic, was thus painstakingly weighed up and given due consideration. The "Gaboons", for example, who were brought over at the beginning of the 19th century, were also assessed from this standpoint: they were considered excellent slaves but apt to kill themselves by swallowing their tongues (H. Koster, 1816: 410). In short, within the slave system itself, there was a minimal undertaking towards slaves which had to be respected.

It thus seems reasonable to suppose that between the dead letter of the written legislation and the living practice of customary law, the latter was much more effective. Why then was there so much reluctance to commit it to writing, to put down on mostly innocuous paper the rules which were already in force? It was a paradoxical situation: a custom which was generally practised was prevented from crystallising into a law which, in any case, would not necessarily have been obeyed. As we have seen, this was not a question of oversight: the law was not silent — it was silenced. Thus, it is not in the text of the law that we can expect to find the logic of this process, but in the silence itself.

It was a political matter, and the 1855 verdict issued by the Section of Justice of the Council of State made it explicit: it was hard, it admitted, to deny a slave the right to pay for his manumission, but reasons of state made it imperative to do so, in order to prevent the slave system from becoming even more dangerous than it already was. If, on the contrary, the slave could only receive his freedom from the hands of his master, not only was the right to property preserved, but the slave's sentiments of obedience and subordination towards his master would be left equally untouched, as would his dependence on the master (C. Mendes de Almeida, 1870: 1074). What this text is referring to, quite explicitly, is personal dependence.

A remark by Perdigão Malheiro, probably dating from 1866, points in the same direction: he recommends that the right to buy freedom should be limited; it should only be permitted when the master wishes to sell the slave because he has need of money, but when selling as a punishment, or exchanging, donating and making dowries, it would not be acceptable to establish this right: "To establish it as an absolute rule would be to give way to the insubordination for which this class [i.e. the slaves] has a natural propensity" (A. Perdigão Malheiro, 1976 (1867), Vol. II: 165, footnote 657).

Thus, subordination comes to the fore once again. In 1871, when the "Free Womb" Law was up for debate as a bill in the Chamber of Deputies, Perdigão Malheiro, who was by then a deputy for Minas Gerais, expressed opposition to the bill, and specifically to including in the legislation the right to paid manumission, even against the master's will. In the reasoning he developed, he was even more explicit regarding the implications of such a measure:

> Even if we leave aside the question of property, as I see it, we shall not be able with impunity *to slacken the relations between slave and master*, which today bind the one so firmly to the other and are *the only moral element* to contain the slaves within this sad condition in which they find themselves ... If we burst these ties violently asunder, not so that they slacken merely but so as to sever them completely, as this Bill would entail (like Alexander cutting the Gordian knot), the consequence will be disobedience, lack of respect and of subjection. This is one of the gravest dangers. Seen in all its context, this Bill tends towards nothing less than the violent rupture of the moral ties which bind a slave to his master.
>
> (F.V. Bruno, 1979 (1871-89): 250 — my emphasis)

At first sight it is surprising that insubordination is brought up in this context. Those who advocated the slave's right to buy his freedom saw it rather as a stimulus to hard work, hoarding and discipline. It was in these terms that in 1816 Koster recommended that this right be recognised in the British colonies. But subordination and discipline are not at all the same thing. Discipline pertains properly to the free labourer, subordination to the dependent. And, as we shall try to show below, the question here is the production of dependents.

In order to understand this, it is necessary to think in terms of the division of political control between the State and private individuals in Brazil at that time. The control of slaves, except in the case of insurrections and sometimes of assassinations, was — traditionally — the responsibility of the slaveowners.

In 1700, the Jesuit Benci reprimanded the Portuguese for considering, "as a matter of pride and honour, that to hand over a delinquent slave to Justice is an offence against the nobility and grandeur of the master" (J. Benci, 1977 (1700): 167). Benci was referring only to slaves sentenced to death; in other words, he did not even discuss whether the other punishments he recommended — whipping and private incarceration — should be left to the discretion of the slaveowners and carried out by them. Nor did he say they should not judge whether or not the slave deserved to die. What he recommended is that the State should be in sole charge of applying the death penalty.

Over a century later, the same rule still held absolute sway in the countryside. And the slaveowners who did not have sufficient power of coercion over their slaves ended up selling any disobedient slaves to those who did (H. Koster, 1816). In the urban centres, however, where there was a proliferation of *escravos de ganho*[7] and of masters who owned only a few slaves, with no overseers or private means of coercion, the State had placed itself purely and simply at the service of the slaveowners' private justice; thus, the *"Calabouço"* was instituted, with the specific function of housing jailed slaves and administering the punishments to which they had been sentenced by their masters. The latter paid the costs of this confinement and of the whippings meted out (J.A. Goulart, 1971: 103ff., 197; P. Aufderheide, 1976: 301).

In the liberal period of the thirties, when the role of the State was reinforced in the legal field, a number of constraints were placed on this subservience of the State with regard to private individuals. The 1830 Criminal Code prohibited more than 50 whiplashes in one day (Art. 60); a master could not order more than 50 blows or leave any slave of his locked up in the *Calabouço* for more than a month without trial (Lei de 3 de novembre de 1831; Decisão no. 67, Justiça, 10 de fevereiro de 1832, in *Colleção das Leis e Decisões do Império do Brasil*)[8]. It was at this time that the then Minister of Justice, Feijó, declared: "The government has decided that the authority of the masters, which is limited to the correction of misdemeanours, should not be extended to the punishment of crimes reserved for Justice. Slaves are men and the Laws encompass them" (Relatório do Ministro da Justiça, 10 de maio de 1832, *apud* J.A. Goulart, 1971: 105).

In reality, these humanitarian measures and declarations of intent did not affect the basic agreement. It was the master's "paternal responsibility" to control both his slaves and his children. The State, theoretically, was expected to control freed and free men alike. Now during these early years of the 19th century, there is no doubt that the non-whites who were not slaves were considered the most dangerous category of all. It is not known exactly how many of them there were: "As regards certain portions of the inhabitants," wrote the American traveller Thomas Ewbank, "it is considered discreet in the authorities to say little; thus no reliable comparison of the numbers of white and free colored are given, on account of the alleged overwhelming proportion of the latter" (Th. Ewbank, 1856: 430). There were thought to be more free men than slaves, but it was known that the non-whites far outnumbered the whites. One source estimates a million whites, around 700,000 free non-whites, an imaginary number of 250,000 "domesticated Indians", and about 1,900,000 slaves; this was on the eve of Independence (A. Balbi, 1822, Vol. 2: 229). This is not the place to discuss these figures — I do so elsewhere (M.C. da Cunha, 1983, ms); what I wish to stress is that the loyalties of the free non-whites carried a crucial political weight. They could well be the decisive factor in maintaining or destroying an equilibrium which was felt by all, especially since the Haiti revolt in 1798, to be precarious and explosive.

Would the State be able to ensure effective control of this population? Nothing could be more dubious. It was the free non-whites, apparently, who were most subject to legal proceedings and imprisonment (P. Aufderheide, 1976: 209-10, 304, 346). They were also the focus for compulsory military recruitment. But desertion[9], banditry and widespread complaints concerning the vagrancy of free non-whites bear witness to the partial nature of such control.

Under these circumstances, it might be supposed that the State was indeed fully prepared to share the task of controlling the free non-white population with the slaveowners. The latter, in turn, as individuals also had an interest in controlling part of this population. It is known today that some agricultural work, even in the sugar- and coffee-producing regions where most of the slave labour was employed, was done by freemen, or more precisely by dependent labourers, with whom a number of arrangements were made: for example, they could receive a piece of land and protection in return for a part of the harvest, personal services — which included defending the master — and seasonal or occasional work (e.g. S. Stein, 1957: 117; P. Eisenberg, 1977). There was a whole range of free labourers, from the most dependent to the seasonal wage-labourers (P. Eisenberg, 1977). The existence of this reserve of free labour, which also supplied villages and towns with subsistence foodstuffs, was essential to the big plantations, in providing for seasonal requirements for cane crushing or coffee picking.

I believe that it is in this context that the question of the manumission of slaves can be cleared up. On condition that manumission was left entirely to the master's discretion, it could play a major role in the constitution of this dependent population.

However closely paid manumission resembled a sale, and although its price was normally determined by the market price of a slave, ideologically speaking nothing was more emphasised than the distinction between the two. In law, manumission was traditionally dealt with under the same heading as donations (A. Perdigão Malheiro, 1976 (1867), Vol. I: 117). No letter of manumission, even if it resulted from a ransom payment, would ever refrain from including a preamble insisting on the generosity of the master or on his affection for his slave, and on its counterpart, the fidelity and the good offices of the slave, which had made him eligible for release from captivity. Trite formulas, perhaps, but revealing ones.

All this implied the existence of moral ties between masters and slaves — ties which were certainly not intended to cease to exist after manumission. An ideology is only worthy of the name if shared by its holders: while freedmen were expected to be grateful and loyal, moral injunctions, basically of protection, also weighed upon the masters.

This matter is also dealt with by the jurist Perdigão Malheiro in a lengthy discussion of the mutual obligations of patrons and their freed slaves. At one time in Roman law one of these precepts was that the patron should inherit his former slave's possessions if the latter died intestate. Perdigão Malheiro takes violent objection to the application of this precept in Brazil. Although it might be supposed that this is a mere theoretical debate, the publication of wills left by freedmen and their analysis by Maria Inês Cortes de Oliveira (1979) makes it clear that, on the contrary, the bonds between patron and freed slave were grounded in customary law: wills often specified the saying of mass for the souls of dead masters and slaves throughout the first half of the 19th century (M.I.C. de Oliveira, 1979: 195, 199, 219, 179); this was sometimes the condition for manumitting slaves laid down in a will (*ibid.*: 210); there were often legacies by freedmen to their former masters, or by patrons to their former slaves (*ibid.*: 178; P. Verger, 1968: 343). There was even a transitivity of the patron's rights and duties. Kiernan (1976: 148) recalls the case of a manumitted black woman from Paraty, Vicência Maria, who, when freeing an African girl, Rosa, in 1814, declared that Rosa owed allegiance and services to Felizarda Maria Espírito Santo, who had freed her, Vicência Maria. On the other hand, should Vicência die before her patron, the latter was to be responsible for bringing up and taking care of Rosa, as the freed slave of her freed slave.

Another indication of what was intended for freed slaves is the famous question of the revoking of manumission for ingratitude; this was so broadly defined that it comprehended even verbal ingratitude in the absence of the patron (A. Perdigão Malheiro, 1976 (1867), Vol. I: 135, §149). It has been doubted whether such a provision was really applied, but I believe there is evidence that it was[10]. Indeed, revocation of manumission for ingratitude also only disappeared with the "Free Womb" Law in 1871. The question of ingratitude is revealing with regard to the expectations which weighed upon the freed slaves: that they should become clients and dependents. In fact, there was very often a clause in letters of so-called "free" manumission referring to a kind of temporary dependence, including services to be rendered over a number of years (K. Mattoso, 1982).

Private control of manumission was thus of crucial importance: it not only maintained the subjection of the slaves but permitted the production of dependent freedmen. It kept hope alive amonst the slaves, however small the statistical probability of attaining freedom[11], and it was an incentive to saving and to the adoption of a work ethic; but it also subordinated freedom to personal relations with the master. For the freedmen, it gave access to the status of dependents, while maintaining the bonds of gratitude and personal debt in return for the patron's protection. Perdigão Malheiro was indeed right, therefore, when he said that the legal right to buy manumission without the master's acquiescence would subvert subjection by weakening the ties between masters and slaves (see quote above).

The policy of subjecting freedmen was not entirely successful: throughout the century there persisted an endemic situation of conflict between slaveowners and dependents. The Frenchman Tollenare speaks of sugar-mill owners in Pernambuco who tremble with fear of their tenants, and of one such owner who dare not journey more than a quarter of a league away from the manor house for fear of them (L.F. Tollenare, 1956 (1818): 96). There are records of conflicts in 1858 between the Baron of Piabanha and his dependents in the coffee-producing Vale do Paraíba (E. Viotti, 1966: 29-30). In the seventies, an official verdict stresses the latent or explicit antagonism of the sugar-mill owner towards his tenants or dependents (J. Nabuco, 1883: 111).

Even more eloquent concerning the imperfections of the policy of constituting a dependent labour force are the eternal complaints of the landowners about the "vagabondage" of the freedmen.

The system may not have been perfect, but neither was it totally unworkable. In alliance with an official policy of suspicion towards freed blacks, and even more so towards freed Africans (see M.C. da Cunha, 1983, ms), it succeeded in realising the settlement of significant contingents of dependents on the big properties. In this early 19th century Brazil, a black, and above all an African with a recognizable accent and ethnic facial marks, had to prove he was no slave to be considered free. For fear of being enslaved again, many freed blacks either settled near the plantations where they had been slaves and where they were at least known to have been manumitted, or went to live with runaway slaves in the *quilombos*. Many freed mulattoes, on the contrary, often preferred to try to pass themselves off in distant regions as *ingênuos*, i.e. as freeborn men (H. Koster, 1816: 440; M.S. de Carvalho Franco, 1974 (1969): 95).

Within this configuration of a State gradually strengthening its hand and acquiring its own means of control, subjected on one hand to direct pressure from the British, who wished to have the slave trade stopped and slavery abolished, and on the other to its real links with the big plantation owners, it is possible to reach a political understanding of the silence of the law. The tacit division of the labour of controlling the "dangerous classes" between State and slaveowners was subverted when manumission, one of the chief devices to ensure private control, became a right inscribed in the law after 1871. This was in fact the landowners' point of view at the time. In this same year of 1871, in two coffee-producing localities, Rio Claro and Campinas, the landowners and tradesmen requested permanent military garrisons to control the slaves (W. Dean, 1977: 125-6).

Until 1871, customary law and positive legislation seem not so much to have been in conflict as to have carved out distinct domains for themselves. The law was written in universalistic terms following the 1830 reform — but its essential domain in reality was that of the humble freemen, the "lower orders". It is they who filled the legal records and it is for them that the courts were chiefly important (P. Aufderheide, 1976: 209-10, *et passim*).

Yet there were two further strata: those above the law and those beneath it. Slaves, free and freed blacks and rich men all appeared before the courts in distinctly lower proportions than their weight in the total population would lead one to expect (P. Aufderheide, 1976: 212 ff.). Both for those who were beneath the law and for those beyond its reach, it was customary law that prevailed, characterised by the lack of formal institutions to sustain it.

But the silence of the law, along with its political function, also had roots in ideology. At its most abstract levels, from the Constitution to the Codes, the law of the Empire had to coexist with the contradiction of using the language of liberalism to describe the rules of a slaveowning society based on personal dependence[12]. The solution lay in the generous use of ample silences. The Imperial Constitution of 1824 is silent even on the very existence of slaves. The Criminal Code of 1830, in which it was endeavoured to make punishments impersonal, by suiting them exclusively to the offences committed, mentions slaves in two articles. It distinguishes them from freemen only in order to state that imprisonment with forced labour is not applicable to slaves — it would have been redundant (Art. 60 and Art. 311). Thus, in the endeavour to attain universalised abstraction, what was finally abstracted was a fundamental part of the population. Other countries opted for separate codes for citizens and slaves. Brazil preferred silence.

The use of these silences was foreseeable. Two examples: the advocates of the exclusive right of masters to manumit their slaves recalled, as seen above, that any legislation sanctioning the opposite would jeopardise the right to property. They argued that the silence of the law showed that exceptions had not been made in favour of that article of property, the slave. On the other hand, Article 179 of the Constitution (§19) had abolished punishment by whipping (without qualification). In this case, however, Perdigão Malheiro explains it was *implicitly* understood that this applied to all "*except to slaves*: for which reason we find it applied only to slaves in the Penal Code" (A. Perdigão Malheiro, 1976 (1867), Vol. I: 41 —emphasis in the original). In fact, whippings for slaves were only abolished in 1886 by a special law (Lei de 15 de outubro de 1886, *Colleção de Leis do Império do Brasil*).

Silence was thus the domain of customary law, of what was really done in practice. But is it true to say that the legislation was a fictitious framework by which society was not regulated? This is what the authors I have referred to imply or affirm. Their keynote is the unsuitability of a false language superimposed on a reality which it is intended to hide. Oliveira Vianna, for example, takes the liberal legislation to task for being suited, he argues, to future generations rather than to the real Brazil. And he suggests the adjustment of Brazilian social reality to its written Code, by making customary law into written legislation (F.J. Oliveira Vianna, 1974 (1949)).

But what I ask is this: would such an adjustment be possible? In other words, was there not a need for this silenced law? Was the other, written, law really false? And adjustment to what? For, after all, the adjustment would have to be twofold: to a country inserted in world capitalism and speaking the common liberal language of the system in which it gravitated and in which the elites understood each other; and to a country which internally organised its production on the basis of a slave system and of personal domination. There is no way to choose which is more real. This duplicity is an essence, and the coexistence of customary law and written law as codes which do not merge seems, on the contrary, to be well suited to the reality of the country's peripheral position. What would be unsuitable would be a system of common law which was continually being adjusted to society and its customs.

The written laws are the way in which the State represents its own authority and competence to itself: they are a self-description. Customary law is an alternative description. The true society of 19th century Brazil is this complex of written and unwritten laws which do not intersect, one affirming relations without privilege between equivalent citizens, the other dealing with private relations of dependence and power. They coexist without hindrance because, as allies, they carve out basically distinct fields of application for themselves: the law, essentially, is for the free poor; customary law is for the powerful, their slaves and their dependent clients. The former is also the external face — international, but not necessarily false — of a system which, domestically, is something else.

Notes

1. From A. Perdigão Malheiro, 1976 (1867), Vol. II, pp. 81, 226-8, 232, 247-8, 256.
2. This was the period when the 1830 Criminal Code was drafted and promulgated; it was the most radical of the Codes introduced under the Empire.
3. Perdigão Malheiro is thus mistaken when he takes this specific privilege granted to a given brotherhood of a particular church in Lisbon for a general rule applicable to any brotherhood of São Benedito (A. Perdigão Malheiro, 1976 (1867), Vol. I: 38, 99).
4. Slaves were incompetent in civil law, and their natural guardians were their own masters (A. Perdigão Malheiro, 1976 (1867), Vol. I: 22, 24, 62).
5. Perdigão Malheiro notes that there were provisions on this subject which appeared to be contradictory (A. Perdigão Malheiro, *ibid.*: 46, footnote 96).
6. The career judges were, during the whole Imperial period, a crucial political link between central government and those who wielded power locally (Th. Flory, 1975). Thus, it was not, as some have argued, simply owing to their class position that they refrained from convicting slaveowners, but owing to their specific political function.
7. These slaves were sent out to work in the streets or hired to others, in order to bring in a money income to their masters.
8. The local authorities were equally unaccountable. In 1837, there was an attempt to oblige the *Juiz de Direito*, also the Chief of Police, to refrain from having slaves summarily whipped, but to give them a proper trial first, after hearing their masters. After a mere 4 months, however, a new Notice cancelled the first and repealed the measures announced in it (Aviso 284 de 10.6.1837/495 de 3.10.1837 in *Colleção das Leis do Império do Brasil*).
9. A document from Bahia dated 1827 mentions that of 271 deserters from the regular troops, 222 were free non-whites (list of deserters by Manuel Alexandrino Machado, July 28 1827, *apud* F.W.O. Morton, 1975: 258).

10. Perdigão Malheiro (1976 (1867), Vol. I: 135) refers to the decisions of the Imperial courts which applied this law. Russell-Wood (1972: 91-2) cites the case of the manumitted slave of the Carmo Convent in Salvador who, in 1795, was sentenced to be enslaved anew for disobeying and slandering his former masters, and was said to have "incurred the legal penalty for ingratitude towards the granting of freedom". Another revocation of freedom for ingratitude is recorded to have occurred at Apiaí, São Paulo Province, early in the 19th century (V.W.F. Daglione, 1968/9: 133).
11. For the 1870s, but with results which he believes to be relevant also to the preceding decades, R. Slenes calculates that the statistical expectation of a 10-year-old slave of being alive and free at the age of 40 was 3.8%, and at the age of 60, 3.9%. In other words, the percentage of slaves who survived the original group of 10-year-olds and would be free by the age of 40 was 6.5%, and by 60, 14.7% (R. Slenes, 1976: 491).
12. This subject has been dealt with by a number of Brazilian authors, from Oliveira Vianna in 1920 to Roberto Schwartz in 1973.

Bibliography

Amaral, Braz do (1957) *História da Independência da Bahia*, Salvador: Livraria Progresso editora.

Almeida, Cândido Mendes de (1870) *Codigo Philippino ou ordenações e leis do Reino de Portugal*, Rio de Janeiro: tipografia do Instituto Philomathico.

Araujo, José P. Nabuco de (1836-1844) *Legislação Brazileira ou Colleção Chronologica das Leis, Decretos, Resoluções de Consulta, Provisões, etc. etc. do Império do Brazil desde o anno de 1808 até 1831*, Rio de Janeiro, 7 vols.

Aufderheide, Patricia (1976) *Order and violence: social deviance and social control in Brazil 1780-1840.* Unpublished Ph.D. dissertation.

Balbi, Adrien (1822) *Essai statistique sur le royaume de Portugal et d'Algarve, comparé aux autres états de l'Europe,* Paris: Rey et Gravier, 2 vols.

Benci, Jorge, SJ (1977 (1700)) *A economia cristã dos senhores no gogerno dos escravos*, Sãn Paulo: ed. Grijalbo.

Bruno, Fábio Vieira, ed. (1979) *O Parlamento e a Evolução Nacional. 1871-1889* (3a série), Brasília: Senado Federal, vol.1.

Cunha, Manuela Carneiro da (1983) *Libertos, um programa de sujeicão*, ms.

Daglione, Vivaldo W.F. (1968-9) "A Lībertação dos escravos no Brasil através de alguns documentos" *Anais de História* **1**: 131-134. Assis.

Dean, Warren (1977) *Rio Claro. Um sistema brasileiro de grande lavoura, 1820-1920*, Rio de Janeiro: Paz e Terra.

Eisenberg, Peter (1977) *Modernização sem musdança. A indústria açucareira em Pernambuco 1840-1910*, Rio de Janeiro: Paz e Terra e Unicamp.

Elkins, Stanley M. (1959) *Slavery: a problem in American institutional and intellectual life*, Chicago: University Press.

Ewbank, Thomas (1856) *Life in Brazil*, New York: Harper.

Flory, Thomas (1975) "Judicial Politics in nineteenth-century Brazil" *Hispanic American Historical Review* **55**.4: 665-692.

Franco, Maria Sylvia de Carvalho (1969) *Homens livres na ordem escravocrata*, São Paulo: IEB.

Galliza, Diana Soares (1979) *O declínio da escravidão na Paraíba 1850-1888*, João Pessoa: Editora Universitaria, Un. Fed. da Paraíba.

Goulart, José Alípio (1971) *Da palmatória ao patíbulo*, Rio de Janeiro: ed. Conquista.

Johnston, Sir Harry Hamilton (1969 (1910)) *The negro in the New World*, New York and London: Johnson Reprint Corp.

Kidder, D.P. and Fletcher, J.C. (1857) *Brazil and the Brazilians*, New York: Childs and Peterson.

Kiernan, James Patrick (1977) *The manumission of slaves in colonial Brazil: Paraty 1789-1822*, Unpublished Ph.D. dissertation, Xerox Microfilms.

Koster, Henry (1816) *Travels in Brazil*, London: Longman & co.

Malheiro, Agostinho Perdigão (1976 (1867)) *A escravidão no Brasil*, Rio de Janeiro: Vozes, 2 vols.

Mattoso, Kátia de Queirós (1979) "Testamentos de escravos libertos na Bahia do século XIX",

Centro de estudos Baianos. *Publ. da Univ. federal da Bahia* No. 85, 53 pp.
Mattoso, Kátia (1982) *Ser escravo no Brasil*, São Paulo: Brasiliense.
Morton, F.W.O. (1975) "The military and society in Brazil, 1800-1824" *Journal of Latin American Studies* 7.2:249-279.
Nabuco, Joaquim (1883) *O abolicionismo*, London: Kingdon.
Oliveira, Maria Inês Côrtes de (1979) *O liberto: o seu mundo e os outros (Salvador 1790/1890)*, dissertação de mestrado, Univ. da Bahia, ms.
Prado Jr., Caio (1963) *Evolução Política do Brasil e outros ensaios*, São Paulo: ed. Brasiliense.
Rodrigues, A. Nina (1976) *Os africanos no Brasil*, Col. Brasiliana. São Paulo: Cia Editora Nacional.
Russell-Wood, A.J.R. (1972) "Colonial Brazil" in D.W. Cohen and J.P. Green, eds, *Neither Slave nor Free: the freedmen of African descent in the Slave Societies of the New World*, Baltimore: Johns Hopkins University Press.
Russell-Wood, A.J.R. (1974) "Black and mulatto brotherhoods in Colonial Brazil: a study in collective behavior" *Hispanic American Historical Review* **54**.4: 567-602.
Scarano, Julita (1976) *Devoção e Escravidão*, Col. Brasiliana 357. São Paulo: Cia Editora Nacional.
Schwartz, Stuart B. (1974) "The manumission of slaves in colonial Bahia, 1684-1745" *Hispanic American Historical Review*: **54**.4: 603-635.
Schwarz, Roberto (1973) "As ideias fora do lugar" *Estudos Cebrap* 3: 151-161.
Tannenbaum, Frank (1963 (1947)) *Slave and Citizen: the negro in the Americas*, New York: Vintage Books.
Seidler, Carl (1980 (1835)) *Dez anos no Brasil*, São Paulo: Itatiaia e EDUSP.
Silva, José Justino de Andrade e (1854-9) *Colleção chronológica da legislação portuguesa, compilada e annotada*, 10 vols, Lisboa: Silva.
Slenes, Robert (1976) *The demography and economics of Brazilian slavery: 1850-1888.* Unpublished Ph.D. dissertation.
Southey, Robert (1810-19) *History of Brazil*, 3 vols, London: Longman a.o.
Stein, Stanley (1957) *Vassouras: a Brazilian coffee county, 1850-1900*, Harvard Historical Studies, 69, Cambridge, Mass.
Tollenare, Louis François (1956 (1818)) *Notas Dominicais tomadas durante uma viagem em Portugal e no Brasil em 1816, 1817 e 1818*, Recife: Livraria Progresso Editora.
Verger, Pierre (1968) *Flux et reflux de la traite des esclaves entre le golfe du Bénin et Bahia de tous les Saints*, Paris-La Haye: Mouton.
Vianna, Francisco José Oliveira (1973 (1920)) *Populações meridionais de Brasil*, vol. I, Rio de Janeiro: Paz e Terra.
Vianna, Francisco José Oliveira (1974 (1949)) *Instituições políticas brasileiras*, Rio de Janeiro: Record.
Viotti, Emilia (1966) *Da Senzala à colônia*, Corpo e Alma do Brasil, São Paulo: Cia Editora Nacional.

Islamic law and the social context of exchange in the medieval Middle East

A. UDOVITCH

Princeton University

Islamic law purports to be unchanging and valid throughout the Islamic world. Nevertheless, a close examination of the medieval Islamic law of sale shows that the concept of local knowledge plays a considerable part in it. On the one hand, the distinction between legitimate exchange and usury depends on the adequacy of the information available to the purchaser of goods or services; on the other hand, this stress on information leads to insistence that transactions must conform to the local custom of the merchants. Local custom thus comes in, as one might say, through a side door as a source of law, without being explicitly recognised as such.

IN A RECENTLY published study on the anthropology of law entitled: "Local Knowledge: Fact and Law in Comparative Perspective," Clifford Geertz characterised both law and ethnography as "crafts of place" that "work by the light of local knowledge".[1] It is not easy to summarise Geertz's enterprise which, in spite of the 'local' in the title, casts a very wide comparative and interpretive net. As always with Geertz, his purpose is not to ferret out commonalities nor to construct an encompassing conceptual framework in which law from different societies can cohabit peacefully; it is, rather, to highlight differences. What is a fact and how does it relate to the construct of the imagination which we call law? This is the precise question Geertz explores. The very different ways in which these components of legal sensibility interact in Malaysia, in Indic Bali or in Islamic Morocco become accessible and comprehensible only in the light of their respective local knowledge.

For medieval Islamic law, especially those segments concerned with economic exchange, this term is particularly felicitous. The notion of "local knowledge" permeates some of its major institutions and is built into its very structure and formulation.

Paradoxically, or maybe not so paradoxically, the simple external (*zahir*) meaning of these texts obscures their local, embedded character. There are

History and Anthropology, 1985
Vol. 1, pp. 445-465
0275-7206/85/0102-0445 $18.50/0

several reasons for this. The most important is that classical Islamic law sees itself as the expression of a universally valid system of law, one whose inspiration, origins and, one might even say, ultimate authorship go back to God. And although God may be local as well, He is first and foremost — at least in a monotheistic system — universal in character. Another reason for obscuring the "local knowledge" in Islamic law is its historical genealogy. No matter how inspired it was by God, it was not created *ex nihilo* in a historical vacuum. Its formulations, forms and substance were much affected by the legal traditions of the world in which Islam made its appearance. Thus Roman law, rabbinic law and canon law all left their imprint on the *sharīʿah*, not necessarily as direct influences but rather as bodies of law which provided a vocabulary, an idiom and an ambiance for the growth of Islamic law.[2]

The point of this paper will be to read beyond the surface meaning of some representative medieval Islamic legal texts dealing with the law of sale and economic exchange in an attempt to uncover its "local knowledge," its assumptions about social and economic life which alone give its operations meaning and vitality. It is also through "local knowledge" and its associated notions that one can perhaps situate Islamic law with respect to a number of theoretical issues of concern to historians and anthropologists of law.

SOME METHODOLOGICAL CONSIDERATIONS

To treat any historical problem from an anthropological perspective presupposes the existence of sources, or some body of data which roughly corresponds in character to the information present day anthropologists compile in the course of their fieldwork. At the risk of oversimplification, this means access to written material, archives or artefacts which reflect actual behaviour and practice permitting one to get behind external forms to actual systems of social relations or systems of meaning of any given society. In the case of the historical study of law, this would mean the availability of court records or firsthand descriptions of some facet of the legal system which would allow us to know the practice of the law as opposed only to its theory. Codes of law would not, at first sight, seem to constitute an adequate source for an enterprise of this kind. One might thus legitimately question the propriety of undertaking an anthropologically oriented study based on early Islamic law, that is on the law produced by Muslim scholars in the Middle East during the medieval period. What we have of early Islamic law are large numbers of law books giving us the theory, the ideal construct of positive Islamic law. What we do not have for this period, or have precious little of, are records or detailed accounts of actual court proceedings of what Weber, in a very different context and with a very different purpose in mind, called "qadi justice."

Medieval Islamic law, in Arabic *sharīʿah*, is actually a system of religious law created by Islamic religious scholars. Orthodox Muslims consider its principles and positive content to derive from several divine or quasi-divine sources: from the Qur'an, the revealed word of God to His ultimate prophet Muhammad, and from a body of oral traditions describing the actions, behavior and declarations of the prophet (the *sunnah* or *hadith*). These are, in turn, elaborated by the hermeneutic techniques of analogy (*qiyas*), and reason (*ra'y*) and the social technique of consensus (*ijmaᶜ*).

Islamic law thus saw itself as an extension of the word of God, as a system of conduct in matters ritual, social, economic and personal, by adhering to which any individual would ensure himself a favorable outcome on the Day of Judgment. This ideal character of Islamic law led generations of scholars to question the propriety of using medieval Islamic legal sources for the purpose of reconstructing social history and social practice. This is not the place to enter into this debate. Suffice it to say that in the past two decades attempts to exploit this vast body of medieval legal literature, dating from the 9th century onward, for understanding the social and economic institutions of the medieval Islamic world have yielded valuable results. However, though Islamic religious law takes all of human behavior within its purview, not every domain of Islamic religious legal literature is equally relevant for actual practice and, consequently, equally valuable for the historian and social scientist. The sections on ritual, on the law of personal status and on commercial law have proved particularly rich for reconstructing otherwise poorly documented aspects of social life.

Islamic legal scholars have been producing compendia of religious law since the 9th century. Each successive generation of legal experts has produced commentaries, reformulations or elaborations of the early compendia. Contrary to prevailing scholarly opinion, their subsequent restatements are not, in most cases, mere repetitions. While the enunciation of positive religious law remains, because of its partially divine derivation, essentially, although not entirely, the same, the justifications and explanations of these legal requirements and rules and, at times, even their adaptations to new realities were not the same from one generation to another nor were these subsequent discussions — especially with respect to commercial law — based strictly on narrow, legal, religious reasoning. What we frequently find are commentaries which, in addition to their religious considerations, are practically oriented, one might even say functional in their interpretations. And, the ensemble of these functional-type statements and commentaries frequently offers us insights on social concerns and social relations which are otherwise denied us.[3]

For the purpose of this study, I have relied primarily upon two 11th century handbooks of the Hanafi school of Islamic law. This school originated in Iraq and spread from there throughout the Fertile Crescent and to many other parts of the Islamic world. The first is the *Mukhtasar* (Abridgement) of Ahmad

b. Muhammad Al-Quduri (d. 1037), a concise summary of Hanafi law which subsequently became one of this school's standard handbooks. The very fact that it is concise and selects only the main points of the law highlights many of its extra-legal concerns. The second is the *Book of Sale* (*Kitab al-bay*ᶜ) from the *Mabsut* of Shams al-Din as-Sarakhsi (d. 1090) written about a half-century later. The *Mabsut* is one of the most remarkable works of classical Islamic law. In this 30-volume compendium of Hanafi law, the author, a brilliant exponent of legal-religious reasoning, often attempts to highlight the internal social and practical logic of the institutions of Islamic law.

Ideally, one should present here a translation of one of these texts, followed by a commentary on its social meaning as well as comparisons with whatever examples and evidence of actual medieval Islamic market behaviour we possess. An article of this nature does not allow for this kind of elaborate exposition. What I propose to do, therefore, is present a brief summary of the law of sale, following Quduri, and then to focus on some of its characteristic features which permits us to recover the assumptions about social relations on which they are based. By drawing on contemporary documentary material and on ethnographic studies of traditional markets of the Islamic world, I will try to reconstruct the social matrix of market exchange.

THE ISLAMIC LAW OF SALE

Construed in its narrowest sense, sale is one of a fairly large number of contracts in the general domain of what in Islamic law is called *mu*ᶜ*amalat* — a term which can be translated as commercial relations or simply as transactions. The Arabic word ᶜ*aqd*, meaning contract, is used in Islamic law; but contract does not constitute a category of law as it does, for example, in other legal systems. The category of legal connections which comprehends most forms of contract is designated as *mu*ᶜ*amalat*, a term which linguistically and grammatically denotes interaction, mutuality and movement in reciprocal directions, thus anticipating on the linguistic level the style of exchange as conceived by Islamic law. In addition to sale, other contracts in this category to which Islamic law devotes separate chapters are hire (*ijara*), partnership (*sharika*) and commenda (*qirad/mudaraba*). As one of the recognised Islamic contracts of obligation, sale shares certain general features with all the others.

Sale is a bilateral transaction which is concluded and made binding by offer (*ijab*) and acceptance (*qabul*). To be licit under Islamic religious law, the transaction cannot involve any arrangement which can be construed as unjustified enrichment; that is, no party to the contract can obtain any advantage without giving some countervalue. This notion of unjustified enrichment is one of the basic features of the Islamic concept of usury (*riba*), any trace of which is thoroughly and consistently excluded from any transaction under Islamic law. In sale, as in other contracts of obligation, Islamic law insists on clarity with respect to the object of the contract as well as the obligations undertaken by each party. Ignorance concerning any of these elements could lead to violating the prohibition against *riba*, as well as to many other undesirable consequences. I shall elaborate on this point at some length presently.

Any person with legal capacity can be a party to a sale or exchange. This excludes minors, individuals with diminished mental or physical capacities and slaves acting without their master's permission. Any licit commodity can be the object of a sale. For a Muslim, this excludes such items as idols, drugs, wine and impure foods and for all parties to a sale it excludes property in the public domain, property belonging to someone else, runaway slaves and the like.

Sale is conceived broadly as an exchange of goods and therefore also includes barter within its purview. Even after a sale is concluded, Islamic law, under certain circumstances, allows for the right of rescission, that is, the ability to cancel or to confirm the exchange unilaterally. For example, the discovery of a defect in the merchandise, i.e., anything that would cause a reduction in its commercial value, is automatically a basis for annulling the transaction. Other bases for rescission are discussed below.

In addition to what we might call "normal" sale — the simultaneous exchange of goods for money, or for other goods at a negotiated price — Islamic law treats in some detail several specific variations of sale. Most prominent among these are the *salam* contract, the ordering of goods to be delivered at a later date for a price paid immediately, and the *murabaha*, the resale of goods with a fixed surcharge above the stated cost, the surcharge in this case representing the seller's profit. In the legal discussions of both of these and of related forms of sale, the chief consideration is the prevention of any conduct which could lead to unjustified enrichment and which might violate either the prohibition against *riba* (usury) or the rules of honest and fair market exchange.[4]

SOCIAL COMPONENTS OF THE LAW OF SALE

Exchange was conceived as a social as well as an economic transaction. The first and indispensable condition for a valid sale, offer and acceptance, presupposes a face to face encounter of some duration. Some early legal authorities even speak of a physical gesture — the *safqa*, a handshake or handslap — which was to accompany the conclusion of a bargain. No specific, single formula is required to express either offer or acceptance. The exchange is not viewed as either formulaic or ritualised. Any number of words, verbs or phrases and even gestures can effectuate a valid exchange as long as their meaning is clear and unequivocal. That this confrontation between exchange partners is not viewed as impersonal or simply pro-forma is confirmed by the notion of *majlis* — a session or seance. The exchange takes place in the course of a meeting, a *majlis*, and is not complete or irrevocable until one of the parties gets up to leave. Even after the offer and acceptance have been duly pronounced, either party still has the option (Arabic *khiyar*) to withdraw from the bargain if the session has not been concluded. This 'option of the seance', *khiyar al-majlis*, is one of a number of such conditions affecting the finality of a sale or transaction. Other possible options include the customer's right to inspect the object of the sale (*khiyar ar ruᶜya*), the right to return it in case of a defect (*khiyar al-ᶜayb*), and the right, if both parties agree, to a three day period in which either party can decide either to finalise or to annul the transaction.

An exchange of words, and sometimes of gestures, precedes the actual exchange of goods. Even though, in the theory of Islamic religious law, some exchange was possible without direct, personal and verbal contact, the model and paradigm for a transaction is the *majlis*, the personal confrontation and face-to-face seance. It is as if the physical presence of both parties and their words not only confer validity on the exchange but also somehow guarantee its reliability, honesty and quality. As we shall see, this element of personal guarantee and oral testimony is suffused throughout Islamic legal and exchange practices.

To be sure, not every exchange in the medieval Near Eastern marketplace entailed these prolonged transactions. This would have been too cumbersome a procedure even for the fragmented traditional bazaar and would have unbearably slowed up the pace of commercial life. That the *majlis* and face-to-face contact nevertheless remained the legal model for market exchanges suggests that these took place in conditions or in an ambiance which preserved the essential features of the *majlis*. So for example, if, as is very likely, exchange was not random but took place between habitual, regular (although not necessarily exclusive) trading partners, this in effect could take the place of the *majlis*; under such circumstances, parties to any transaction would presumably have sufficient acquaintance and familiarity with each other and with the market to assure the reliability and durability of the exchange. On the one hand, the law assumed that such a familiarity between trading partners existed, and on the other, it insisted on the creation of a minimal familiarity by means of the *majlis* and the various forms of option in order to protect those who might be outside the system.

What information we do possess on the actual operation of medieval Islamic commerce and the marketplace (mostly from the Cairo Geniza documents) confirms that exchange operated within the framework of established, fairly stable networks in which people's knowledge of each other or of each other's friends and relatives guaranteed the flow of goods, cash and credit. Ethnographers who have studied traditional markets in different parts of the Islamic world have described and analysed the same phenomenon.[5]

While Islamic law assumes a social situation in the marketplace in which people know something about each other, it does not explicitly require such knowledge. However, it does insist very prominently and consistently on clear and detailed knowledge concerning virtually every other aspect of the transaction.

INFORMATION AND EXCHANGE

One can dip into a medieval Islamic text discussing the law of sale almost at random and be sure of finding reasoning which insists that one or another aspect of the transaction must be clearly known (*maᶜruf*) for the transaction to be valid or, conversely, a statement that some exchange is excluded because one of its essential elements is unknown (*majhul*), and ignorance (*jahala*) in such matters leads to disputes, discord and inequity.

This compulsion for "knowing" and this abhorrence of "ignorance" in economic exchange is both a requirement of Islamic law, an inherent principle emerging from its inner dynamic, and a reflection of the day-to-day transactions in the marketplace. That is, it is a reflection and a recognition that in the marketplace, as Geertz observes for Sefrou in the past half century, it is not only goods which are being exchanged but also information. Thus, in the traditional Islamic market, both the acquisition and the withholding of information could be advantageous in exchange, instrumental in making a good deal and in achieving profit.[6]

One could argue that this is true in almost any exchange situation — East, West, North or South. Information can be translated into economic gain, just as lack of information can submit one to economic peril. But in the setting of the Islamic market as reflected in the law texts and as seen from other documents, the role of information and knowledge was more than simply functional in terms of accomplishing economic goals; it was intertwined with the process of exchange itself. In Islamic commercial law generally, and in the law of sale in particular, the insistence on local knowledge, the abhorrence of local ignorance and the concern for the protection of the locally ignorant correspond to the two fundamental categories which, from a legal and religious point of view, structure the field of economic exchange: *tijara* = trade = licit exchange; and *riba* = usury =unfair gain = ignorance on the part of one or both of the parties to the exchange.

One particular form of exchange to which Islamic law books devote a great deal of attention is the *salam* — a sale which involves immediate payment in return for the future delivery of a given commodity. This arrangement was a source of considerable uneasiness for medieval Islamic lawyers as it involved the transfer of an object or product which was "absent" (*maᶜdum*) and which was not even yet owned by the seller. By skillful interpretation of Qur'anic verses and prophetic traditions as well as on the basis of customary practice and economic necessity, this form of exchange is declared licit. But according to Sarakhsi who bases himself on a statement of Abu Hanifa, the founder of the Hanafi school of Islamic law, the following seven conditions must be fulfilled for a valid *salam* exchange:

Information concerning the category/species (*jins*) of the commodity to be delivered; information concerning its type/variety (*nawᶜ*); information concerned its quantity (*qadr*); information concerning its quality (*sifa*), information concerning the time period (*ajl*) within which it will be delivered; information concerning the place (*makan*) at which it will be delivered including the cost of transportation and incidental expenses; and information concerning the exact sum of money (*ra's al-mal*) which is the counterpart of the quantity of goods to be delivered. The basis for these stipulations is the tradition relating that the messenger of God, may God preserve him and pray for him, instructed that the quantity (of money and goods) be made known, since the absence of this information can lead to disputes which prevent the seller from delivering the goods and receiving payment. This proves that any element of ignorance (*jahala*) which can prevent the consummation of the transaction must be replaced by information.[7]

Sarakhsi concludes this particular discussion by pointing out that accurate and full information is necessary not only to avoid discord but

because the goal of this contract is the achievement of profit and the latter cannot be known except through a knowledge of the precise amount of the market value (of the goods being exchanged) and the market value varies with the variation of the category, type, quality and quantity (of the goods). There must be information on all these aspects in order to achieve the goal of each party (to the transaction).[8]

Sarakhsi's justification for requiring so much information is cast in rational, functional terms. His contention is simple and persuasive: the more that is known about any transaction, the less likely any social discord and the more likely a satisfactory, profitable outcome for all the parties concerned. Nevertheless, this functional interpretation, interesting as it may be in its own terms, is not by itself sufficient to explain the insistence of Islamic law, not only in the *salam* contract, but for all contracts of economic exchange and association, on a maximum of precise information.

In the institutions of Islamic commercial law, the preoccupation with knowledge and information and the presumption that these are, or should be, accessible to most of the actors in the marketplace are expressed on different levels. On the most obvious, one might say literal level, as in the cases discussed on the preceding pages, we encounter the insistence that the object and terms of the exchange be spelled out as clearly as possible. However, there is also a level on which local knowledge is built into the very credibility and viability of certain sanctioned forms of exchange. Most prominent among these is the *murabaha* or fixed profit sale.

Islamic law discusses in great detail three forms of sale which have as their starting point the cost of the sale object to the seller. These are: the *tawliya*, resale at the stated original cost with no profit or loss to the seller; the *wadīʿa*, resale at a discount from the original cost; and the *murabaha* which receives the most detailed — almost exclusive — attention of the Islamic lawyers and which was undoubtedly the most widespread in actual commercial practice.

In any system recognizing the legitimacy of the profit motive in a comparatively free and open market — as was generally the case in the medieval Islamic world — the entire notion of the *murabaha* seems somewhat unreal and illogical. It does seem a bit odd for the seller to have to guarantee to the buyer — or even to offer him any information concerning — the cost of a commodity, and to make the accuracy of this information a condition of the validity of the exchange. It is no wonder, then, that as eminent an authority as Joseph Schacht expressed his perplexity at the exact economic function these institutions, especially the *murabaha*, fulfilled in trade.[9]

The medieval legal texts themselves suggest that the purpose of these arrangements was prophylactic, intended to protect the innocent general consumer lacking expertise in the various items of trade from the wiles and stratagems of sharp traders. By basing the sale price on the original cost of the item to the seller, the customer was provided with a modicum of protection against unfair exploitation.[10]

How was this to be achieved? By providing clear, honest and unambiguous information concerning the transaction. As Sarakhsi puts it:

> Since the *murabaha* sale is an exchange based on trust, any hint of suspicion or dishonesty must be excluded, and (the seller) must be wary of using any falsehood or equivocal speech which conduces to vagueness. It is not permitted to employ such language in concluding a *murabaha* transaction.[11]

The chief concern was to avoid any fraud on the part of the seller by setting out detailed guidelines regarding the considerations that are to enter into determining the cost of any item. Foremost among these, of course, is the price paid by the seller for the goods in question. A variety of expenses connected with the maintenance, improvement and transport of the goods may be included in the cost which forms the basis for the *murabaha* sale. As a basis for determining what to include in the cost price, Islamic religious law had recourse to "the custom of the merchants." The general rule emerging from the numerous cases discussed is that money expended directly on the goods, or on services indispensable to their sale (e.g., brokerage fees) may be included, whereas the personal expenses of the merchant and other expenses not directly involved with the goods are not to be figured into the stated original cost on which the *murabaha* transaction is based. As an additional protection to the customer, the law books insist that the seller avoid any misleading statements. He must be scrupulous over the designation of the sum serving as the basis of the *murabaha*. If he includes various additional expenses in this sum, he may not, directly or indirectly, lead the buyer to believe that the *murabaha* is based solely on the purchase price, but must use some expression indicating that this is what it cost him and not that this is what he paid for it. So Sarakhsi:

If the seller bought some cloth, he is allowed to include in the base price whatever he spent on having it sewn and on transportation. But, he must say: 'this is what it cost me,' and he must not say, 'I bought it for this amount,' for the latter would be false. In a *murabaha* transaction, the custom of the merchants (*ᶜurf at-tujjar*) is taken into account. Whatever this customary practice allows as an addition to the cost can be added by the merchant; whatever is excluded, he is to exclude as well.[12]

Whatever its role in commerce and exchange, and the evidence from documents and from legal sources suggests a multiplicity of roles including that of a commission sale, the first question to be confronted is: How was it possible for this form of transaction to be practised at all? To the extent that merchants kept written accounts, these were neither very orderly nor were they open to inspection by customers. Thus, there was no possible formal way in which a buyer could verify the cost of goods being purchased or the accuracy of the seller's assertions. In any case, procedures of this kind are virtually inconceivable in the conditions of a traditional Near Eastern market in which almost all transactions, including those of fairly large volume, were concluded orally even when credit arrangements were involved. Fixed profit sales, i.e., *murabaha* exchanges, were possible along the general lines indicated in Islamic law books because of the economic and social structure of the markets. Markets, even in large cities, were of relatively small size, the trade in any given commodity was usually concentrated in one small section of the market and the exchange partners constituted a fairly regular, stable network of individuals. Most significantly, as far as the *murabaha* was concerned, the current prices of the most important commodities were known and disseminated. From the documents of the Cairo Geniza, dating from the 11th and 12th centuries, we now know that on trading days the price level of major commodities was informally established periodically and announced throughout the market. And while commodities in a given category did not necessarily all trade for the identical price, transactions varied within a comparatively small percentage range. In addition to the announced price levels, merchants avidly accumulated information about prices, quantities of goods, movements of men, boats and commodities from distant places through travellers, couriers and correspondence. Commenting on the voluminous commercial correspondence of the 11th century Mediterranean trade from the Cairo Geniza, S.D. Goitein tells us:

We find, indeed, that the greatest concern of the writers of the writers of the Geniza letters was business intelligence. The term used for it, *akhbar*, 'information,' was identical with that of the intelligence services of the government and the police. One inquired first about prices, of course, but then also about many other things such as the volume of business, the availability of capital, the movements of ships and caravans, the arrival and departure of merchants, the general situation in a country, and the safety of communications.[13]

More than fifty percent of the content of an average business letter from the Geniza is taken up with commercial information and gossip which frequently are not directly related to the precise business between the two correspondents. Given this almost insatiable hunger for business information and its ample supply, one can understand how *murabaha* type exchanges were not only possible but also made some sense.

THE "LOCAL" COMPONENT OF LOCAL KNOWLEDGE

Islamic commercial law, as I hope we have demonstrated by now, placed a high premium on knowledge concerning the goods being exchanged and concerning the people exchanging them. For a transaction to be valid and binding, the minimum of information required was considerable. *What* must be known is spelt out clearly and in detail in the legal treatises. This information might be characterised as generic in nature, falling into well-known, recognised categories such as genre, quality, quantity, price, etc. *How* things are to be known, *how* they are to be determined and judged is frequently not clearly delineated, but is relegated by the religious lawyers without any qualms or hesitations to the domain of custom (*ᶜurf*), or to "the practice of the merchants" (*ᶜadat at-tujjar*). Large chunks of commercial conduct and the legality of many of its practical details are left unexplored and uncharted, relinquished by Islamic legal theory to the omnipresent but substantively amorphous custom and practice of the merchants.

Even such widespread traditional practices as advance payment to an artisan for the manufacture to order of clothes or other products, or the payment of an entrance fee for the privilege of using a bathhouse (*hammam*) confront rather formidable legal barriers which, surprisingly, can be surmounted only by abandoning legal theory and seeking refuge in customary practice.

If a man orders from another the manufacture of a pair of shoes, or of a headdress (*qalansuwwa*), or of a washbasin, or of a jug, or of a copper vessel, then, on the basis of legal analogy (*quiyas*), this transaction is not permissible. The reason is that the object ordered for manufacture was sold while it was non-existent and the sale of a non-existent object is not permissible. For the prophet forbade the sale of anything which is not in the seller's possession. That is, even when the object is existent but not owned by the party to the contract, its sale is prohibited; *a fortiori*, then, when the object is non-existent.

However, we declare that in this case we abandon the application of legal analogy on the basis of the fact that people conduct exchanges of this kind and that they have been transacting their business in this way from the time of the messenger of God, may God bless and keep him, until this very day without anyone gainsaying this practice. Uncontested transactions of people constitute an important source (of law). Witness the statement of the prophet, may God bless

> him and keep him: "Anything which the Muslims consider appropriate is also appropriate in the eyes of God." He, may God bless him and keep him, also said: "My people will never agree on an error."
>
> This situation is similar to the case of paying a fee for entrance into the bathhouse. This is permissible on the basis of its (continued) practice among people, even though the length of one's stay in the bathhouse and the amount of water one will use is unknown (*majhul*). The same is true when one pays a penny (*fals*) for a drink from the water carrier.[14]

This passage is a rather bold statement of the primacy of established customary practices over the requirements of legal reasoning. It is all the more surprising — and revealing — since Islamic jurisprudence does not recognise custom as a formal source (*asl*) of law, nor does it accord custom any privileged theoretical position in the development and formulation of the law. In the passage just cited the confrontation between theory and practice is stark, and theory retreats in the face of long-established practice. While this is not always the case in Islamic law, neither is it an isolated example, especially in the Hanafi version of Islamic commercial law. However, in most comparable examples of potential conflict between Islamic legal theory and actual practice, the outcome is less clear-cut than that enunciated in the case discussed by Sarakhsi and compromises of a more nuanced kind are generally proposed.

It is not only theory and custom that are in conflict in this case of *istisnaᶜ* (commissioning an object to be made to order). Two levels of knowledge and information with divergent requirements confront each other here: on the one hand, the formal, explicit aspects of commercial information which could be specifically required by the law (size, weight, duration of work, etc.), and on the other the informal, implicit personal knowledge manifested in a situation of *istisnaᶜ* in which a client commissions the manufacture to personal specifications of a product from an artisan. One might say that in this case the social realities of the marketplace are brought to the surface. They are here raised from their usual status of unspoken assumptions underlying and complementing the legal institutions of exchange to be cited as an explicit argument and justification for the validity of certain commercial practices which seem *prima facie* to conflict with legal theory.

It is in matters of practical detail that custom, and particularly local custom, is most frequently invoked as a criterion for the actual conduct of exchange. For example, yoghurt or sour milk can be the object of a *salam* sale; but the manner in which its quantity is designated — by weight or by volume — depends on "the customary practice of their region (*ᶜurf diyarihim*)."[15] When it comes to determining the manner in which the information about various aspects of exchange is to be expressed and made known, Abu Yusuf, one of the founders of the Hanafi school declares: "The criterion in all of these things is custom (*ᶜurf*)."[16]

It is not only local custom which determines the forms of exchange, but also local experts.

The buyer in a *salam* contract stipulated the future delivery of a garment of excellent quality. The seller subsequently delivered a garment which he claimed was of the stipulated quality, while the buyer claimed that it was not. The judge (or arbitrator, Arabic: *al-hakim*) should then show it to two members of this particular craft. Since he (i.e., the judge) does not, himself, have expert knowledge in this regard; and when the parties disagree, he must have recourse to those who do possess such knowledge.[17]

With respect to weights and measures, with respect to credit, to means of transportation, to appointing agents to carry out purchases or sales, to the meaning of descriptive terms when applied to certain commodities, it is custom (*ᶜurf*), the habitual practice of the merchants (*ᶜadat at-tujjar*) the usual practice of people (*al-mutaᶜarif bayna an-nas* or *taᶜamul an-nas*) or the general manner of commerce (*wajh at-tijara*) that is invoked as a final arbiter.[18] All of this might seem hardly noteworthy, and simply a common-sense way to proceed with problems of this sort. However, the numerous references to custom, to proximate people and proximate information as criteria for the validity of economic behaviour combine to form a thick, crowded web of "local knowledge" surrounding the operations of exchange in the medieval Islamic Near East.

In the case of the *murabaha*, the fixed-profit sale, not only the practical details, but the very core of the transaction is explicitly dependent on local custom. In this transaction, the crucial issue is determining the legitimate cost to the seller of any given commodity, for it is on the basis of that cost that the fixed-profit is calculated. The single most important guideline for establishing this cost, according to Hanafi law, is local, customary practice.

If a master incurred expenses in teaching his slave a craft, he cannot add this sum to the cost, since there is no explicit customary practice (*ᶜurf zahir*) in this regard. The same applies to funds expended to teach the slave Arabic poetry or singing, or for the tuition costs of teaching him the Qur'an or arithmetic. However, if there is an explicit custom on any of these matters in a given place which permits the owner to add such expenses to the cost (literally: capital, *ra's mal*), then he may indeed do so.[19]

In the theory of Sunni Islamic jurisprudence, the Qur'an, the prophetic traditions (*hadith*), the application of analogy (*qiyas*) and scholarly consensus (*ijmaᶜ*) are the four recognized sources of law. Custom is not in theory an accepted source of positive law. Yet, as should be clear from the passages just cited, in the actual elaboration of the law, especially in the Hanafi school and especially in the sphere of economic life, the resort to custom as a guide to, and as a criterion for, proper economic conduct is prominent indeed. One might risk the proposition that *de facto*, if not *de jure*, custom constituted a source for Islamic commercial law. And, if the opposition of *maᶜruf*, known and therefore valid, to *majhul*, unknown and therefore invalid, highlighted the importance of knowledge and information in the Islamic law of exchange, the frequent recourse to *ᶜurf* and *ᶜada*, custom and usage, highlights the importance of the local component of this knowledge.

In a system of religious law such as that of Islam, it is rather remarkable that, so frequently, the ultimate reference for what is or is not meant by God's word is local custom, and that the arbiters of its application are the local experts.

THE LAW OF EXCHANGE — A CONSTITUTION FOR THE MARKETPLACE

In medieval Islamic urban society, the marketplace and the mosque were the two principal, recognised loci of extra-familial sociability. To be sure, there were other places and other occasions (festivals, ceremonies and public and private celebrations), but it was religion and economic exchange that provided the primary and ongoing opportunities for sociability. If we join this social reality to the ideological ambition of Islamic law which saw itself as all-embracing, as an absolute, divine norm for behaviour in this world and as a guide for entry into the next, then it is perhaps not surprising that the treatment of commercial law in Islamic legal compendia becomes more than just a technical discussion, taking on the dimension of a philosophy of economic life and an Islamic constitution for the marketplace.

It is in this light that one should view the preamble to the *kitab al-bay*ᶜ in Sarakhsi's legal compendium, the *Mabsut.* Sarakhsi introduces his "Book of Sale," the core-book of Islamic commercial law, with a philosophical and sociological comment:

> God, may he be praised and exalted, has made material goods (*mal*) the basis for sustaining man's well-being in this world, and He has devised the path of commerce as the lawful means of acquiring them. The goods which people need to live are not to be found ownerless (*mubahan*), and acquiring them by coercive means would constitute an iniquity disapproved by God. And it is to this end that God, may He be praised and exalted, intended his statement: "O believers, consume not your goods between you in vanity, except that there be trading, by your agreeing together." (Qur'an, IV:33)[20]

The purpose of trade and exchange (*tijara*) is not only to provide for mankind's material sustenance, but also to do so in a manner which is socially harmonious and avoids aggression and conflict. Emphasis is placed on the Qur'anic phrase "*tijara ᶜan taradin minkum,*" exchange which grows out of mutual agreement, in which the circulation and transfer of wealth is peaceful, non-violent and, on the whole, free from constraints.

Here again, exchange as conceived by Islamic law is not simply or narrowly an economic transaction. One might even go so far as to say that in the eyes of the *shari*ᶜ*a*, an exclusively economic exchange is virtually inconceivable; every exchange in the marketplace necessarily partakes of a social and moral quality. For it was God himself, in His benevolence, who not only sanctioned commerce, but made its practice necessary and inevitable for mankind. Given this view of the place of exchange in God's sub-lunar world, it is no wonder that throughout the legal discussions, the term for sale — *bay*ᶜ — has an entirely positive connotation.

> Trade (*tijara*) is of two kinds: the permissible type, which in the law is designated as 'sale' (*bay*ᶜ), and the prohibited type which is designated as 'usury' (*riba*). Each of these two types is within the general realm of commerce.[21]

Thus, the term for sale is not neutral; it connotes the entire domain of licit, approved exchanges. The antonym of 'sale' in this context is neither purchase (*shira'*), nor barter, nor any comparable term, but rather *riba* — usury — a term comprehending a large category of illicit forms of exchange.

The insertion of economic activity into an overall Islamic scheme which includes social, moral and religious life takes place according to a model in which trade and exchange are viewed as positive pursuits in which the quality of conduct has impact on many levels of society. Just as a person who engages in trade is more pleasing in the eyes of God than a person who spends all his time praying,[22] so those who practice *riba* are, to use one of Sarakhsi's more colorful phrases, engaging in a sin more grievous than thirty-three adulteries.[23] Even if somewhat hyperbolic, this metaphor serves to illustrate the connection in the eyes of Islamic law between economic interactions and the general commonweal.

The marketplace and the activity that transpired there were seen as a kind of microcosm of society as a whole and the religious and ethical values by which it was supposed to live. In describing the purpose of 'The Book of Sale' within the context of Islamic religious law, Sarakhsi writes:

> The aim of this book is the clarification of that which is permitted, in other words, lawful sale, and that which is forbidden, in other words, usury (*riba*). In this regard Muhammad ash-Shaybani (one of the founders of the Hanafi school) was asked: 'How is it that you have not written anything concerning abstemious behavior (*zuhd*) in your compendium of Islamic law?' He replied: 'I have already composed The Book of Sale.' What he meant to say was: 'In the Book of Sale I have explained that which is permissible and that which is forbidden, and *zuhd* (abstemiousness/asceticism) consists in nothing more than the avoidance of that which is forbidden and striving for that which is permitted.[24]

The rather remarkable assertion being attributed to Shaybani here is that all the religious, moral and social qualities implied by the notion of *zuhd* are identical with honest and lawful behavior in the sphere of exchange. Asceticism and abstemious behavior in the eyes of God and in the eyes of Shaybani are to be sought not in any form of self-denial, or poverty, but simply in pursuing one's livelihood within the broad and spacious confines of the law.

LOCAL KNOWLEDGE AND PERSONAL GUARANTEE

Underlying the prominence of local knowledge and localised information in the Islamic law of exchange is the notion that the ultimate guarantee for the stability and effectiveness of economic transactions passed through individual persons and what they knew about each other rather than through institutions. This appreciation of the realities of social relations and social structure found its expression in other realms of Islamic law, and conferred a certain cultural style on the economic practices of the medieval near East.

In a famous passage of the second Surah of the Qur'an the followers of the Prophet are enjoined as follows: "Oh ye who believed, when ye contract a debt one to the other for a stated term, write it down" (*Qur'an* II:282). Yet, in spite of this divine recommendation — one might even say explicit instruction — to record one's obligations in writing, written agreements and contracts have a rather dubious status in Islamic law. They are not required for any legal transaction in Islamic commercial law. A written document gives rise to no obligation, nor does it constitute competent evidence in the event of litigation. In Hanafi law, a written document can acquire legal force only through the verification of its contents by the oral testimony of qualified witnesses. It is the oral testimony which is the decisive factor in determining the existence and nature of an obligation. The existence of a document constitutes, at best, only corroborative evidence. This gave rise to a system of professional witnesses who also acted as scribes, a practice designated by Geertz as "normative witnessing."[25]

Despite their devaluation by legal theory, written documents continued in use, as Sarakhsi puts it, "from the time of the Prophet to our own very day." Evidence from the Arabic papyri of the 8th to 10th centuries and of the Geniza documents of the 11th through 13th centuries bear ample testimony to the importance of documents in exchange, in commercial and in credit operations. However, in the administration of justice, it was not the document which gave credence to the person's claims, but rather the person who conferred credibility (and validity) on the document.[26] In other words, claims, in Islamic law, can be neither abstract nor abstracted; they are always incarnated. Not only are they incarnated, but they are incarnated in people about whom something is known and whose worth and word have received a consensual certification.

Thus in matters of witnessing and testimony as in matters of daily market exchange, we find Islamic law giving preference to personal knowledge, to what is known about a man, to his probity and reliability, to the worth of his personal guarantee rather than to any formalised procedure for sustaining the authenticity of claims. Here again, we find a form of local knowledge triumphant.

THE DISCOURSE OF ISLAMIC LAW — BETWEEN SOUND AND SILENCE

On many of the issues which preoccupy historians and anthropologists of law, Islamic law seems to occupy an intermediate position. While the *sharīʿah*, as expounded by the religious lawyers, was the only officially recognised system of law, it was flanked on the one side by the state's control of administrative practices in the domains of criminal, fiscal and political law, and on the other by a body of *ad hoc* customary practices and mechanisms for adjudicating the minor disputes and conflicts generated by everyday life. The relationship of Islamic religious law — that is, of its bearers and practitioners, the religious scholars who elaborated it and the judges who applied it — to the state — that is, those who controlled the institutions of political coercion — was ambiguous. Qadis were, indeed, appointed and could be removed by kings, princes and governors; but the body of law which the qadis administered was one elaborated by themselves and their confreres and not legislated or decreed by any secular or political authority. Generally speaking, the coercive power at the qadi's disposal to enforce his decisions was minimal. During the middle ages, qadis did usually have some form of gendarmerie under their control, but it was rather by consensus and through the recognition of their legitimacy that their rulings were effective.

The qadis and their associates controlled, or even monopolised the discourse of the law; however, they controlled the language much more than the speech of the law and only imperfectly mastered the actions associated with the law. Put somewhat differently, the discourse of Islamic religious law was on the whole free from the restraints or influences of power relationships as embodied in the state. It is not only that state authorities permitted legal experts a virtually free rein in elaborating legal doctrine, but the "secular" power-holders were explicitly excluded from tampering with the discourse of the law. In return, religious-legal experts (*ʿulemaʾ/fuqahaʾ*) tacitly ceded practical control of large segments of social and political life (e.g., criminal law, fiscal and administrative law) to the powers that be while never relinquishing their claim to their own theoretical rectitude and authority in all of these domains. In terms of power relationships, one finds, once again, medieval Islamic religious law occupying an intermediate and ambiguous position: it did not function simply as an agent or organ of the state, but neither was it totally independent of it.[27]

To sustain its legitimacy, medieval Islamic law had recourse to a two-tiered strategy: on the one hand, invocation of its direct ascendance to the divine word and, on the other, reaching down to accommodate custom, local practices and local knowledge. Contrary to what many have thought and said, Islamic law did not avert its gaze from custom and pretend that it did not exist. Paradoxically, *because* of its universal claim, and not in spite of it, Islamic law was propelled to make room for custom and to stretch its theoretical postulates in order to bridge the gaps and discrepancies between theory and practice.

The example of *istisnaᶜ* discussed above demonstrates the distance which the Hanafi branch of Islamic law was willing to traverse in order to accommodate accepted practices, even when doing so ran counter to its jurisprudential theory. It did not do so in every case in which customary practice opposed legal theory, and custom did not always enter Islamic law through the front door. More frequently, Islamic law absorbed custom either as a slight modificaton of its theoretical positions, or as a basis for settling details. Thus, custom, whether discordant or not with theory, was not greeted with silence; neither, of course, was it received into the body of the holy law with a "haute voix." It was rather by a whisper, by a silent gesture pointing to the "custom of the merchants," or the "usual practice of the People" of this or that place or profession that practice was incorporated into the framework of Islamic law.

LOCAL KNOWLEDGE AND LOCAL RATIONALITY

It was, apparently, precisely this ambiguous quality in Islamic law which so impressed Max Weber. To the best of my knowledge, no one has thus far investigated the empirical data upon which Weber made his judgments about Islamic law, nor why he singled it out as a source for designating his famous category of 'qadi-justice', a category which comprehends not only the legal conduct of the Islamic world, but also legal phenomena as culturally and chronologically disparate as Attic people's courts, rabbinic law, English common law and the jury system.[28] For Weber, 'qadi-justice' included any legal system, or parts of a legal system in which decisions were not exclusively oriented toward fixed rules of formally rational law, but were diluted by ethical, religious, political or other expediential considerations.[29] The rationality which Weber found lacking in the administration of Islamic 'qadi-justice' coincides largely with the uniformity, consistency and predictability of its decisions. It is what he termed 'formal rationality'. Legal provisions, whether in Islamic or other 'qadi-justice' legal systems, even when they make good practical or contextual sense are, in the absence of formal rational principles, at most accorded the status of 'substantive rationality'.

Although he formulated it somewhat differently, Weber was attuned to the phenomenon of 'localism' in Islamic law, and particularly in Islamic commercial law.

> As a status group law, the sacred law applies only to the Muslim but not to the subject population of unbelievers. As a consequence, legal particularism continued to exist not only for several tolerated denominations, which were privileged partly positively and partly negatively, but also as local or vocational custom. The scope of the maxim that "special law prevails over

> the general law of the land", although it claimed an absolute validity, was of doubtful application whenever particular laws happened to conflict with sacred norms, which themselves were subject to thoroughly unstable interpretations. The commercial law of Islam developed from the legal techniques of late antiquity a variety of norms, quite a few of which were directly taken over by the West. In Islam itself, however, the validity of these commercial norms did not derive from enactment or from stable principles of a rational legal system. Their guarantee consisted in nothing but the merchant's sense of honesty and economic influence. The sacred traditions rather threatened than promoted most of these particularistic institutions. They existed *praeter legem*.[30]

That various non-Muslim religious denominations in the abode of Islam possessed their own legal systems, which *de facto* or *de jure* governed many aspects of their lives, is a historically accurate and theoretically important observation. From Weber's point of view, of course, this contributed yet another element of 'irrationality' to an already insufficiently uniform legal system. Having other denominations with their own laws and courts is a nightmare for anyone who conceives of rationality as largely equivalent to consistency.

In spite of the 'status group law' characteristic of Islamic law and in spite of the 'legal particularism' resulting from the diverse make-up of the society, all the groups shared certain basic cultural and social values. They shared ideas about the mode of social and economic relations which made their legal-economic institutions — even if different in detail — quite similar in flavor. In the marketplace of traditional Islamic societies, including, of course, those of the medieval period, the business dealings of Christians, Muslims and Jews — even if they adhered in part to different judicial jurisdictions — were based on the same assumptions and even had the same form. The point is that this diversity, whether within the Muslim community or between Muslims and non-Muslims, did not, in practice, result in uncertainty, or confusion or unpredictability. The situation was not subject to arbitrariness.

Legal particularism within the framework of universal norms, or sacred norms which claimed universal validity, was a fact of medieval Islamic society. Indeed one might say, contrary to what Weber implies in this passage, that it is precisely the presence or availability of this legal particularism which made the system work. The problem was not simply or primarily one of the conflict of 'particular laws' with 'sacred norms'. First of all, there were no particular laws. What there was, was custom. Local custom, regional custom, general custom. Consequently, the problem was how to reconcile, absorb or adapt custom and practice to the 'sacred norms' whose interpretation, while exhibiting some flexibility, was not nearly as unstable as Weber seems to believe. On the contrary, once interpreted, these norms achieved a fair degree of acceptance, and their repetition and diffusion guaranteed a large measure of stability.

Those areas which were within the purview of religious courts were areas in which custom was, one way or another, absorbed or accommodated into the law in a way which was known and recognised. The customs may have varied from one place to another, but this was of little importance, since most significant things in life were local and consequently it was the 'local knowledge' that counted.

Notes

1. Geertz 1983: 167.
2. On the various, often conflicting, views concerning the formation and development of Islamic law during the first two centuries of the Islamic period, see: Schacht 1950; 1964: 6-75; Coulson 1964: 9-73; Juynboll 1983.
3. On the relationship of the theoretical prescriptions of Islamic law to medieval Islamic practice and on the use of Islamic legal treatises for social and economic history, see Schacht 1964: 76-85; Coulson 1964: 75ff.; Udovitch 1970: 249-261.
4. For summaries of the Islamic law of sale, see: article *Bay*ᶜ in the *Encyclopaedia of Islam* (1960), 2nd edition, Leiden: Brill, Vol. I, pp. 1110-1113; Schacht 1964 : 145-160. For a translation of a Hanafi text dealing with the law of sale, see Grady 1963: 211-317. Even though this translation is slightly archaic, it conveys both the flavour and the essential substance of the Islamic law of sale.
5. Goitein 1967: 192 ff.; Geertz 1979: 205ff.
6. Goitein 1967: 200-201; Geertz 1979: 198-229.
7. Sarakhsi, *al-Mabsut*, 30 vols., Cairo: n.d., Vol. XII, p. 124.
8. *Ibid*, p. 125.
9. Schacht 1964 : 153-54.
10. Al-Marghinani, *Al-Hidaya*, 4 vols., Cairo: n.d., Vol. III, p. 56.
11. Sarakhsi, *Mabsut*, XIII, p. 78.
12. *Ibid*, XIII, p. 80.
13. Goitein 1967: 201.
14. Sarakhsi, *Mabsut*, XII, p. 139.
15. *Ibid*, XII, pp. 140-41.
16. *Ibid*, XII, p. 142.
17. *Ibid*, XII, p. 153.
18. *Ibid*, XII, pp. 196, 197, 199, 203, 214.
19. *Ibid*, XII, p. 83.
20. *Ibid*, XII, p. 108.
21. *Ibid*, XII, p. 107.
22. al-Ghazzali (n.d.), *Ihya ᶜulum al-din*, 4 vols., II, Cairo, p. 64.
23. Sarakhsi, *Mabsut*, p. 110.
24. *Ibid.*
25. Geertz 1983: 190-91.
26. Wakin 1972: 1-29; Rosen 1980-81: 219-20; Schacht 1964: 193-4.
27. On the position and power of qadis, see the article *kadi* in the *Encyclopaedia of Islam*, 2nd edition, Vol. IV, pp. 373-75. On the relationship of Islamic religious learning —including, of course, the law — to the groups who wielded political power, see the very perceptive discussion of H.A.R. Gibb in Gibb 1962: 10-17. See also, R.P. Mottahedeh 1980: 7-31.
28. Weber 1978 Vol. II, p. 813.
29. Weber, *ibid*, II, p. 806, note 40 and p. 976.
30. *Ibid*, II, pp. 821-22.

Bibliography

Coulson, N.J. (1964) *A History of Islamic Law*, Edinburgh: Edinburgh University Press.

Geertz, Clifford (1979) "Suq: The Bazaar Economy in Sefrou," in C. Geertz, H. Geertz, L. Rosen, *Meaning and Order in a Moroccan Society*, Cambridge: Cambridge University Press.
Geertz, Clifford (1983) "Local Knowledge: Fact and Law in Comparative Perspective," in Geertz, *Local Knowledge, Further Essays in Interpretive Anthropology*, New York: Basic Books, pp. 167-234.
Gibb, H.A.R. (1962) *Studies on the Civilisation of Islam*, Boston: Beacon Press.
Goitein, S.D. (1967) *A Mediterranean Society*, Vol. I, *Economic Foundations*, Berkeley: University of California Press.
Grady, S.G., ed. (1963) *The Hedaya or Guide: A Commentary on the Mussulman Laws*, translated by Charles Hamilton, Lahore: Premier Book House.
Juynboll, G.H.A. (1983) *Muslim Traditions: Studies in Chronology, Provenance and Authorship of Early Hadith*, Cambridge: Cambridge University Press.
Mottahedeh, R.P. (1980) *Loyalty and Leadership in an Early Islamic Society*, Princeton: University Press.
Rosen, L. (1980-1) "Equity and Discretion in a Modern Islamic Legal System" *Law and Society Review* **15**: 217-245.
Sarakhsi, *Kitab al-mabsut*, 30 vols, Cairo, n.d.
Schacht, J. (1950) *The Origins of Muhammadan Jurisprudence*, Oxford: Oxford University Press.
Schacht, J. (1964) *An Introduction to Islamic Law*, Oxford: Oxford University Press.
Udovitch, A.L. (1970) *Partnership and Profit in Medieval Islam*, Princeton: Princeton University Press.
Wakin, J.A. (1972) *The Function of Documents in Islamic Law*, Albany: State University of New York Press.
Weber, Max (1978) *Economy and Society*, 2 vols., eds G. Roth and C. Wittich, Berkeley: University of California.